Digital Privacy, Terrorism and Law Enforcement

This book examines the UK's response to terrorist communication. Its principle question asks, has individual privacy and collective security been successfully managed and balanced? The author begins by assessing several technologically-based problems facing British law enforcement agencies, including use of the Internet; the existence of 'darknet'; untraceable Internet telephone calls and messages; smart encrypted device direct messaging applications; and commercially available encryption software. These problems are then related to the traceability and typecasting of potential terrorists, showing that law enforcement agencies are searching for needles in the ever-expanding haystacks. To this end, the book examines the bulk powers of digital surveillance introduced by the Investigatory Powers Act 2016. The book then moves on to assess whether these new powers and the new legislative safeguards introduced are compatible with international human rights standards.

The author creates a 'digital rights criterion' from which to challenge the bulk surveillance powers against human rights norms. Lord Carlile of Berriew CBE QC in recommending this book notes this particular legal advancement, commenting that rightly so the author concludes the UK has fairly balanced individual privacy with collective security.

The book further analyses the potential impact on intelligence exchange between the EU and the UK, following Brexit. Using the US as a case study, the book shows that UK laws must remain within the ambit of EU law and the Court of Justice of the European Union's (CJEU's) jurisprudence, to maintain the effectiveness of the exchange. It addresses the topics with regard to terrorism and counterterrorism methods and will be of interest to researchers, academics, professionals and students researching counterterrorism and digital electronic communications, international human rights, data protection, and international intelligence exchange.

Simon Hale-Ross is a Lecturer in Law at Leeds Law School, Leeds Beckett University, UK.

Routledge Research in Terrorism & the Law

Available titles in this series include:

Gender, National Security and Counter-terrorism
Human rights perspectives
Margaret L. Satterthwaite and Jayne Huckerby

Surveillance, Counter-Terrorism and Comparative Constitutionalism
Fergal Davis, Nicola McGarrity and George Williams

Homeland Security, its Law and its State
A Design of Power for the 21st Century
Christos Boukalas

Anti-Terrorism Law and Normalising Northern Ireland
Jessie Blackbourn

The Impact, Legitimacy and Effectiveness of EU Counter-Terrorism
Fiona de Londras and Josephine Doody

Preventive Detention of Terror Suspects
A New Legal Framework
Diane Webber

Domestic Counter-Terrorism in a Global World
Post-9/11 Institutional Structures and Cultures in Canada and the UK
Daniel Alati

Anti-Terrorism Law and Foreign Terrorist Fighters
Jessie Blackbourn, Deniz Kayis, and Nicola McGarrity

Digital Privacy, Terrorism and Law Enforcement
The UK's Response to Terrorist Communication
Simon Hale-Ross

For more information about this series, please visit: www.routledge.com/Routledge-Research-in-Terrorism-and-the-Law/book-series/TERRORISMLAW

Digital Privacy, Terrorism and Law Enforcement

The UK's Response to Terrorist Communication

Simon Hale-Ross

Routledge
Taylor & Francis Group
LONDON AND NEW YORK

First published 2019 by Routledge

2 Park Square, Milton Park, Abingdon, Oxfordshire OX14 4RN
52 Vanderbilt Avenue, New York, NY 10017

Routledge is an imprint of the Taylor & Francis Group, an informa business

First issued in paperback 2020

British Library Cataloguing-in-Publication Data
A catalogue record for this book is available from the British Library

Library of Congress Cataloging-in-Publication Data
Names: Hale-Ross, Simon, author.
Title: Digital privacy, terrorism and law enforcement : the UK's response to terrorist communication / Simon Hale-Ross.
Description: New York, NY : Routledge, 2018. | Series: Routledge research in terrorism and the law | Includes bibliographical references and index.
Identifiers: LCCN 2018005520 | ISBN 9780815360186 (hardback)
Subjects: LCSH: Terrorism–Great Britain. | Electronic surveillance–Law and legislation–Great Britain. | Privacy, Right of–Great Britain. | Computer security–Great Britain. | Digital communications–Security measures. | Internet–Law and legislation–Great Britain. | Law enforcement–Great Britain.
Classification: LCC KD8039 .H35 2018 | DDC 345.41/052–dc23
LC record available at https://lccn.loc.gov/2018005520

ISBN: 978-0-8153-6018-6 (hbk)
ISBN: 978-0-367-58886-1 (pbk)

Typeset in Galliard
by Taylor & Francis Books

Contents

Foreword vi
Other ix

Introduction: approaching terrorism 1

1 The United Kingdom's legal definition of terrorism 11

2 The 21st Century terrorist threat: how terrorist groups and terrorists communicate and the unknown threat 44

3 The necessity of bulk communications data surveillance 60

4 The necessity of pre-emptive legal counterterrorism measures 97

5 Implications of the UK's legal response: striking the right balance between individual privacy and collective security in the digital age 113

6 The international nature of the 21st Century terrorism threat: preserving international intelligence exchange and the implications of the UK leaving the European Union 137

Conclusion 156

Bibliography 161
Index 187

Foreword

The pace, nature and technical sophistication of terrorist communications changes almost as quickly as the reading of a book. In the years since the invention of the mobile telephone and the initial years of the World Wide Web, the potential for lethal and secret communication has risen exponentially and fast. Instructions to make a mass killing can be given in less time than it takes to blink an eye. The dark web, the passing of messages through games and other concealed means, and the use of multiple cell phones acquired anonymously and paid for untraceably, are among the means that facilitate the ruthless.

To devote a book to this issue of communications is timely. It is also brave, in that it opens up the sometimes raw debate about the relationship between private rights on the one hand, and protection of the public by the State on the other.

There is no doubt that it has become accepted, and rightly so, that citizens, even including the criminal and malevolent, have the right to communicate privately with one another, subject to proportionate restrictions by the State for the prevention of crime and for the protection of those whose lives might otherwise be damaged and even shattered by serious criminality. Terrorist offences are the most serious of crimes, possessing the capacity to undermine our accepted democratic system and the freedoms that are an accepted part of our lives, through often indiscriminate attacks on soft targets.

In assessing what is the true nature of the private rights to be protected, we do well to remind ourselves that, voluntarily, we have surrendered a great deal of our privacy. Online grocery companies know our tastes and remind us of them regularly; online clothes retailers know our vital statistics; online dating agencies have a cache of intimate information; online therapists know our weaknesses. All that information is subject to perversely so-called privacy policies operated by the Internet providers, which in reality allow them to disseminate for profit vast amounts of what we used to regard as private information. In my view, the reach of the British State under counter-terrorism legislation such as the Investigatory Powers Act is much exaggerated when compared with the reach of the private sector. However, that view should not be used as an excuse for the State to snoop into our online activity without clear protection against the abuse of administrative action.

This book examines the range of communications affected by the law, including encrypted materials. It reminds us that the authorities often are searching for an electronic needle in a huge haystack, and that this has been used as a reason for allowing the interception and examination of bulk data. The author helps us in this hunt by starting from a black letter rule of law approach: this is not a political book by any stretch of the imagination. It sets out a full legal toolkit, and leaves any political conclusions to the reader. In this sense, it is a book of true legal scholarship, enabling primary sources such as legislation and secondary sources such as case law and academic analysis to be the raw materials for any broader social science conclusions that readers may wish to reach.

Chapter 5 is of particular note. In developing the digital rights criterion, it focuses on human rights norms, testing the Investigatory Powers Act against UK jurisprudence and also that of the Court of Justice of the European Union (CJEU) and the European Court of Human Rights (ECtHR). The authors challenges the Act, tests it, and correctly concludes that, since its enactment, the UK has managed suitably and proportionately to balance collective security with individual data privacy.

Chapter 6 tackles one of the major challenges posed by the UK's exit from the European Union. The current information sharing agreement between the UK and the US is used to illustrate how bilateral arrangements can be used effectively to ensure necessary cooperation in the public interest. The same applies to multilateral compacts, such as the *Five Eyes*.

The establishment by the UK Government of an Extremism Commission will lead to further important developments. Will the Commission advise the Government to criminalise more precursor offences, even more distant from actual terrorism acts than the present inchoate offences? It has been suggested by the governing Conservative Party that it should be an offence if, without reasonable excuse (the evidential burden of proof of which is transferred to the accused) a person repeatedly logs on to radicalising jihadist or extreme right-wing sites. If such laws were introduced, they would broaden the range of terrorism related criminality, and might well bring the UK into conflict with the CJEU and ECtHR jurisprudence. The book emphasises the importance of the retention of an internationally acceptable standard of law and interpretation, within which reflective judgement of proposed new laws can be reached. It also warns against the danger that we might criminalise many expressions of support for armed resistance against a brutal or repressive regime.

In practical terms, this contemporarily relevant book offers lawyers and students an understanding of the extra-territorial effect of UK counter terrorism laws, reminding us that international agreements, and also necessity, demand an international response to violent extremism. The author reminds us that this can be achieved in a developing human rights context, in which legislation has become more flexible in its capacity to address the remarkable speed of the electronic revolution. We are reminded of the multiple levels of scrutiny applied to interception and investigation, of the importance of review of the actions of those necessarily operating in the interests of justice in secret and sometimes ungoverned spaces, and of the necessity to use a wise critical faculty in fervently hunting down those who decry our democratic polity in the name of heretical and oppressive religious or political ends.

I recommend this book as required reading for those who are committed to sound legal learning and balanced judgement in what is recognised widely as a challenging area of law and policy. I foresee several editions in the future.

Lord Carlile of Berriew CBE QC
House of Lords, London, SW1A 0PW

Other

First, I must express my sincerest appreciation to Lord Alex Carlile of Berriew for providing the foreword for this book, and additionally for the level of dedication shown throughout his life to his craft. I can only hope this work meets the high level of faith his Lordship has positioned.

I would like to express gratitude to my Director of Studies Dr David Lowe for his continuous support throughout my research and academic career. He has always been the immeasurable proprietor of knowledge, particularly regarding terrorism, and he has shown great patience and dedication throughout my career. My thanks also go to my PhD examiners Professor Stuart Kirby, Dr Julian Richards and Dr Yarin Eski.

The sheer level of indebtedness is increased exponentially by the exuberant amount of time and effort spent by my friend and colleague Richard Ridyard in reading the entire manuscript and providing a high level of elegance and prose. His support has been unwavering.

Finally, I would like to thank my parents and my fiancée Charlotte for all their support and encouragement. Without you all this work would simply not have been possible. Put simply, I cannot thank you enough.

Introduction: approaching terrorism

> terrorism is a generic concept covering a wide range of phenomena, with important political, philosophical, psychological, historical, ethical and legal dimensions.[1]

Terrorism, as a topic of study, is expansive. It is also a term of legal art. I want to begin by explaining my position on the balance between state counterterrorism and surveillance powers and human rights, namely the right to privacy, which in this case is tapered to centre upon digital privacy.

The right to life

An 8-year-old girl accompanies her mother and father to a concert in Manchester, England, where her favourite singer is to perform. She is so excited. The doors to the venue open at 6pm; the show is set to start at 7:35pm. As the family arrive, all seems well in this memory-producing moment.

In the intervening period, between the time of the doors opening and the show starting, unknown to them, a grave warning appeared on social media. At 6:28pm and 6:32pm on the 22 May 2017, user name @owys663 posted,

> you forgotten our threat? This is the just terror #ISLAMICSTATE #manchesterarena #UK #British … We have more … #manchesterarena.

The 8-year-old girl was one of 22 people killed some four hours later by Salman Abedi, a British born 22-year-old man who detonated a bomb at the entrance to the concert hall, killing himself in the process. The girl's mother, one of 50 people seriously injured, did not learn of her daughter's death until she woke following critical surgery.

In 1993, aged 14 , I witnessed the aftermath of the Irish Republican Army's terrorist bombing in Warrington, England. Two young boys were killed and many more injured. Throughout the late 20th Century, moving into the 21st Century, the terrorist threat faced by the UK has continually increased. In fact the only

1 Wilkinson, P. cited in R. Jackson and S. J. Sinclair (2012) *Contemporary Debates on Terrorism* (Routledge) p.11.

static element of terrorism has been the loss of life and serious life-altering injury inflicted on citizens, for a cause. Of course, in the digital age where the average age of the terrorist is 24, the terrorists have the ability to use the Internet, expertly, to recruit and radicalise others into joining their cause, as well as fashioning new high-tech malware. They are also experts at using 21st Century electronic communications technology, such as commercially available encryption. The terrorist threat posed to the UK has increased throughout this period, with this expert use of technology often becoming the driving force behind organised action and recruitment.

A number of questions present themselves. First, could the 2017 Manchester attack have been prevented? Could or should UK law enforcement agencies have seen the warning on social media and intervened, potentially saving lives? Should law enforcement be able to police and monitor the Internet in real time? And the digital age prompts another question: how far are citizens willing to allow law enforcement state agencies to screen their retained data, in an attempt to find the ever-elusive terrorist, thereby saving lives and eliminating terrorist threats? For me, the right to life is the most sacred human right of all. It is a right protected by Article 2 of the European Convention on Human Rights 1950 (ECHR), and also by Article 2 of the Charter of Fundamental Rights of the European Union 2000 (CFR).

The capabilities gap and privacy

The right to privacy has collided with legitimate advances in technology in the 21st Century. We now see, with the continuing decline in postal communication and landlines, a preference for various means of electronic communication. This allows private conversations to be secure through encryption technology. The use of the Internet is continually expanding, as is the growth and use of commercially available encrypted direct messaging applications, largely used legitimately and extensively by smartphone users. What often follows legitimate technological growth, however, is criminal exploitation. It has become increasingly easy for terrorist groups to communicate and circulate their propaganda, and for individual terrorists to communicate freely. Given the average age of the terrorist, most have grown up with the Internet and smart technology and are therefore proficient in its use. Cyber-crime has vastly escalated along with the use of the darker side to the Internet, named the 'darknet'. The capabilities presented to a potential terrorist by the darknet are perhaps the most concerning, allowing those who mean to do serious harm anonymity and access to weaponry, including firearms, ammunition and explosives.

This has opened an investigatory capabilities gap, increasing the pressures on UK law enforcement agencies in fulfilling their task of protecting national security and safeguarding citizens' right to life. In response to such pressures, the UK and the European Union (EU) have enacted new laws allowing the monitoring of electronic communications data. For example, the British Government recently enacted the Investigatory Powers Act 2016 (IPA), which introduces and preserves the ability to bulk collect, retain electronic communications data and attain the operator's assistance in decryption. Although the IPA is sensitive to human rights, the bulk interception of electronic communications data and ability to retain data is contentious. Additionally, concerns surround the introduction of 'backdoors' into encrypted online services, and bulk interception and equipment interference warrants, which weaken the security and individual data protection and privacy rights of, potentially, the entire population.

The Court of Justice of the European Union (CJEU) has been the most influential judicial body in terms of individual data protection through its key judgments in *Digital Rights Ireland Ltd v Minister for Communications, Marine and Natural Resources and others and the conjoined case of Kärntner Landesregierung, Michael Seitlinger, Christof Tschohl and others (Digital Rights Ireland)*. The CJEU has done this by asserting the EU's constitutional and legal facility in defending data protection, through, for example, Article 8 of the Charter of Fundamental Rights, the Data Protection Directive in 1995 and the e-Privacy Directive in 2002. Focusing on the EU rather than the ECHR is essential given the EU's constitutional and legislative direct impact on UK data privacy laws and policy.

To close the capabilities gap faced by law enforcement, the British Government must reconcile UK law with the jurisprudence of the CJEU and of course the European Court of Human Rights (ECtHR). The courts focus on various elements, shaped by the Conventional rights, with the CJEU focused on data protection and the ECtHR on Article 8 right to privacy. To strike an appropriate balance between individual privacy and collective security, a focus on human rights is required, with particular emphasis placed on the following aperçu: one cannot assert privacy rights if one's right to life is not fully protected in the first place.

The consequence of the UK's broadly drafted counterterrorism legal framework is to criminalise almost any expression of a view that an armed resistance to a brutal or repressive anti-democratic regime could, in certain circumstances, be justifiable. However, although the current counterterrorism structure is broad, the UK and the EU, additionally through surveillance legislation, allow for the policing of the Internet and remove any safe spaces used by criminals and terrorists. The IPA fashions a way to achieve this, but because it can be aimed at the whole population, subject to authorisation checks and balances, it is likely to receive continual CJEU and ECtHR judicial scrutiny. Post the UK's exit from the EU, however, the CJEU may become less important, leaving the ECtHR to conduct the analysis. At present, the UK must follow CJEU rulings when the matter concerns EU law, whereas ECtHR decisions are merely recommendatory.

State counterterrorism and surveillance powers v international human rights

This leads us to consider the legally and emotively charged principles in conflict. Advocates on either side of the debate show signs of force and dogma. What is at stake is often framed as: powers versus rights; collective security versus individual freedoms. It is not, however, an either or problem. One can reasonably state that there are instances when state powers should impede privacy but there should always be a presumption of privacy rights.

This position is redolent of Lord Hoffmann's judgment in *A and others v Secretary of State for the Home Department*, where he illustrated the dichotomy between terrorism, the resulting restrictive laws and human rights:

> In my opinion, such a [counterterrorism] power in any form is not compatible with our constitution. *The real threat to the life of the nation, in the sense of a people living in accordance with its traditional laws and political values, comes not from terrorism but from laws such as these.* That is the true measure of what terrorism may achieve. It is for Parliament to decide whether to give the terrorists such a victory.[2] [My emphasis]

Although dealing with the then powers of indefinite detention of foreign nationals without judicial processes under the Anti-Terrorism, Crime and Security Act 2001, this statement provides much needed illumination. The focus has since shifted to another increasingly controversial area: bulk electronic communications data surveillance, and bulk equipment interference.

Rather than exploring counterterrorism measures that affect the few, these new measures are aimed at the population as a whole. And this is where the CJEU's decision in *Digital Rights Ireland* becomes important, given it repeals the EU's 2006 Directive, with the parties concerned having successfully challenged the UK's Data Retention and Investigatory Powers Act 2014 (DRIPA).[3] The 21st Century terrorist threat faced is extraordinarily different from previous experiences, particularly following al-Qaeda's terrorist attack on the United States on 11 September 2001.[4] The use of communication technology by stateless terrorist organisations, such as al-Qaeda and, more recently, Islamic State (IS), in conducting covert and organised action, and influencing and recruiting others to their cause, illustrates the need for legislative measures.

The UK Government's approach

This book examines a number of issues. It uses a legal perspective to analyse the surveillance of electronic communications data, UK counterterrorism legislation and the impact of such laws on society. Before that, the UK Government's approach to legislating for counterterrorism must be explored. Legislation must be

2 [2004] UKHL 56, [97]. Although beyond the ambit of this chapter Hoffmann was referring to sections 21 and 23 of the Anti-Terrorism, Crime and Security Act 2001 (ATCSA) which allowed for the indefinite detention of foreign nationals, without having been formally charged or having gone through due process.

3 *Digital Rights Ireland Ltd v Minister for Communications, Marine and Natural Resources and others and the conjoined case of Kärntner Landesregierung, Michael Seitlinger, Christof Tschohl and others* delivered on 8 April 2014 and reported at [2015] QB 127. Hereinafter referred to as *Digital Rights Ireland*.

4 *Ibid.*

aimed at combatting the 21st Century terrorist threat whilst ensuring human rights protections.[5] Clearly the UK's current counterterrorism structure has been built up, incrementally, over time, which significantly curtails human rights and civil liberties.[6] Many of these counterterrorism laws lack full and complete pre-legislative and legislative scrutiny, which has created a fractured relationship between the judiciary and the executive when conducting post-legislative scrutiny.[7] Compounding a controversial area of law with controversial legislation is certainly damaging on a number of fronts, not only to human rights but to legitimate law making and the reputation of the Government. The UK Government appear to have recognised this during the passing of the IPA in 2016.

Focusing on the UK's counterterrorism legal framework research shows that the laws in this area are comprehensive and interlinked with other regulatory laws not entirely terrorism focused, such as the IPA and the Regulation of Investigatory Powers Act 2000 (RIPA). It was around this time in particular that the UK Government introduced numerous broadly worded Acts – the reach of which have only been moderated by unelected executive departments such as the Department of Public Prosecutions.[8] This is an important point because these broadly worded Acts fashioned a repeated movement between the UK Government and the jurisprudence of the ECtHR.[9] Changes in UK legislation are often prompted by judicial decisions against the Government. However, if the Government would implement recommendations made by others, such as their own various Parliamentary committees and appointed independent reviewers of anti-terrorism legislation, the situation could potentially be eased at an earlier stage.

The UK Government has enacted unprecedented levels of counterterrorism legislation since the introduction of the Terrorism Act 2000, which re-defined an act of terrorism. The rationale behind this is that such laws have been aimed at policing the changing nature and methods of terrorism, thereby attempting to reduce the terrorist threat posed. Some of these legislative measures, such as the

5 D. McKeever (2010) The Human Rights Act and Anti-Terrorism in the UK: One Great Leap Forward by Parliament, but Are the Courts Able to Slow the Steady Retreat that Has Followed?, *Public Law*, January, 110–139, 111.

6 *Ibid.*

7 The Anti-Terrorism, Crime and Security Act 2001 was enacted 33 days after the first reading in Parliament. See the Report on the Anti-Terrorism, Crime and Security Bill 2001 (2001–02 HC 351), and Reports on the Anti-Terrorism, Crime and Security Bill (2001–02 HL 37, HC 372) and (2001–02 HL 51, HC 420). Also the Prevention of Terrorism Act 2005 was enacted within 17 days of the first reading in Parliament. See the Joint Committee on Human Rights, Prevention of Terrorism Bill (2004–05) (2005) HL 68 Paragraph 1, 'The rapid progress of the Bill through Parliament has made it impossible for us to scrutinise the Bill comprehensively for human rights compatibility in time to inform debate in Parliament.

8 For example, the Sexual Offences Act 2003.

9 For example, sections 1 and 2 of the Terrorism Act 2006, enacted in a reactionary fashion to the 7 July 2005 terrorist attack on London. Another example is the Anti-Terrorism, Crime and Security Act (ATCSA) that was presented to UK Parliament on 12 November 2001 and enacted on 14 December 2001, in response to the terrorist attack on the US on 11 September 2001.

Prevention of Terrorism Act 2005, which was superseded by the Terrorism Prevention and Investigation Measures Act 2011 (TPIMs), and particularly sections 1 and 2 of the Terrorism Act 2006, have not been as effective as the UK Government had hoped. Indeed, advances in technology have been quick to provide means to circumvent counterterrorism laws. The activities of Islamic State, whose digital communications strategy has been very effective, illustrate that current legislation remains lacking. The problem therefore remains: How can the UK's legal response to the way in which terrorists communicate in the 21st Century balance individual privacy rights whilst ensuring collective security?

The rationale and rule of law

The book starts by exploring restricted activities. This is important because of the impact these counterterrorism laws have, conferring special restrictions upon individual citizens and providing special executive powers to the State. The activity, terrorist action, is distinguishable from other forms of violent criminal aggression. This is because terrorist action ultimately results in the indiscriminate killing of innocent civilians, with whom the perpetrators have no relationship other than the fact they are there at the time. It is importantly motivated chiefly by the desire to gain publicity for their cause.[10] Used by groups and individuals, terrorist action has been described as triadic rather than dyadic in terms of the effectual relationship, reaching far beyond the immediate victims involving other observers and the media.[11] Forming an integral part of the success of a terrorist attack is the placement of fear in the population, by effecting a spectacular event causing death and serious injury. Essentially aimed at undermining democracy, states are forced to take legislative action in seeking to prevent and pre-empt further episodes.

Whilst there is little international agreement on the accurate ascription of the terrorist label, the rule of law demands clarity and precision to enable the State to deal effectively with the problem.[12] The importance of the rule of law is worth emphasising since the legislature, the executive and law enforcement staff must all work within it. Legal definitions ought to be precise and, insofar as possible, representative of the problems they are designed to address.[13] Much difficulty lies in trying to formulate a legal definition of terrorism. Part of this

10 *R v F* [2007] EWCA Crim 243, [29], the very nature of terrorism is indiscriminate. See also C. H. Simmons and J. R. Mitch (2001) Labelling Public Aggression: When Is It Terrorism?, *The Journal of Social Psychology*, 125(2), 245–251, 245.

11 F. J. Hacker (1980) Terror and Terrorism: Modern Growth Industry and Mass Entertainment, *Studies in Conflict and Terrorism*, 4, 143–159. Hacker argues most aggression is dyadic, involving the attacker and victim only, whereas acts of terrorism are described as triadic due to the dramatisation of the events, involving observers and the media. See also C. H. Simmons and J. R. Mitch (2001) Labelling Public Aggression: When Is It Terrorism?, *The Journal of Social Psychology*, 125(2), 245–251, 246.

12 *Ibid* as per C. H. Simmons and J. R. Mitch (2001), 245.

13 Analysis drawn from Lord Carlile of Berriew QC (2007a) Independent Reviewer of Terrorism Legislation, *The Definition of Terrorism*, March 2007, Cm7052, p.21.

difficulty is tied up in the subjectivity of the term. It is also apt to be pejorative and political.[14] Internationally and domestically its use is dependent on the legislators or definers' viewpoint, and is often ascribed opportunistically rather than representing a factually accurate description of a tactic.[15] Fashioning a 'one size fits all' legal definition of terrorism is extraordinarily difficult given that globally there are a large number of groups labelled as terrorist, all with different grievances, employing different tactics.[16]

An issue that repeatedly comes to light is the low threshold and broadly worded nature of the definition of terrorism under section 1 of the Terrorism Act 2000. Independent reviewers of anti-terrorism legislation have recommended the threshold be raised, such as from 'influence' to 'intimidate'. This is due to the view that 'influence' serves to unnecessarily expand the applicability of the terrorist label. Despite what seem modest suggestions, the UK Government have failed to implement such changes. For Gale this is representative of the UK remaining in a permanent state of emergency, and as a result measures are increasingly encroaching upon UK citizens' rights, protected under the ECHR and the CFR.[17] However, the definition serves its purpose well in practical terms, where law enforcement agencies use it to determine if an activity they are investigating is terrorist in nature. This has been particularly important when determining if the electronic communications data is of a terrorist character or not. As signalled earlier, technological advances constantly evolve and progress, and it is therefore essential the UK legislature change its approach from reactionary to progressive. If legislators could stay one step ahead, then this would help ensure law enforcement does not continue to suffer from the capabilities gap.

14 B. Hoffman (2006) *Inside Terrorism* (2nd Edition, Columbia University Press) pp.1–44: The term 'terrorism' has changed from the revolutionary view in the 1970s, to the pejorative present-day view implying moral and social judgement. This change in direction has been driven by political will. See also R. Jackson, L. Jarvis, J. Gunning and M. B. Smyth (2011) *Terrorism: A Critical Introduction* (Palgrave Macmillan) p.101.

15 *Ibid.*

16 A. Martyn (2002) *The Right of Self-Defence under International Law – the Response to the Terrorist Attacks of 11 September*. Australian Law and Bills Digest Group, Parliament of Australia, available at http://www.aph.gov.au/About_Parliament/Parliamentary_Departments/Parliamentary_Library/Publications_Archive/CIB/cib0102/02CIB08 accessed 30 March 2018.

17 C. J. S. Gale (2006) The UK Response to Terrorism: Human Rights and a Wider Perspective, *Working Paper Series*, No 06/01. See also J. Welch and S. Chakrabarti (2010) The War on Terror without the Human Rights Act – What Difference Has It Made?, *European Human Rights Law Review*, (6), 593–600, 594. Measures include those such as sections 57 and 58 of the Terrorism Act 2000 that criminalise the collection of terrorist documentation, and section 59 covering incitement. The Terrorism Act 2006 was then enacted to attempt to fill the vacuum between phrases such as 'incitement' and 'encouragement', but all attempts have been unsuccessful in preventing terrorist groups from spreading their propaganda through the Internet.

The IPA

The IPA is an essential element in the UK Government's approach, assisting in the determination of which members of the public are friend and which foe. The proliferation of terrorist communication through the Internet and social media means that the Internet must be monitored if the dangerous and destructive nature of a terrorist attack is to be averted. The monitoring is aimed at far more than the gathering of bulk data and the accruing of other statutory powers littered throughout the surveillance legal framework. In addition, the IPA introduces the ability to decrypt messages sent through instant messaging applications, such as Whatsapp.[18] The possible outcome of increased state presence online, which may result in a sudden growth of the availability of anonymity software and services, seems to have been pre-empted by the Government. At the back of the IPA lies section 253, which offers such pre-emption allowing the Secretary of State to issue an operator with a technical capability notice, requesting all assistance in the removal of electronic protection. Such a notice was ascribed in April 2017. It may, however, prove difficult to police given the international nature of the Internet and the locality of service and application providers.

To reassure and gain public support for this legal initiative, a human rights and civil libertarian approach must be taken in concert with open and honest governance. Utilising the CJEU's jurisprudence, this book has developed a new criterion from the *Digital Rights* case, by which to test the IPA. It comprises of the following:

1 Primary legislation must lay down clear and precise rules governing the scope and application of the measure;
2 Minimum safeguards must be imposed sufficiently reducing the risk of abuse or unlawful access to the data;
3 Access to the data must be expressly provided for, limiting the number of persons authorised to have such access and restricted to the purpose of preventing and detecting precisely defined serious criminal offences;
4 Access to the data will only be granted after a prior assessment has been made by an independent administrative body or court, with the primary focus on human rights and proportionality of the measure;
5 Retained data will be deleted after 12 months unless an independent administrative body or court decides otherwise, having weighed the evidence and conducted a proportionality test.[19]

18 Investigatory Powers Act 2016, Part 6 for Bulk Powers, and s 253(5)(c): The Secretary of State may impose an obligation on the service provider to remove electronic protection, i.e. encryption.
19 *Digital Rights Ireland.*

Building public trust

The passing of this test and the focus on the building of trust is crucial given that the IPA has passed through the UK Parliament, resulting in the public's belief that they are being constantly subjected to online surveillance, effectively removing the majority of available online privacy. Human rights groups such as Liberty perpetuate this belief.[20] There are at least two reasons to doubt such a belief. First, law enforcement agencies have finite resources and simply cannot physically conduct surveillance on the entire population.[21] This is apparent where they have struggled to keep careful watch of targeted individuals, such as the killers of Fusilier Lee Rigby.[22] Although the IPA allows retained electronic communications data to be stored for 12 months, and legislative pre-emptive measures that criminalise neutral behaviour are littered thought the UK's counterterrorism framework, this book argues that neither affect individual privacy rights in the way portrayed by groups such as Liberty. The doctrinal and non-doctrinal methodology highlights that mass data retention does not equate to mass data surveillance, and pre-emptive measures are not 'pre-crime' measures. They are in fact, criminal offences.[23]

Secondly, the Home Secretary must first sanction the use of bulk powers, which is then subject to independent judicial approval, and reviewable by the Independent Investigatory Powers Commissioner.[24] This 'double lock' system provides a new, proactively pervaded human rights agenda. With this in mind, the book argues that the balance in the UK between collective security and individual data privacy is reasonably steady because of the role of judicial review, judicial independence and the overarching scrutiny provided by commissioners and parliamentary committees.

The method

Against a backdrop of international human rights standards, this book will look at the current 21st Century terrorist threat and assess some of the many UK laws enacted to combat it. Whilst the majority of academic research approaches the subject of terrorism from a sociological perspective, this book approaches the subject from a legal doctrinal and non-doctrinal view.[25] This is perhaps the most

20 See https://www.liberty-human-rights.org.uk accessed 30 March 2018.

21 First Sitting Committee Debate Session 2015–2016, Investigatory Powers Bill, Publications on the Internet, Column 23, 24 March 2016, available at http://www.publications.parliament.uk/pa/cm201516/cmpublic/investigatorypowers/160324/am/160324s01.htm accessed 30 March 2018.

22 The Rt. Hon. Sir Malcolm Rifkind MP, *Report on the Intelligence Relating to the Murder of Fusilier Lee Rigby*, Intelligence and Security Committee of Parliament, HC 795, 2014, p.81.

23 See Terrorism Act 2006 ss 1–3.

24 See https://www.gov.uk/government/uploads/system/uploads/attachment_data/file/473744/Factsheet-Investigatory_Powers_Commission.pdf accessed 30 March 2018.

25 *Ibid.*

traditional methodology for a legal study, which permits significant analysis with an interdisciplinary approach. It means that I focus on the legalistic, concentrating on the letter of the law. Some might argue this doctrinal approach marginalises discussion on political, ethical, moral and societal impact. There is a grain of truth in this. However, using a non-doctrinal approach allows me to adequately consider various problems, policy and law reform as a baseline for the research. The book therefore reflects the great tradition of legal scholarship and uses mainly primary sources such as legislation found in UK statute books and case law, which is reported. This approach fits within the broader picture of social science theory and methodologies, and whilst a substantial amount of secondary data is relied upon, it remains empirical.

The impact of my method will be highlighted throughout the book, which has allowed me to dispel certain socio-political phrasing used by other researchers in this area. Fabricated phrases such as 'pre-crime' and 'mass surveillance' that are shorn of meaning in law have been shown to confuse citizens. They are, in turn, incorrectly used by some organisations to scare the public into supporting their agenda. Focusing for the moment on the 8-year-old girl at the concert and the foreshadowing of social media, I would challenge such groups to defend their agenda to the victims of a terrorist attack and the families of those killed.

The bulk powers under the IPA, which forms part of the focus of this book, have received and will undoubtedly continue to receive legal challenges by such organisations. With the aim of protecting life and finding the would-be terrorist (needle) within ever-expanding 21st Century technological growth (haystacks), this book will highlight the necessity of the bulk powers in reducing the threats posed. The analysis ultimately leads to the abrasive individual human rights versus collective security scenario.

1 The United Kingdom's legal definition of terrorism

Introduction

Terrorism is distinguishable from other forms of criminal activity and aggression by the indiscriminate killing of innocent civilians, the lack of nexus between the victims and perpetrators and by the motivational aspect to gain publicity.[1] The threat posed by terrorism to national security and to the public in the 21st Century is sufficiently serious to give grounds for specialist counterterrorism legislative powers and increased powers of electronic communications data surveillance.[2]

This chapter delineates the 21st Century understanding of the concept of terrorism, sketching out the need for specialist permanent counterterrorism legislation. UK law enforcement and the courts use the legal definition of terrorism to determine if the crime being investigated is, in fact, terrorist related. It legally defines what actions amount to terrorism and introduces an extra-jurisdictional provision, illustrating the international nature of the threat. By considering certain prominent cases, this chapter reveals that the UK's legal definition of terrorism presents numerous shortcomings, such as the relative lack of resolute definitions for certain phrases used, which has led to malleable judicial application. These undefined phrases have also resulted in rather low thresholds, which expands the term 'terrorism' beyond international comparisons. Discussion will then focus on what this lack of legislative uncertainty means for the rule of law.[3] Alternative options to the phrases currently used in the UK will be analysed. It is suggested that harmonisation with international law is desirable as it may result in a more comprehensive understanding of terrorism and be grounded in a greater degree of fairness.

The aim of this chapter is not to offer a complete exploration of the historical changes surrounding the term 'terrorism', rather it focuses on the legal definition

1 *R v F* [2007] EWCA Crim 243, [29]. See also C. H. Simmons and J. R. Mitch (2001) Labelling Public Aggression: When Is It Terrorism? *The Journal of Social Psychology*, 125(2), 245–251, 245.
2 D. Anderson QC (2014) *The Terrorism Acts in 2013* (The Stationary Office) p.84.
3 Legal terms must be clear and precise, analysis drawn from Lord Carlile of Berriew QC (2007a) Independent Reviewer of Terrorism Legislation, *The Definition of Terrorism*, March 2007, Cm7052, p.21.

of terrorism and presents a commentary on the phrases used within the legislation. The inconsistencies brought to light herein can be described as a legislative failure due to the higher currency fixed to the political value of terrorism in the UK. Concededly, it is not feasible to entirely remove this political value because UK Parliamentarians create law, and terrorism is, after all, a political crime. This chapter therefore advocates for a *permanent* definition of terrorism that is as shorn as practically possible from ambiguous phrasing, focusing on the wrongful nature in line with international law.

Terrorism: the concept

Before considering the law in this area, it is helpful to briefly explore the concept of terrorism and to understand the need for specialist legislation. Terrorism is a unique form of criminality. It often results in the indiscriminate killing of innocent civilians, and is increasingly complex to investigate. Terrorists' capabilities have increased, particularly in the digital age, which has allowed them to remain unknown to the policing and security services until the moment of attack.[4] This goes some way to justify specialist legislative powers.[5] Wilkinson defines terrorism as: 'coercive intimidation or more fully as the systematic use of murder, injury, and destruction or threat of same to create a climate of terror, to publicise a cause, and to coerce a wider target into submitting to its aims'.[6]

It is clear that 'without being noticed terrorism would not exist', meaning the act of killing alone fails to create a terrorist act.[7] The acts to which are assigned the terrorist label are deliberate terrifying events, but without their horrified witnesses, they would be rendered as 'pointless as a play without an audience'.[8] For Wilkinson, the general public understanding of terrorism in the 21st Century includes bombing campaigns, shootings and hostage takings, hijackings and threats of carrying out these actions, aimed at the civilian population.[9] Conceptually and empirically, terrorism can be distinguished from other violent crimes by the following characteristics:

- Premeditated and designed to create a climate of extreme fear;
- Directed at a wider target than the immediate victims;
- Inherently involves attacks on random or symbolic targets, including civilians;

4 J. Klausen (2009) British Counter-Terrorism After 7/7: Adapting Community Policing to the Fight against Domestic Terrorism *Journal of Ethnic and Migration Studies*, 35(3), 403–420, 404. See also *supra* as per The RT Hon Lord Lloyd of Berwick (1996) paragraph 1.7.

5 *Supra* as per D. Anderson QC (2014) p.84.

6 P. Wilkinson (2006) *Terrorism versus Democracy: The Liberal State Response* (2nd Edition, Routledge) pp.20–21. Professor Paul Wilkinson is the former chairman of the Centre for the Study of Terrorism and Political Violence at St Andrew's University.

7 *Ibid.*

8 M. Juergensmeyer (2000) *Terror in the Mind of God: The Global Rise of Religious Violence* (University of California Press) p.139.

9 *Supra* as per P. Wilkinson (2006) p.1.

- Considered by the society in which it occurs as 'extra-normal', that is, in the literal sense that it violates the norms regulating disputes, protest and dissent;
- Used primarily, though not exclusively, to influence the political behaviour of governments, communities or specific social groups.[10]

Since terrorism is directed towards a wider target than the immediate victims, the relationship is different from traditional ideas on violent criminal behaviour. Usually, one would know one's victim, and simply aim the violent criminal aggression towards that person. Hacker recognises this and describes the terrorist relationship as 'triadic', reaching far beyond the immediate victims, involving other observers and the media. Whereas traditional criminal activity is 'dyadic' in nature, meaning that the aggression is limited involving only the attacker and the victim.[11] The placement of fear in the population forms an integral part to the success of a terrorist attack. Essentially aimed at undermining democracy, states are pressured into taking legislative action as they seek to prevent and pre-empt further episodes by providing law enforcement agencies with sufficient powers. Former British Home Secretary Jack Straw registered this in 1999, when he defended to the UK Parliament why special powers and restrictions were desirable, stating: 'Terrorism differs from crime motivated solely by greed in that it is directed at undermining the foundations of government'.[12] This statement brings to the fore the rationale behind the introduction of the Terrorism Act 2000, and within this context, captures terrorism's danger to democracy.[13] Existing criminal law is shown to be inadequate, which points towards the adoption of specialist terrorist offences, especially when considering the international nature of terrorism and the UK's obligations under international law.[14]

The UK Government's former independent reviewer of anti-terrorism legislation, David Anderson QC, supports this contradictory view that terrorist violence is not necessarily worse than ordinary crime, and has therefore recommended a review of criminal law specifically in the area of national security, focused primarily the extent to which it is necessary to supplement ordinary rules and procedures.[15] He seems to advocate for a review of criminal law due to the amount of counter-terrorism legislation that is aimed at early intervention, enacted to safeguard against the worst-case scenario. This is an important point given that, currently, the law criminalises the disseminating of what is deemed terrorist publications,

10 *Ibid.*

11 F. J. Hacker (1980) Terror and Terrorism: Modern Growth Industry and Mass Entertainment, *Studies in Conflict and Terrorism*, 4, 143–159. See also *supra* C. H. Simmons and J. R. Mitch (2001) 246.

12 Jack Straw MP, the then Home Secretary, The Terrorism Bill, Second Reading HC 14 December 1999, col, 152.

13 C. Walker (2009) *Blackstone's Guide to the Anti-Terrorism Legislation* (2nd Edition, Oxford University Press) p.10.

14 *Supra* as per The RT Hon Lord Lloyd of Berwick (1996) Chapter 2, paragraph 2.2 and 2.3.

15 *Supra* as per D. Anderson QC (2014) p.83.

through the use of electronic communications data surveillance. This would have otherwise fallen short of a prosecutable offence under the ordinary criminal law of inchoate offences.[16] McKeever takes this argument further and suggests that action captured by counterterrorism laws is significantly below the standard required by ordinary UK criminal law, whereby 'only that action which goes beyond mere preparation for the commission of the offence, is criminalised as attempt'.[17] The threshold for attempt is extremely high where the suspect must only have the actual crime left to commit.[18] Given the potentially devastating nature of a successful terrorist attack, law enforcement and the courts must be able to intervene *before* this point. Waiting, for example, until the suspect has his finger hovering over the trigger is not a viable option. This is why it is argued that Anderson is potentially incorrect in advocating that counterterrorism laws must be closely associated with ordinary criminal law.[19] Regardless the UK Government has failed to undertake such a review.

It is also worth highlighting that the serious implications of being convicted and labelled a terrorist remain with that person for the rest of their lives. This is because the term has become increasingly pejorative, particularly in the 21st Century, where the terrorist label has a dehumanising effect on the person convicted. This could be due to the inhumane nature of the acts committed by terrorist groups such as al-Qaeda and IS. They are depicted in the graphic and disturbing media released by the group, showing the beheading of non-combatant Western citizens and combatant captives. Justice Collins pointed out the pejorative nature of the label in *R (CC) v Commissioner of Police of the Metropolis and another*, stating:

> once a terrorist always a terrorist whether or not the person in question has renounced his past or circumstances have changed (for example where the acts of terrorism occurred in a country whose government, perhaps because dictatorial and oppressive, has since been overthrown). Indeed, the terrorist may have become a respected and respectable member or even leader of the new government of that country. Nevertheless, he is still a terrorist within the meaning of the [Terrorism Act] 2000.[20]

The law in the UK: the Terrorism Act 2000

The naval stone to the UK's current specialist legislative counterterrorism framework is the Terrorism Act 2000. It legally defines what actions amount to an act

16 Terrorism Act 2006, ss1, 2.
17 D. McKeever (2010) The Human Rights Act and Anti-Terrorism in the UK: One Great Leap Forward by Parliament, but Are the Courts Able to Slow the Steady Retreat that Has Followed?, *Public Law*, January, 110–139, 119.
18 Criminal Attempts Act 1981 s 4(3).
19 *Supra* as per D. Anderson QC (2014) p.83.
20 [2011] EWHC 3316, [5].

of terrorism and is used by UK law enforcement as well as the courts to determine if the criminal action is terrorist related.[21] Under section 1 of the Terrorism Act 2000, for an action to be deemed as terrorist, three collective elements are required: the action or threat of action, the target and the causes.[22] The use or threat of action must involve[23] serious violence against a person,[24] serious damage to property,[25] endanger a person's life,[26] create a serious risk to the health and safety of the public or a section of the public[27] or be designed to seriously interfere with or seriously disrupt an electronic system.[28] The use or threat must also be designed to influence the government or an international organisation[29] or to intimidate the public or section of the public.[30] The second element, however, is expressly made redundant by way of an exclusionary provision when such action or threat of action involves the use of firearms or explosives.[31] In satisfying the causes element, the use or threat must be made for the purpose of advancing a political, religious, racial[32] or ideological cause.[33]

Comparatively, overall the international perspective is not very different in terms of the words used to define an act of terrorism.[34] Although the international community has not entirely succeeded in defining terrorism, the United Nations (UN) Member States have adopted a series of conventions, which attempt to define and criminalise terrorist activities.[35] In 1994 the UN General Assembly condemned terrorist acts as:

> Criminal acts intended or calculated to provoke a state of terror in the general public, a group of persons or particular persons for political purposes are in any circumstance unjustifiable, whatever the considerations of a political,

21 It has also been described as a lynch pin in *R v F* [2007] EWCA Crim 243, [962], a cornerstone [963], and central to counterterrorism legislation [967].
22 *Supra* as per D. Anderson QC (2014) p.75.
23 Terrorism Act 2000, s 1(1)(a).
24 *Ibid* s 1 (2)(a).
25 *Ibid* s 1 (2)(b).
26 *Ibid* s 1 (2)(c).
27 *Ibid* s 1 (2)(d).
28 *Ibid* s 1 (2)(e).
29 International organisation was added to section 1 of the Terrorism Act 2000 by an amendment brought in by the Terrorism Act 2006, s 34(a).
30 Terrorism Act 2000, s1 (1)(b).
31 *Ibid* s 1 (3).
32 The racial element was added to section 1 of the Terrorism Act 2000 by an amendment brought in by the Counter-Terrorism Act 2008, s 75(1).
33 Terrorism Act 2000, s 1(1)(c).
34 *Al-Sirri v Secretary of State for the Home Department (United Nations High Comr for Refugees intervening) DD (Afghanistan) v Same (Same intervening)* [2012] UKSC 54 [25G].
35 A. Martyn (2002) *The Right of Self-Defence under International Law – the Response to the Terrorist Attacks of 11 September*. Australian Law and Bills Digest Group, Parliament of Australia available at http://www.aph.gov.au/About_Parliament/Parliamentary_Departments/Parliamentary_Library/Publications_Archive/CIB/cib0102/02CIB08 accessed 30 March 2018.

philosophical, ideological, racial, ethnic, religious or any other nature that may be invoked to justify them.[36]

Similar to the international situation, the UK's legal definition of terrorism is essential in condemning violations of human rights by other citizens and to ensure adequate protection of both the state and its citizens.[37] It is also argued that 'without a definition of terrorism it is impossible to formulate or enforce international agreements against terrorism'.[38] This is representative of the fact that terrorism is no longer a local problem but an international issue requiring an international unified response. An example of the need to define terrorism in line with other nation states concerns the extradition of terrorists. For Ganor, extradition for political purposes is often expressly forbidden as per the many bilateral and multilateral agreements. However, this can be achieved for the committing of a crime.[39] Although these are important aims, in practical terms the UK's legal definition does nothing more than clarify what actions and causes must be met for the UK executive to use it in determining if an individual's actions amount to terrorism, and thereby seek prosecution, and for the judiciary to then interpret and determine if the case before them amounts to terrorism.

The Terrorism Act 2000 was enacted specifically to provide some permanence to the counterterrorism structure and in order to combat the emerging international Islamist terror threat. This was identified by the research carried out by Lord Lloyd of Berwick working with an inquiry team, where the threat was highlighted as directly affecting the UK, given that many Islamist supporters were permitted direct entry into the UK through the means of asylum in the late 1980s and 90s.[40] Governmental scrutiny of applications was lacking at that time because the UK's primary focus was directed towards Irish-related terrorism.[41] Internationally, it became a well-known fact that Islamist supporters were free to openly fundraise for international terrorist groups and causes, which inevitably led

36 United Nations General Assembly Resolution, 49/60 (1994) Declaration on Measures to Eliminate International Terrorism A/Res/60/49.

37 B. Saul (2008) Defining 'Terrorism' to Protect Human Rights, *Sydney Law School Legal Studies Research Paper* No. 8–125, p.1. See also R. Jackson (2008) An Argument for Terrorism, *Perspectives on Terrorism,* 2(2), 1–12, 1.

38 B. Ganor (2002) Defining Terrorism: Is One Man's Terrorist Another Man's Freedom Fighter? *Police Practice and Research: An International Journal*, 3(4), 287–304, 300.

39 B. Ganor, (2014) Defining Terrorism: Is One Man's Terrorist Another Man's Freedom Fighter? In D. Lowe, A. Turk and D. K. Das, *Examining Political Violence: Studies of Terrorism, Counterterrorism and Internal War* (CRC Press) pp.18–19.

40 G. Joffe (2008) The European Union, Democracy and Counter-Terrorism in the Maghreb, *Journal of Common Market Studies,* 46(1), 147–171, 155.

41 R. S. Leiken (2005) Europe's Mujahideen: Where Mass Immigration Meets Global Terrorism, April 2005, *Center for Immigration Studies*, available at http://cis.org/EuropeMujahideen-ImmigrationTerrorism accessed 30 March 2018. See also *Legislation against Terrorism, A Consultation Paper* (1998) (The Stationary Office Cm 4178) paragraph 4.

French intelligence to describe London as 'Londonistan', the international jihadist/Islamist hub.[42]

In addition to this emerging threat, the UK and the EU fashioned multilateral agreements in a joint effort to combat it, recognising an international threat required an international response, and cooperation.[43] Commonwealth countries and the EU have all provided similar definitions of terrorism within their own legislative frameworks, highlighting this fact. Canada and Australia for example have the same causes, reflecting the international nature and response required to combat the terrorist threats. Although the UK's Terrorism Act 2000 is easily understood by policing and security agencies and the executive, and therefore could be said to serve its purpose well, it has been criticised for being too broad with terms undefined.[44] The words 'threat' and 'influence', and the proliferation of potential causes represent the main contentious issues.

The causes

Let us deal first with the causes. The idea of introducing more potential causes was fashioned by Lord Lloyd in his 1996 report titled 'Inquiry into Legislation Against Terrorism', commissioned by the UK Government of the time.[45] Lloyd's mandate was to assess the potential types of terrorist threats moving forward into the future, and to assess whether permanent counterterrorism legislation would be required, following, at the time, the potential peace settlement in Northern Ireland. Lloyd's research findings led him to conclude that as the Northern Ireland threat would decrease, a new emerging international Islamist threat would increase, rendering the then legal definition under section 20(1) of the Prevention of Terrorism (Temporary Provisions) Act 1989, inadequate. This definition read: '"terrorism" means the use of violence for political ends and includes any use of violence for the purpose of putting the public or any section of the public in fear'.[46] For Lloyd this definition was aimed solely towards dealing with the Irish-related threat, and would therefore prove to be unsatisfactory should a terrorist act be carried out for a single-issue religious or ideological cause rather than a straightforward political cause.[47] Ensuring that the legal definition of terrorism captures *all* terrorist activities, and taking cues from the US Federal Bureau of Investigations (FBI) definition of terrorism, Lloyd recommended social and

42 R. Pantucci (2010) A Contest to Democracy? How the UK has Responded to the Current Terrorist Threat, *Democratization*, 17(2), 251–271, 253, and see also S. Hewitt (2008) *The British War on Terror* (Continuum Books) p.33.

43 A. Kaczorowska (2013) *European Union Law* (3rd Edition, Routledge) pp.17–21.

44 Lord Carlile of Berriew QC (2007a) Independent Reviewer of Terrorism Legislation, *The Definition of Terrorism*, March 2007, Cm7052, p.22.

45 The RT Hon Lord Lloyd of Berwick (1996) *Inquiry into Legislation against Terrorism*, Volume One, (The Stationary Office Cm3420) Chapter 5, paragraph 5.21.

46 Prevention of Terrorism (Temporary Provisions) Act 1989 and the Prevention of Terrorism (Additional Powers) Act 1996.

47 *Supra* as per The RT Hon Lord Lloyd of Berwick (1996) Chapter 5, paragraph 5.21, and Chapter 6, paragraph 6.13.

ideological causes be introduced in addition to a political cause.[48] The UK Government of the time largely agreed, but declined to take on his recommendation for the inclusion of a social cause, opting instead for a religious cause due to the breadth of non-terrorist style crimes it could capture, such as blackmail or extortion.[49] The UK Government's response is confusing for two reasons. First, it seems to imply a generalised terrorist crime exists despite there being no such general criminal offence of terrorism *per se*. Secondly, it is questionable why an ideological cause is included if a social cause was seen as too broad. After all, there appears to be very little difference between the two terms. The impact of the expanded use of these causes is to broaden the definition of terrorism and ultimately serves to cast the net wider, encapsulating a broad range of behaviours.

Specifying the use or threat of action must be for a political, religious, racial or an ideological cause is not unique to the UK. Countries within the Commonwealth have taken a similar approach. Canada, for example, covers the same causes apart from racial.[50] This is also seen in Australia where the Criminal Code 1995 was amended by the Security Legislation Amendment (Terrorism) Act 2002, meaning that the action must be taken for advancing a political, religious or ideological cause, aimed at influencing or intimidating a government, Australian or foreign, or intimidating the public or a section of the public.[51] What is interesting is that the EU's approach differs from that of the UK and other Commonwealth nations insofar as it does not include potential causes in its legal definition of terrorism, whereby specific types of actions must be fulfilled to be determined as terrorist:

> attacks upon a person's life which may cause death, attacks upon the physical integrity of a person, kidnapping or hostage taking, causing extensive destruction to a government or public facility, a transport system, an infrastructure facility, including an information system, a fixed platform located on the continental shelf, a public place or private property likely to endanger human life or result in major economic loss, seizure of aircraft, ships or other means of public or goods transport, [the] manufacture, possession, acquisition, transport, supply or use of weapons, explosives or of nuclear, biological or chemical weapons, as well as research into, and development of, biological and chemical weapons, release of dangerous substances, or causing fires, floods or explosions the effect of which is to endanger human life, interfering with or disrupting the supply of water, power or any other fundamental natural resource the effect of which is to endanger human life.[52]

48 *Ibid* at Appendix E Part 1.
49 *Supra* as per *Legislation Against Terrorism, A Consultation Paper* (1998) 3.16 and 3.17.
50 See the Canadian Criminal Code R.S.C.1985, c. C-46, s 83.01(1)(a) and (b)(i)(A) and (B). Code can be viewed at http://laws-lois.justice.gc.ca/eng/acts/c-46/page-12.html#h-26 accessed 18 March 2018.
51 Criminal Code 1995, s 100.1(b) and (c)(i) and (c)(ii).
52 *Ibid.*

The causes are, however, a

> useful way of categorising non-state terrorist movements or group by their political motivation; ethno-nationalist groups, for example Euzkadi Ta Askatasuna (ETA) in Spain, or ideological motivation, for example the Red Brigades in Germany whose aim was of creating a neo-communist state and socio-economic system.[53]

Wilkinson goes somewhat further than the law provides, detailing a more academic typology of terrorism to include five types:

- Nationalist;
- Ideological;
- Religiopolitical;
- Single-issue;
- State-sponsored and state-supported.[54]

Definition of causes

What does not help is the fact that the UK Government failed to offer an explicit definition of what these new causes *actually* mean, despite the fact that legal discourse and the rule of law demands clarity to ensure denotations are not used or interpreted interchangeably, thereby providing a safe and secure legal framework. It could be argued the causes were not defined for the very reason that it allows for the interpretation to change over time, allowing law enforcement and the UK courts a degree of flexibility when applying the law. Either way, questions regarding the differences between religious and political, racial and ideological can therefore be legitimately raised.[55] As a direct result, the judiciary, applying normal rules of statutory interpretation, have been afforded the task of providing a definition that for Walker has in turn occasioned malleable application. It would appear dissemination by the courts turns on the practicality and evidence put forward, where the terrorist group is in essence placed in a category dependent upon the predominate cause.[56]

The political cause

An example of predominantly political terrorist groups is the various denotations and factions of the Irish Republican Army (IRA), which carried out many terrorist attacks on the British mainland during the Irish Troubles (1969–1997). Its aim

53 *Supra* as per P. Wilkinson (2006) p.4.
54 *Ibid* pp.19–21.
55 Nicholas Ryder (2007) A False Sense of Security? An Analysis of Legislative Approaches Towards the Prevention of Terrorist Finance in the United States and the United Kingdom, *Journal of Business Law*, November, 821–850, 824.
56 *Supra* as per C. Walker (2009) p.10.

was, and still is, to have the British Government relinquish its control over the six northern counties to the Dail in Dublin, unifying Ireland's 32 counties. The threat posed by republican dissident groups remains set at 'severe' in Northern Ireland, and 'substantial' for the UK mainland.[57] The political cause element remained dominant during the Irish Troubles, despite recorded religious intolerance, and therefore proved adequate within the old definition of terrorism under the Prevention of Terrorism Act 1974 (PTA).[58] And the political meaning has not been expressly altered by Parliament under section 1 of the Terrorism Act 2000. As a result, it appears that neither has the judicial approach to the term. It could be argued therefore that the judiciary could potentially widen the term rendering the additional causes redundant. This would serve to bring the law into line with Ganor's research findings, namely that terrorism is always political regardless of the underlying ideological or religious reasons.[59] Walker labours this point, arguing that the UK definition of terrorism is too broad and should focus on the chief cause of terrorist action, being political.[60] What comes through clearly is that the goal of terrorism is to effect political change, which may be underscored by an ideological or religious view.[61] Comay adds currency to this point, proposing political terrorism is in fact always driven by social or ideological ambitions.[62] Ganor has contended the same position where he refers to a statement by Duvall and Stohl, in Schmid's book titled *Political Terrorism*:

> Motives are entirely irrelevant to the concept of political terrorism. Most analysts fail to recognise this and, hence, tend to discuss certain motives as logical or necessary aspects of terrorism. But they are not. At best, they are empirical regularities associated with terrorism. More often they simply confuse analyses.[63]

57 https://www.mi5.gov.uk/threat-levels accessed 30 March 2018.

58 Irish-related terror still remains a threat to the UK's mainland, evidenced by the increase in threat level set by the Joint Terrorism Analysis Centre and the Security Service (MI5), from moderate to substantial in May 2016 https://www.gov.uk/terrorism-national-emergency/terrorism-threat-levels accessed 20 March 2018. See also http://www.bbc.co.uk/news/uk-36267052 accessed 30 March 2018. See also Continuity IRA Claims Responsibility for Dublin Boxing Weigh-in Shooting at Regency Hotel, 30 March 2018, http://www.belfasttelegraph.co.uk/news/republic-of-ireland/continuity-/-claims-responsibility-for-dublin-boxing-weighin-shooting-at-regency-hotel-34433366.html accessed 30 March 2018. For IRA/32CSM see http://www.belfasttelegraph.co.uk/news/republic-of-ireland/continuity-ira-claims-responsibility-for-dublin-boxing-weighin-shooting-at-regency-hotel-34433366.html accessed 30 March 2018.

59 *Supra* as per B. Ganor (2014) p.12.

60 *Supra* as per C. Walker (2009) p.10.

61 *Supra* as per B. Ganor (2014) p.12.

62 M. Comay (1976) Political Terrorism, *Mental Health and Society*, 3, 249–261. See also *supra* as per C. H. Simmons and J. R. Mitch (2001) p.246.

63 A. P. Schmid (1984) *Political Terrorism* (Amsterdam and Transaction Books) p.100. See also *supra* as per B. Ganor (2002) p.294.

The concept of political cause is sufficiently broad, effectively removing the need for other causes.[64] When reviewing this area of law, Lloyd recognised this and in light of it discussed the possibility of retaining the definition under the PTA.[65] The UK Government's response to Lloyd's recommendations illustrated this point, which begs the question as to why other causes were added in the first place: 'The Government notes that Irish, domestic, and international terrorist groups are driven by the same desire to achieve political change by violent means'.[66]

Anderson suggested that the causes elements be 'trimmed' to make the definition clearer and more precise.[67] Trimming the causes is not the same as removing the causes all together. The corollary of this is that it could leave the definition of terrorism even broader, applicable to almost any given criminal offence, unless the potential terrorist offences are *specifically* outlined.[68] It could be argued therefore that the additions of the religious and ideological cause along with the racial cause are unnecessary and problematic, since terrorism is always political.[69]

Contrary to this view, the UK is currently faced with a terror threat inspired by, and based upon, a religious interpretation. Groups such as al-Qaeda and IS want to alter the cast of the Western world by imposing their religious interpretation and strict Sharia law. This, on the face of it, does not appear entirely political. Therefore the religious cause element *is* necessary to capture terrorist action taken under such a cause.

Political or religious cause: the difference

The UK has a deep laying history of dealing with politically inspired terrorism. Religiously inspired terrorism is quite a different story since the UK courts' approach turns on evidential matters in determining the right cause.[70] It must be remembered that the judiciary can apply no real substantive tests because

64 B. Saul (2010) *Defining Terrorism in International Law* (Oxford University Press) p.45. See also B. Xhelili (2012) Privacy & Terrorism Review: Where Have We Come in 10 Years? *Journal of International Commercial Law and Technology*, 7(2), 121–135, 129.

65 *Supra* as per The RT Hon Lord Lloyd of Berwick (1996) Chapter 6, paragraph 6.13: Lord Lloyd stated, 'the existing definition in PTA section 20 "the use of violence for political ends ..." could be retained, subject to the addition of the word "serious" before "violence", and an amplification of what is meant by "political ends"'.

66 *Supra* as per *Legislation against Terrorism, A Consultation Paper* (1998) 3.6.

67 *Supra* as per D. Anderson QC (2014) p.81.

68 *R v Khawaja* [2006] 214 C.C.C. (3rd) 399. Canadian Criminal Code s 83.01(1)(b)(i)(A): the motive clause defines terrorist activity as 'an act or omission, in or outside Canada, that is committed in whole or in part for a political, religious or ideological purpose, objective or cause'. See also *supra* as per C. Walker (2009) p.10. See also *supra* as per D. Anderson QC (2014) p.81.

69 *Supra* as per B. Ganor (2014) p.12. See also discussion on religious tolerance and the rule of law in Lord Bingham (2007) The Rule of Law, *Cambridge Law Journal*, 66 (1), 67–85, 82.

70 *A and Others v Secretary of State for the Home Department* [2004] UKHL 56, [199].

no definition of the causes exists within the Terrorism Act 2000. This was seen in *R (CC) v Commissioner of Police of the Metropolis and another* where Justice Collins refers to the causes listed under the Terrorism Act 2000.[71] The same can be said of all terrorism cases, where the judiciary illustrate this reliance.[72] In *R v G* and *R v J* the House of Lords (now called the UK Supreme Court) heard evidence that J had in his possession a digital file containing documents entitled 'How Can I Train Myself for Jihad?', '39 Ways to Serve and Participate in Jihad' and another called the 'Al Qaeda Training Manual'.[73] Similarly in *R v Zafar*, although much more complex, the fact remained the defendants 'were charged under section 57(1) of the 2000 Act, with possessing computer disks and hard drives containing extreme political and religious material', which the prosecution alleged 'were part of a settled plan to commit a terrorist act or acts in Pakistan'.[74] Academically, Schmid traces the courts' difficulty in assessing whether the terrorist action was inspired by political or religious causes. He argues that 'since terrorists generally challenge the monopoly of violence of the state and its ability to protect its citizens', terrorist acts obtain political significance even when the motivation for them is not primarily political but religious.[75]

Although the UK's Crown Prosecution Service charged *G* and *J*, and *Zafar* with having political and religious motivations, research shows that religious terrorism is inherently different from political terrorism.[76] Pantazis and Pemberton argue that terrorism inspired by a religious cause represents new terrorism and therefore new challenges, stating:

> The *new* terrorism can be differentiated in terms of different actors, motivations, aims, tactics and actions from the *old* twentieth-century concept of terrorism. For instance, the *new* terrorists are inspired by religious extremism and ethnic-separatism (rather than political or ideological causes) and are not predisposed to political negotiation ...[77] [My emphasis]

The difference between religious and political causes becomes more palpable when looking at this issue from a wider context. Research shows that in an exclusively religious context, a key feature of religious practices is the ritual of

71 [2011] EWHC 3316, [3].
72 See *Gillan and Quinton v United Kingdom* [2010] 50 E.H.R.R. 45, [28], and *R (on the application of Lord Carlile of Berriew QC and others) v Secretary of State for the Home Department* [2014] UKSC 60, [17], [118].
73 [2009] UKHL 13, [26]–[27].
74 [2008] 2 WLR 1013.
75 A. P. Schmid (2004) Frameworks for Conceptualising Terrorism, *Terrorism and Political Violence*, 16(2), 197–221, 200.
76 A. Richards (2014) Conceptualizing Terrorism, *Studies in Conflict & Terrorism*, 37 (3), 213–236, 225.
77 C. Pantazis and S. Pemberton (2009) From the "Old" to the "New" Suspect Community: Examining the Impacts of Recent UK Counter-terrorist Legislation, *British Journal of Criminology*, 49(5), 646–666, 650.

making sacrifices.[78] The impact of this line of reasoning means that the terrorist attack and victimisation is often perceived by the terrorist as a *legitimate* sacrifice, in a positive sense, consisting of both attacking innocent citizens viewed as the enemy, and the physical act of killing oneself and becoming a martyr.[79] Human rights violations are rationalised and invoked by a divine law that supersedes man-made laws.[80] The French philosopher Blaise Pascal noted in the 16th Century, 'Men never do evil so openly and contentedly as when they do it from religious conviction.'[81]

The UK courts require substantive evidence to make their assessments. This is where information regarding the particular group(s) that the defendant is accused of having links with, or having been inspired by, become important. The IS terrorist group highlights the ambiguity inherent in the undefined terms, in assessing whether the group is political or religious.[82] Although predominantly religious and following its own extreme interpretation of Islam, the group has evidenced some political aspirations having proclaimed a caliphate in June 2013 crossing the borders of Syria and Iraq.[83] IS appears to satisfy the additional factors needed to exist in order to fuse religion with political violence as laid out by Schmid.[84] The forming of a caliphate sets them apart from other terrorist groups who have a predominantly religious cause, such as al-Qaeda, Jabhat Fatah al-Sham (formally called al-Nusra and aligned with al-Qaeda) and Al-Shabaab, who follow a similar extreme interpretation of Islam

78 D. Young (1999) *Origins of the Sacred: The Ecstasies of Love and War* (St. Martin's Press) p.208.

79 M. Juergensmeyer (2000) *Terror in the Mind of God: The Global Rise of Religious Violence* (University of California Press) p.167: 'The idea of martyrdom is an interesting one. It has a long history within various religious traditions, including early Christianity. Christ himself was a martyr, as was the founder of the Shii′ Muslim tradition, Husain. The word martyr comes from a Greek term for 'witness', such as a witness to one's faith. In most cases, martyrdom is regarded not only as a testimony to the degree of one's commitment, but also as a performance of a religious act, specifically an act of self-sacrifice'.

80 A. H. Cook and M. O. Lounsbery (2011) Assessing the Risk Posed by Terrorist Groups: Identifying Motivating Factors and Threats, *Terrorism and Political Violence*, 23(5), 711–729, 724. See also Hazel Blears in the Counter-Terrorism and Security Bill, House of Commons third sitting, 16 December 2014, Columns 1312–1313.

81 R. S. Robins and J. M. Post (1997) *Political Paranoia: The Psychopolitics of Hatred* (Yale University Press) p.144.

82 The so-called 'Islamic State' is a Salafi Islamist group following an Islamist Wahhabi and Takfiri doctrine developed historically from Sunni Islam. See G. Kepel (2002) *Jihad: The Trail of Political Islam*, (Harvard University Press) pp.219–222. See also S. G. Jones (2014) *A Persistent Threat: The Evolution of al-Qaiada and Other Salafi Jihadists* (RAND National Defense Research Institute) available at https://www.rand.org/content/dam/rand/pubs/research_reports/RR600/RR637/RAND_RR637.pdf accessed 30 March 2018. See also M. Haider (2013) European Parliament Identifies Wahabi and Salafi Roots of Global Terrorism, *Dawn*, available at http://www.dawn.com/news/1029713 accessed 30 March 2018.

83 See http://english.al-akhbar.com/node/20378 accessed 20 March 2018.

84 *Supra* as per A. P. Schmid (2004) p.212.

and enforcement of their religious beliefs through the implementation of Sharia Law.[85]

Although the religious cause was added in response to the rise in the international Islamist threat, its inclusion could now be debatable in light of greater understanding of the Islamic religion, together with the fact that religion for many is very personal and subjective.[86] UK MP's Yasmin Qureshi and Dr Lewis made a similar point during the passing of the Counter-Terrorism and Security Act 2015.[87] Placing this highly contextual term into a piece of legislation is perhaps quite hazardous, especially when considering the UK Government's aim of prevention, and has been seen to damage community relations within the UK.[88] Since the 1990s it has been clear many Muslims perceive that they are treated as a suspect community and targeted by law enforcement agencies due to their religion, and those few who commit terrorist actions, in the name of Islam.[89] It was the early Prevent strategies under the UK's CONTEST policy that proved most divisive, raising these issues whereby the religious cause element was seen as commensurate with Islamophobia.[90] Non-violent and violent extremism here was linked directly to Islamist ideology.[91] The Muslim community subsequently felt, and still feel, discriminated against and demonised for the actions of a few terrorists, using

85 H. Mustapha (2014) The al-Nusra Front: From Formation to Dissension, Policy Analysis Series, *Arab Centre for Research and Policy Studies*, pp.3, 10, 14 and 20. See also S. J. Schulhofer, T. R. Tyler and A. Z. Huq (2011) American Policing at a Crossroads: Unsustainable Policies and the Procedural Justice Alternative, *Journal of Criminal Law & Criminology*, 101(2), 335–374, 369. The al-Nusra groups have now changed their name to al-Sham, for further information see http://edition.cnn.com/2016/08/01/middleeast/al-nusra-rebranding-what-you-need-to-know accessed 30 March 2018.

86 R. Douglas (2010) Must Terrorists Act for a Cause? The Motivational Requirement in Definitions of Terrorism in the United Kingdom, Canada, New Zealand and Australia, *Commonwealth Law Bulletin*, 36(2), 295–312, 303 (3.4). See also M. Elliott (2004) Parliamentary Sovereignty and the New Constitutional Order: Legislative Freedom, Political Reality and Convention, *Legal Studies* 22, 340–376, 322.

87 Counter-Terrorism and Security Bill, House of Commons Second Reading, 2 December 2014, Column 253 for Dr Lewis, and 2 December 2014: Column 262 for Yasmin Qureshi.

88 Counter-Terrorism and Security Bill, House of Commons Second Reading, 2 December 2014, Column 263 as per Jeremy Corbyn MP. See also T. Choudhury and H. Fenwick (2011) The Impact of Counter-terrorism Measures on Muslim Communities, *Equality and Human Rights Commission Research Report 72*, (Durham University), p.8.

89 *Ibid.*

90 D. Batty (2016) Prevent Strategy 'Sowing Mistrust and Fear in Muslim Communities', *Guardian*, 3 February 2016, available at https://www.theguardian.com/uk-news/2016/feb/03/prevent-strategy-sowing-mistrust-fear-muslim-communities accessed 30 March 2018.

91 See *Countering International Terrorism: The United Kingdom's Strategy*, HM Government, July 2006, Cm 6888 at section 3. Although developed from 2003, the revised version was available from 2006.

the name of Islam incorrectly, in their view. This, in turn, challenges integration and the creation of a British and European identity.[92] It has been suggested that this negatively impacts on the positive nature of strong Muslim identity, offering empowerment and allowing them to challenge cultural practices within their own religion.[93] Although politically rather than religiously inspired, in Hillyard's view during the Irish Troubles many Irish Catholics and British born Catholics of Irish descent felt similarly discriminated against by UK counterterrorism legislation aimed at prevention.[94]

In contrast to the above, Pantazis and Pemberton dispute there is any empirical evidence to suggest that the police are currently targeting individuals based needlessly on their religious identity.[95] In any case, the fact remains that IS and al-Qaeda have a religious foundation, made up from an extremist ideology which has, in recent times, been the main terrorist threat, hence why the UK's international terrorist threat level is 'severe'. And as a result the figures show, from 2001 to 2010 there were 237 convictions in the UK for terrorist-related activity, with 87 per cent of these citizens being Muslim.[96]

92 *Supra* as per T. Choudhury and H. Fenwick, (2011) p.8. Also note despite this point being heavily questioned by the Chair, Keith Vaz, at the recent Home Affairs Select Committee hearing on Countering Extremism, Karim and Dad asserted that IS and other similar groups interpret the Quran into their own perverse ideology. They confirmed this ideology is under no circumstances to be regarded as religious, see House of Commons Home Affairs Select Committee, Countering Extremism, Oral Evidence, 2 February 2016, HC428, available at https://www.parliament.uk/business/committees/committees-a-z/commons-select/home-affairs-committee/inquiries/parliament-2015/countering-extremism/publications accessed 12 March 2018.

Evidence heard from Zulfiqar Karim, Bradford Council for Mosques (18 Mosques), and Fazal Dad, Senior Imam, Abu Bakr Mosque, Bradford, 12 January 2016, BBC Parliament Channel viewed 19 February 2016. See also: https://sjiyad.wordpress.com/2014/07/24/7-reasons-why-daesh-are-not-muslim-actually-conflict-with-islam-and-go-against-the-quran accessed 30 March 2018.

93 J. S. Carpenter, M. Levitt and M. Jacobson (2009) Confronting the Ideology of Radical Extremism, *Journal of National Security Law & Policy*, 3, 301–327, 322.

94 See P. Hillyard (1993) *Suspect Community: People's Experience of the Prevention of Terrorism Act in Britain* (Pluto Press).

95 *Supra* as per C. Pantazis and S. Pemberton (2009),

96 *Supra* as per T. Choudhury and H. Fenwick (2011) p.75. See also I. Mandoza (2012) What's in a Name?: Challenging the Word "Islamist", *The Chicago Monitor*, Critical Perspectives on Mainstream Media, available at http://chicagomonitor.com/2012/05/whats-in-a-name-challenging-the-word-islamist/ accessed 30 March 2018. See also P. Beinart (2015) What Does Obama Really Mean by 'Violent Extremism'? *The Atlantic*, available at http://www.theatlantic.com/international/archive/2015/02/obama-violent-extremism-radical-islam/385700 accessed 30 March 2018. See also https://lawyerssecularsociety.wordpress.com/2015/05/01/is-there-really-any-difference-between-islam-and-islamism for debate on the terms used, Islam, Islamism, Islamic and Islamist, accessed 30 March 2018.

Religious or ideological cause?

The former UK Prime Minister David Cameron frequently stated that the IS group is not based on Islam, or Islamic, but on an extremist Islamist ideology.[97] These Islamist groups are based on an extreme view of Sunni Islam, known as Salafi and Wahhabism, upon which the doctrine of Takfir rests. Such a political statement conforms with Neumann's theory surrounding radicalisation, which posits that two elements are always present.[98] First, there must be a grievance, usually rooted in political discontent, and secondly, an ideology.[99] Anderson provides evidence for this, relying on Neumann's theory, confirming that a quarter of all terrorists currently serving custodial sentences in the UK are Muslim converts.[100] Perhaps then, they are not practising religious beliefs at all, but rather an ideological belief founded from the religion, as suggested by Cameron's assertion. This suggests a greater political understanding of the 21st Century terrorist threat and perhaps a move away from utilising the religious cause element. Emphasis is placed on the political value of the terrorist label. Rather than having definitive legal definitions for such phrases, politicians can effectively remove all references to ny of them, or alter the meaning of the phrases to suit their particular needs at any given time, thereby applying them malleably.

Pantucci indicates this is the case by putting forward a rather negative argument that by adding a religious cause into the UK legal definition of terrorism, the Government can effectively decide who are good Muslims and who are bad, by their own engagement within their communities.[101] However, it could be argued that rather than the negative viewpoint put forward here by Pantucci, it is simply a matter of UK law enforcement and the Government, making their way through a new threat that they did not entirely understand. In the early days of the Islamist threat, UK policing and security agencies were learning about this new threat first hand and serious questions required answering, such as who they were and what type of threat they pose.[102]

97 O. Crowcroft (2015) What's the Correct Name for the World's Most Dangerous Terrorists? *International Business Times*, available at http://www.ibtimes.co.uk/why-isis-hate-being-called-daesh-whats-correct-name-worlds-most-dangerous-terrorists-1531506 accessed 30 March 2018. See also http://www.dnaindia.com/world/report-isis-is-not-islamic-call-them-daesh-david-cameron-2151363 accessed 30 March 2018.

98 P. R. Neumann, opinion cited in M. Sedgwick (2010) The Concept of Radicalisation as a Source of Confusion, *Terrorism and Political Violence*, 22(4), 480.

99 A. P. Schmid (2013) *Radicalisation, De-Radicalisation, Counter-Radicalisation: A Conceptual Discussion and Literature Review* (International Centre for Counter-Terrorism – The Hague (ICCT)), p.3.

100 Home Affairs Select Committee, Countering Extremism. Evidence heard from David Anderson QC, Independent Reviewer of Anti-Terrorism Legislation, 19 January 2016, BBC Parliament Channel viewed 19 February 2016.

101 R. Pantucci (2010) A Contest to Democracy? How the UK has Responded to the Current Terrorist Threat, *Democratization*, 17(2), 251–271, 262.

102 C. Andrew (0000) The Rise of the Islamist Terrorist Threat, Security Service MI5, available at https://www.mi5.gov.uk/the-rise-of-the-islamist-terrorist-threat accessed 12 March 2018.

The ideological cause, in particular, is perhaps better referred to as a 'catch-all' cause. The problem here is the broadness of the term 'ideological' which could potentially capture anything such as animal rights groups' activity or anti-abortion groups not normally associated with the 21st Century general understanding of terrorism.[103] During the drafting stages of the Terrorism Act 2000 Parliamentarians raised concerns about the inclusion of the ideological cause. The then Home Secretary Jack Straw was questioned as to whether or not industrial strike action would amount to an act of terrorism, as per the definition, which was topical at the time given the UK fire fighters were on national strike.[104] Such action could have been perceived as influencing the Government for an ideological cause, to alter its policy on pay and working conditions, and subsequently be found to be endangering people's lives by withdrawing labour.[105]

Although the Home Secretary unequivocally confirmed that although industrial action would be omitted from capture, this fact is not reflected in the legislation, despite his assurances the ideological cause was aimed at action by eco-terrorism, anti-abortion groups and animal liberation groups mentioned above. Without legislative certainty, the suggestion is transmitted that there is little in place to legitimately stop a successive government deeming such action as terrorist. Furthermore, industrial action has been expressly omitted from the legal definition of terrorism in Canada and Australia. In addition to omitting industrial action, the Canadian legal definition of terrorism does not include an act or omission committed during an armed conflict, as in accordance with customary international law, or the activities by military forces or a state in exercise of their duties, as discussed further below.[106]

The causes and freedom of expression

There is perhaps little to deny the effectiveness of the causes element when looking into the terrorist offences introduced, for example, under sections 1 and 2 of the Terrorism Act 2006. Enacted in the aftermath of the 7 July London bombings in 2005, the provisions were introduced to deal with religious extremist hate preachers and the sheer amount of extremist religious text available in print and online that served to influence others to become a terrorist. To this end, section 1 criminalises the encouragement of terrorism and section 2 the distribution of terrorist publications, which may inspire terrorist action.[107] In practice, this broadly phrased Act can then be used by policing and security agencies when differentiating between freedom of expression and expression that crosses the line into potential terrorist activity, when carrying out electronic communications data surveillance under an Investigatory Powers Act 2016 (IPA) authority.

103 *Supra* as per P. Wilkinson (2006) p.4.
104 *Supra* as per C. Walker (2009) p.10.
105 *Ibid.*
106 *Ibid.*
107 These can be committed recklessly, which certainly has an impact on Article 10 Freedom of expression under the ECHR.

Utilising this authority, if law enforcement, monitoring electronic communications data through the IPA authority, discovered, for example, a citizen planning to carry out attacks in the name of the Irish republican cause, then this may satisfy the political element. Similarly, if a person were to advocate serious violence with the aim of preserving animal rights by attempting to force the UK to keep the Hunting Act 2004 in place, this may raise law enforcements alarm when picking up electronic communications data that could be seen as potentially terrorist acts, satisfying the ideological element. This is further emphasised by the fact that the provisions in the Terrorism Act 2006 rely on the definition of terrorism under the Terrorism Act 2000, as raised prior to the enactment, in the Third Report of Session 2005–2006 of the Joint Committee of the House of Lords and House of Commons on Human Rights.[108] The breadth of the Terrorism Act 2006 mixed together with the broad definition of terrorism raised serious concerns for the Committee where they found

> the creation of the offence of encouragement of terrorism defined as broadly as in section 1 of the Terrorism Act 2000 is to criminalise any expression of a view that armed resistance to a brutal or repressive anti-democratic regime might in certain circumstances be justifiable, even where such resistance consists of campaigns of sabotage against property, and specifically directed away from human casualties.[109]

Former Home Secretary, John Reid MP, admitted this was the effect of the offence, but went on to defend the scope saying: '[T]here is nowhere in the world today where violence can be justified as a means of bringing about political change.'[110] The Committee remained concerned and called for urgent changes to the definition of terrorism to be brought in line with the EU Council Framework Decision and the UN Security Council Resolution 1566, 'to avoid a high risk of such provisions being found to be incompatible with Article 10 ECHR freedom of expression and related Articles'.[111] Other low threshold parts to the definition of terrorism were pointed out to this regard, such as the phrase 'influence'.

Even putting the scope to one side, the 2006 Act has not been particularly successful for the UK given there have only been a few convictions. This could be due to the high threshold of evidence required, and could also be in part because these types of terrorist activities take place on the Internet. Now that the IPA has been passed, the chances of law enforcement's alarm being raised by such behaviour are set to arguably increase exponentially. Testing whether or not the line into terrorist activity has been crossed, the IPA's bulk interception, bulk acquisition and bulk equipment interference powers, discussed in Chapter 3, will play a

108 HL Paper 75-I, HC 561-I.
109 *Ibid* paragraph 12.
110 *Ibid.*
111 *Ibid,* In attempting to satisfy the Committee's concerns, the then Home Secretary announced Lord Carlile of Berriew would undertake a review of the definition of terrorism.

huge role in the 21st Century, in the digital age. This, in turn, could generate a surge in use of the Terrorism Act 2006.

The threshold of influence

The word influence is extraordinarily broad particularly when taken together with 'the ideological cause'. It does not fit comparatively with other jurisdictions, especially when the fact that protests and industrial actions are not expressly safeguarded under UK legislation.[112] Illustrative of the UK's ability to 'gold-plate' EU law and international law, utilising catchall phrasing of this nature has been criticised by Anderson as setting the bar 'remarkably low'.[113] In Anderson's analysis, he draws on comparable definitions from the EU, Council of Europe, the UN, Commonwealth countries and the US, where the standard is set higher, substituting the word influence for 'compel,[114] unduly compel,[115] influence by intimidation,[116] coerce,[117] intimidate,[118] and force'.[119] Lord Lloyd, in drawing from the FBI's definition suggested, 'to intimidate or coerce a government' should become the set standard.[120] In attempting to satisfy the concerns raised in the Third Report of Session 2005–2006 of the Joint Committee of the House of Lords and House of Commons on Human Rights, the then Home Secretary John Reid MP announced Lord Carlile of Berriew would undertake a review of the definition of terrorism. Carlile inevitably agreed with Lloyd and pressed the point in his 2007 report to the then Government: 'The existing law should be amended [to ensure] actions cease to fall within the definition of terrorism if intended *only to influence* ... ' [my emphasis].[121]

112 See the Canadian Criminal Code R.S.C.1985, c. C-46, s 83.01(1)(b)(ii)(E).
113 *Supra* as per D. Anderson (2014) p.85.
114 Canadian Criminal Code R.S.C.1985, c. C-46.
115 Council Framework Decision on combating terrorism 2002/475/JHA.
116 Uniting and Strengthening America by Providing Appropriate Tools Required to Intercept and Obstruct Terrorism Act of 2001, s 2331, Part 1 Chapter 113B (ii) of the United States Code 18. However, when assessing domestic terrorism the threshold is lowered to 'influence the policy of a government', under Part 5B(ii).
117 The Federal Bureau of Investigation's US Code of Federal Regulations, see http://www.fbi.gov/about-us/investigate/terrorism/terrorism-definition accessed 30 March 2018.
118 *Ibid.*
119 *Supra* as per D. Anderson QC (2014) p.86.
120 *Supra* as per The RT Hon Lord Lloyd of Berwick (1996) Appendix E, Part 1. See also G. Joffe (2008) The European Union, Democracy and Counter-Terrorism in the Maghreb, *Journal of Common Market Studies*, 46(1), 147–171, 155. The FBI's US Code of Federal Regulations defines terrorism as, 'the unlawful use of force and violence against persons or property to intimidate or coerce a government, the civilian population, or any segment thereof, in furtherance of political or social objectives'. The FBI's US Code of Federal Regulations, see http://www.fbi.gov/about-us/investigate/terrorism/terrorism-definition accessed 30 March 2018.
121 *Supra* as per Lord Carlile of Berriew QC.(2007) p.47.

This made little difference in the end as John Reid defended the existing law in his reply to Carlile, explaining he did not see the use of the word influence as setting the bar too low. It would appear that despite the reservations over this low threshold, not only advanced by the independent reviewers but also the judiciary and academic community, the Government remains unwilling to change it.[122] According to Anderson's findings, the rationale behind the unwillingness to raise the threshold to 'intimidate', for instance, is that the phrase itself removes the possibility of argumentation being raised surrounding whether or not the Government can actually be intimidated by terrorist actions or threat of actions.[123] An example of hostage taking was posed, whereby the release negotiated by the Government, or an international organisation, would come more readily within the ambit of influence, rather than intimidate.[124] Anderson was not swayed by this argument and, valorising his position, it is suggested that the phrase 'unduly compel' should serve as the replacement for 'influence'. Considering that influencing the Government is the legitimate aim of all political activity, such as the recent strike action by junior doctors in 2016, it is unsafe for the UK Government to continue its use in counterterrorism legislation.[125] As to whether or not the Government can actually be intimidated or influenced, or indeed the life of the nation threatened merely by an act of terrorism, this was raised in *A and Others v Secretary of State for the Home Department* where Lord Hoffmann made it clear that citizens' lives are incomparable with the life of the nation:

> its institutions and values, endure through generations … England is the same nation as it was at the time of the first Elizabeth or the Glorious Revolution. The [Spanish] Armada threatened to destroy the life of the nation, not by loss of life in battle, but by subjecting English institutions to the rule of Spain and the Inquisition. The same was true of the threat posed to the [UK] by Nazi Germany in the Second World War. This country, more than any other in the world, has an unbroken history of living for centuries under institutions and in accordance with values which show a recognisable continuity.[126]

The EU's approach certainly seems to raise the threshold. Article 1 of the EU Council Framework Decision on combating terrorism provides that terrorism includes:

122 *Supra* as per D. Anderson QC (2014) p.88.
123 *Ibid.*
124 *Ibid.*
125 P. Crish (2016) Junior Doctors' Strikes Will Continue as Minister Plans to Impose New Contracts, CIPD available at http://www.cipd.co.uk/pm/peoplemanagement/b/weblog/archive/2016/02/12/junior-doctors-39-strikes-will-continue-as-minister-plans-to-impose-new-contracts.aspx accessed 30 March 2018.
126 *A and Others v Secretary of State for the Home Department* [2004] UKHL 56, [91].

1 seriously intimidating a population;
2 unduly compelling a Government or international organisation to perform or abstain from performing any act;
3 seriously destabilising or destroying the fundamental political, constitutional, economic or social structures of a country or an international organisation.[127]

The actions that amount to terrorism are similar to those in the UK and Commonwealth countries.[128] The phrases used, however, appear to raise the threshold in terms of what aims amount to terrorism. As opposed to the UK's 'intimidate the public' and 'influence a government', the EU's model stipulates that the action must 'seriously intimidate a population' and 'unduly compel a government'.[129] This is a much more thorough definition. No counterterrorism legislation existed in the EU prior to al-Qaeda's terrorist attacks on the US on 11 September 2001. The EU responded to this attack by introducing the framework decision previously mentioned.[130] The purpose was to ensure Member States responded to the transnational threat and to enable cooperation between them supported by EU policy programmes.[131] The then EU's Justice and Home Affairs Council confirmed that the protection of the lives and property of its citizens, within the area of citizenship, freedom, security and justice, is the core task providing legitimacy to extensive public powers and policies, where EU citizens expect EU action to protect their health and safety.[132] Canada uses similar language in its approach to defining terrorism where section 83.01(1) and (b) of the Canadian Criminal Code defines terrorism as:

> as an act or an omission, inside or outside Canada that is committed for a political, religious or ideological objective or cause, and with the intention of *intimidating* the public or a segment of the public, or *compelling* a person, government or organisation to do or to refrain from doing any act, whether inside or outside of Canada.[133] [My emphasis]

127 *Supra* as per EU Council Framework Decision (2002/475/JHA).
128 *Ibid.*
129 *Ibid.*
130 C. C. Murphy (2015) *EU Counter-Terrorism Law: Pre-Emption and the Rule of Law* (Hart Publishing) p.17.
131 European Commission (2007) Report from the Commission based on Art 11 of the Council Framework Decision of 13 June 2002 on combatting terrorism, Brussels, COM(2007)681 6 November 2007, p.10.
132 European Council (2005b) *Communication from the Commission to the Council and the European Parliament*, Brussels COM(2005)124 6 April 2005, p.2. See also Council of the European Union (2005) The European Union Counter-terrorism Strategy 14469/4/05 30 November 2005.
133 See the Canadian Criminal Code R.S.C.1985, c. C-46, s 83.01(1)(a) and (b)(i)(A) and (B). See also R. Douglas (2010) Must terrorists act for a cause? The motivational requirement in definitions of terrorism in the United Kingdom, Canada, New Zealand and Australia, *Commonwealth Law Bulletin* 36(2), 295–312, 295.

Although the 'compelling' element raises the threshold, the addition of 'person' arguably balances this. The UK specifies that 'serious' violence is required, against mere 'violence' here, albeit that intentionally:

> causes death or serious bodily harm to a person, endangers a person's life, causes a serious risk to the health or safety of the public or any segment of the public, causes substantial property damage, whether to public or private property, if causing such damage is likely to result in the conduct or harm referred to in any of clauses (A) to (C), or, causes serious interference with or serious disruption of an essential service, facility or system, whether public or private, other than as a result of advocacy, protest, dissent or stoppage of work that is not intended to result in conduct referred to in any of clauses (A) to (C).[134]

The Canadian definition explicitly includes: 'conspiracy, attempt or threat to commit any such act or *omission*, or being an accessory after the fact or counselling in relation to any such act or omission'[135] (my emphasis). The Australian definition is also similar in its approach, where the Criminal Code 1995 was amended by the Security Legislation Amendment (Terrorism) Act 2002, meaning that the action must be taken for advancing a political, religious or ideological cause, aimed at influencing or intimidating a government, Australian or foreign, or intimidating the public or a section of the public.[136] The Australian legislation, similar to the Canadian model, also omits action taken by way of protest, dissent or industrial action.[137] Serving to lower the UK's threshold further and effectively remove the necessity for an action to influence the Government or international organisation is section 1(3) of the Terrorism Act 2000. It contains an exclusionary provision for the use of firearms and explosives.[138] The UK's definition of terrorism thus changes to: 'the use or threat of action, involving firearms or explosives, made for the purpose of advancing a political, religious, racial or ideological cause'.

At first glance, the importance of this provision might be questioned given the obviousness that such destructive methods and action must be terrorism. It is argued, however, that this serves to overcomplicate the definition of terrorism, as it is irrelevant and unnecessary given that such action would most certainly serve to intimidate the public, or section of the public in any regard.[139] Similar to the proliferation of causes, it adds further convolution to an already complex definition, unnecessarily stretching the applicability of the terrorist label.[140] As an example, should a citizen decide to threaten (i.e. the use or threat of action) a bank manager with a firearm (i.e. involving firearms or explosives) for the purposes

134 See the Canadian Criminal Code R.S.C.1985, c. C-46, s 83.01(1)(a) and (b)(i)(A) and (B), (ii)(A) to (E).
135 *Ibid.*
136 Criminal Code 1995, s 100.1(b) and (c)(i) and (c)(ii).
137 Criminal Code 1995, s 100.3(a).
138 Terrorism Act 2000, s 1(1)(b).
139 R. English (2010) *Terrorism: How to Respond* (Oxford University Press) p.4.
140 *Supra* as per C. H. Simmons and J. R. Mitch (2001) p.246. See also *ibid* p.90.

of having the bank cancel all existing debt of all local citizens (i.e. made for the purpose of advancing an ideological cause), the terrorist label here could potentially be ascribed. Thus one could argue the provision removes the triadic nature of terrorism, thereby supporting Hacker's earlier assertion that the terrorist label could move to the dyadic.[141]

Anderson would disagree that this provision unnecessarily stretches the applicability of the label. He also believes that although the significance of this provision may be small, to effectively remove the target provision would directly counter the intention of the Terrorism Act 2000.[142] Anderson did, however, go on to recommend the removal of this provision in his 2014 report, noting he was not swayed by the argument put forward by the then Home Secretary Charles Clarke: '[section 1(3)] … is to cover for instance, an assassination in which the terrorist's motive might be less to put the public in fear, or to influence the Government, than to "take out" the individual …'.[143]

Anderson further explains that there is no reason as to why such action should be seen as terrorism, and not simply murder. Critically, he appears to have overlooked the fact that this provision fits within the rather historical rationale used by the international community in attempting to define an act of terrorism.

Extra-jurisdictional effect of UK law: an international threat needs an international response

The similarity between the legal definitions of terrorism between nation states within the Commonwealth and the EU illustrates the international nature of the 21st Century terrorism threat and the fact that international security is as important as national security.[144] Simply put, 21st Century terrorists do not recognise borders, rendering such provisions essential within the guise of international cooperation.[145] This legal similarity is pertinent when the policing and security services are monitoring electronic communications data between members of the same group communicating in different parts of the world, for example, UK IS fighters in Iraq communicating with UK IS members encouraging or planning attacks in the UK.

To this end and similar to other nation states, an extra-jurisdictional approach is introduced by way of section 1(4) of the Terrorism Act 2000, stating that an act of terrorism applies to one committed or planned in any state in the world, not just the UK. The definition of Government came under judicial scrutiny in *R v F* and *R v Gul*, where the UK Court of Appeal held that the phrase was not restricted to representative or democratic governments, applying to all countries, additionally and controversially, to those governed by

141 *Supra* as per F. J. Hacker (1980) pp.143–159.
142 *Supra* as per D. Anderson (2014) p.89.
143 *Ibid.*
144 *Supra* as per The RT Hon Lord Lloyd of Berwick (1996) Chapter 2, paragraph 2.4.
145 *Ibid.*

tyrants and dictators.[146] It may be the case that the apprehension of the UK being known internationally as a safe haven for terrorists and supporters made its way from Parliamentarians to the judiciary.[147] Focusing on *Gul*, his appeal against conviction for terrorist offences was based on a number of factors. Overall *Gul's* legal argument turned on his assertion that section 1 of the Terrorism Act 2000 was too broad given its inheritance:

1 The Terrorism Act 2000 intended to give effect to the UK's international treaty obligations and the concept of terrorism in international law does not extend to military attacks by a non-state armed group against state, or inter-governmental organisation, armed forces in the context of a non-international armed conflict, and that this limitation should be implied into the definition in section 1;
2 Rather closely connected, the second argument was based on the fact that it would be wrong to read the Terrorism Acts of 2000 or 2006 as criminalising in the UK an act abroad, unless that act would be regarded as criminal by international law norms;
3 The third argument raised by the appellant was that some qualifications must be read into the very wide words of section 1 of the Terrorism Act 2000.[148]

Unlike comparative nation states, the UK does not omit action taken during an international armed conflict. The first argument therefore is largely correct. The International Convention for the Suppression of Terrorist Bombings in 1997 and the International Convention for the Suppression of the Financing of Terrorism in 1999 excludes attacks by insurgents on military forces during non-international armed conflicts.[149] Additionally, the 1977 Additional Protocol I to the 1949 Geneva Conventions (protection is afforded within Article 14 of the UN Charter) relates to international armed conflict, which has the effect of somewhat indemnifying insurgents fighting against occupation in exercising self-determination during international armed conflicts.[150]

Despite previous international attempts at creating a definition of terrorism, in 2012 the UN General Assembly still could not agree on the differences between terrorism and a 'legitimate struggle of peoples fighting in the exercise of their right to self-determination'.[151] For McKeever, it is difficult to reconcile 'both the

146 *R v F* [2007] EWCA Crim 243, [9], [16], and *R v Gul* [2012] EWCA Crim 280, [23], [51], and *R v Gul* [2013] UKSC 64, [42], and the Terrorism Act 2000 s 1(4)(d), ' "the government" means the government of the United Kingdom, of a Part of the United Kingdom, or a country other than the United Kingdom'.
147 *R v F* [2007] EWCA Crim 243, [16] and *R v Gul* [2012] EWCA Crim 280 [51].
148 [2012] UKSC 64, [24].
149 [2012] UKSC 64, [52]. See also Terrorism Act 2000 ss 62–64 that formed the basis of *Gul's* argument, that the Terrorism Act 2000 and by extension the Terrorism Act 2006 should conform to the international norm, given they were enacted under the UK's international obligations. The second part focused on the criminalisation of terrorist actions being more comprehensive and wider in the UK than required by international norms, [2013] UKSC 64, [43], and *R v Gul* [2012] EWCA Crim 280, [19](i)(ii).
150 *R v Gul* [2012] EWCA Crim 280, [28].
151 *R v Gul* [2013] UKSC 64, [45]–[47].

general abhorrence for violence which is indiscriminate and/or actively targets civilians, with the acknowledgment that some forms of political oppression may be so unjust as to legitimate violent action by the oppressed'.[152] To deal with the freedom fighter conundrum and to secure an effective move forwards, the International Community has attempted to focus on the wrongful nature of terrorism, rather than on the intent.[153] As a result, subsequent conventions have adopted an operational definition of a specific type of terrorist act, without referring to underlying motivational aspects, or causes, be it for political or ideological purposes.[154] The primary focus is concentrated on non-state actors adopting a criminal law enforcement model to address the problem, with emphasis on increasing global cooperation.[155]

Returning to the UK, the Supreme Court rejected the idea of judicial intervention that would effectively serve to introduce legislative change allowing for some sort of freedom fighter exclusion.[156] The Court decided that the nature of the broad definition was known to Parliament prior to enactment and it has had the opportunity to revisit it, as a result of the various independent reviewers of anti-terrorism legislation conclusions and recommendations.[157] Another point worth signalling is that the UK's legislative measures and the judicial response may have been different if the EU Council's Framework Decision in 2002 contained similar freedom fighter type exclusions. As accepted by the Supreme Court, the UK Parliament is supreme and able to legislate on any matters it chooses.

In his analysis written prior to the UK Supreme Court's findings, Coco supports *Gul's* arguments and raises several important issues, proposing the UK Court of Appeal should have interpreted the UK domestic legislation in light of current international frameworks.[158] However, his analysis appears to fall on the pretence that the UK Parliament cannot gold-plate international law and that UK courts, although not requested to do so in this case, can question the validity of Acts of Parliament. Theory surrounding UK Parliamentary Sovereignty suggests the UK Parliament is capable of gold-plating and constructing law on any matter it chooses.[159] It is important to note the capability of the UK Parliament in creating

152 *Supra* as per D. McKeever (2010) p.114.

153 A. Gioia (2006) The UN Conventions on the Prevention and Suppression of International Terrorism. In G. Nesi (ed.), *International Cooperation in Counter-terrorism: The United Nations And Regional Organizations in the Fight Against Terrorism* (Ashgate) p.4.

154 A. Byrnes (2002) Apocalyptic Visions and the Law: The Legacy of September 11, a professorial address by Byrnes at the ANU Law School for the Faculty's Inaugural and Valedictory Lecture Series.

155 *Ibid.*

156 [2013] UKSC 64, [33]–[38].

157 *Ibid*, [39].

158 A. Coco (2013) The Mark of Cain, *Journal of International Criminal Justice* 11(2), 425.

159 *R v Gul* [2012] UKSC 64, [53]. See also K. Syrett (2011) *The Foundations of Public Law, Principles and Problems of Power in the British Constitution* (Palgrave Macmillan) p.100, 'Gold-plating' is the exercise that refers to the UK Government legislating further than is required by international law.

unfettered extra-territorial provisions.[160] This has been seen in other types of statues, such as section 72 of the Sexual Offences Act 2003 and section 1 of the War Damages Act 1965.[161] The only time an Act of Parliament may be challenged by the courts is if the legal matter in question relates to an EU provision, or the UK statute contravenes the ECHR as per the Human Rights Act 1998.[162]

Unlike other comparative jurisdiction there is no defence in the UK, freedom fighter style or otherwise available for an accused to use within the terms under the Terrorism Act 2000, which does not exempt what could be termed 'terrorism in a just cause'.[163] The Canadian judiciary in *R v Khawaja* tested the Canadians' armed conflict exclusion, where *K* claimed that the situation in Afghanistan since 2002 represented a war within the legal definition and therefore his actions were carried out during an armed conflict and in accordance with international law.[164] However, because *K*'s actions involved acts of violence in the UK and Pakistan, and were based on a violent Islamist ideology, the Court found his actions went beyond the Afghanistan conflict. The Court also held the conflict in Afghanistan represented an armed insurrection carried out based on violent jihad against the newly appointed Afghan Government, and non-Islamic regimes and civilians.[165] This illustrates that even when a state has a freedom fighter style defence, the tests applied by the judicial authority appear to be stringent and protective of maintaining the status quo. This fits with Netanyahu's postulation that freedom fighters are in fact not capable of perpetrating terrorist acts:

> For in contrast to the terrorist, no freedom fighter has ever deliberately attacked innocents. He has never deliberately killed small children, or passers-by in the street, ,merely associated ethnically or religiously with the people of that area ... The conclusion we must draw from all this is evident. Far from being a bearer of freedom, the terrorist is the carrier of oppression and enslavement.[166]

The facts discussed in *Gul* however, highlight that even if a freedom fighter exclusion did exist within the UK's legislative framework, it would have made little difference to the outcome. It also suggests the unimportance of the UK Court seeking advice as to whether or not the conflicts were to be regarded as an international armed conflict, given *Gul* posted a video containing not only attacks on

160 *R v Gul* [2012] EWCA Crim 280, [56], and *R v Gul* [2013] UKSC 64.
161 *Madzimbamuto v Lardber-Burke* [1969] 1 AC 645, [723], See also *supra* as per K. Syrett (2011) p.104.
162 See *Mccartys Ltd. v Smith* [1980] ECR 1275 (Case 129/79) for EU law, and see *Gillan v UK* [2010] 50 EHRR 45 (4158/05) (ECHR) for ECHR.
163 *Ibid*, [27]. See also *supra* as per D. McKeever (2010) p.113.
164 [2012] SCC69, [2012] 3 S.C.R. 555.
165 *Ibid*, [100], [102].
166 B. Netanyahu (1985) *Terrorism: How the West Can Win* (Farrar, Strauss and Giroux) p.27.

Coalition forces, but also civilians that were in the US twin towers on 11 September 2001 at the time of al-Qaeda's attack. It also included other attacks on civilians and excerpts from martyrdom videos with symbols associated with proscribed organisations listed under Schedule 2 of the Terrorism Act 2000.[167] Despite these facts the Court thought the need to elucidate further, confirming international law had developed insofar as criminalising terrorism in times of peace.[168] International Humanitarian Law and International Criminal Law specifically refer to civilians and organised groups within their definition, and cover acts of terrorism during an international armed conflict.[169] Defining terrorism as an act carried out primarily against civilians, international rules such as those provided by article 33(1) of the Fourth Geneva Convention, effectively ban terrorism, with other conventions considering it to be a war crime.[170]

What is clear from the UK court's decision in not allowing a freedom fighter defence is that it finds the idea of branding some types of terrorism as officially acceptable unpalatable:

> acts by insurgents against the armed forces of a state anywhere in the world which seek to influence a government … made for political purposes are terrorism. There is no exemption for those engaged in an armed insurrection and an armed struggle against a government.[171]

Although this statement may add some weight to Coco's argument, it seems to suggest the courts have universal jurisdiction over terrorism.[172] In response to such criticism the UK Court of Appeal relied on the *Lotus* case presided over by the Permanent Court of International Justice. This affirmed that its jurisdiction was not questionable given the lack of explicit prohibitions against labelling as terrorism non-state armed groups' attacks on state armed forces, in non-international armed conflicts.[173] Furthermore, although the evidence given by the former UK Foreign Secretary confirmed the conflicts in Afghanistan and Iraq during 2008 and 2009 were regarded as non-international armed conflicts, thereby rendering *Gul's* argument weightless, the impact of the judicial decision reinforces the UKs Government's commitment to the international effort to combat terrorism and serves to prevent individuals from planning action to take place on foreign soil

167 *R v Gul* [2012] EWCA Crim 280, [6], [20](1)(2). See also Terrorism Act 2000, s 3 (1)(a) and Schedule 2.
168 *Ibid*, [33].
169 A. Cassese (2008) *International Criminal Law* (2nd Edition, Oxford University Press) p.171.
170 Fourth Geneva Convention 1949: 'terrorist acts are prohibited if perpetrated by civilians or organised groups in occupied territories or in the territory of a party to the conflict'. See also Second Additional Protocol 1977, Articles 4(1), 4(2)(d), 13(2), 51 (2). See also *ibid* pp.171–173.
171 *R v Gul* [2012] EWCA Crim 280, [16].
172 *Supra* as per A. Coco (2013).
173 *S. S. Lotus (France v Turkey)* [1927] PCIJ Series A, No 10, [44], and *R v Gul* [2012] EWCA Crim 280, [47]–[49].

from the UK.[174] This mirrors the approach taken by the UK Government at the time of drafting the Terrorism Act 2000. Seeking to protect foreign governments from terrorism planned and organised in the UK was additionally reinforced by the Crime (International Co-operation) Act 2003 that confirms a resident in the UK would be guilty of an offence if actions abroad would constitute an offence within the UK under the Terrorism Act 2000.[175] It would be instructive to see where the UK Government would stand should a citizen return from fighting in Syria or Iraq with Kurdish forces against IS, given this has not been recognised as an international armed conflict.[176] At the time of writing, many UK citizens are fighting alongside Kurdish forces, who are currently battling for Mosul against IS's stronghold.[177] For some states, such as Turkey, the British citizens fighting with the People's Protection Units (YPG) are classed as terrorists, but in the UK they are not.[178] This is dependent upon which group or organisation citizens join. For example, in relation to Turkey, which has been in conflict with the Kurdish group the Kurdistan Workers' Party (PKK), where the PKK are looking for the independence of Kurdish territory from Turkey, under section 3 and Schedule 2 of the Terrorism Act 2000, the PKK are a proscribed group in the UK. As such they are seen as a terrorist organisation, yet the YPG and the Women's Protection Units (YPJ) in Syria, which are the army factions of the Syrian Kurds currently fighting IS and the al-Assad regime are not proscribed, and as such any UK citizen who joins the YPG/YPJ would not be deemed to be a terrorist and neither are the actions of this group seen as terrorist action in the UK.[179] Turkey, on the other

174 *R v F* [2007] EWCA Crim 243, [9], [16], and *R v Gul* [2012] EWCA Crim 280, [20], [23], [28], [51], and *R v Gul* [2013] UKSC 64. See also A. Murray (2012) Acts of War or Acts of Terrorism? Case Comment, *Journal of Criminal Law*, 76(4), 298–302, 299.

175 Crime (International Co-operation) Act 2003, s 63A-E. Terrorism Act 2000 ss 54, 56–61.

176 E. Saner (2015) Brits Abroad: Is It against the Law to Fight ISIS? *Guardian*, 25 February 2015, available at https://www.theguardian.com/world/shortcuts/2015/feb/25/brits-abroad-against-law-fight-isis accessed 30 March 2018.

177 See http://www.bbc. co.uk/news/world-middle-east-33083213 and http://www.bbc.co.uk/news/world-middle-east-33083256 accessed 30 March 2018.

178 S. Sharma and A. MacDonald (2016) British Volunteers in Syrian Kurd Forces are 'Terrorists', Turkey Says. *Middle East Eye*, 1 September 2016, available at http://www.middleeasteye.net/news/turkey-british-ypg-terrorist-syria-874419624 accessed 30 March 2018. See also I. Drury (2015) Public Schoolboy Who Quit City to Fight ISIS Returns Home: Briton Who Spent Five Months Alongside Kurdish Forces Says He Can Justify Actions if Questioned by Police, *Mail Online*, 10 June 2015, available at http://www.dailymail.co.uk/news/article-3119071/ISIS-fighting-city-trader-returns-home-UK.html accessed 30 March 2018.

179 For current list of UK proscribed organisations see https://www.gov.uk/government/uploads/system/uploads/attachment_data/file/578385/201612_Proscription.pdf. See also C. Davies (2015) Girl Becomes First Briton Convicted of Trying to Join Fight against Islamic State in Syria, *Guardian*, 20 November 2015, available at https://www.theguardian.com/uk-news/2015/nov/20/girl-becomes-first-briton-convicted-of-trying-to-join-fight-against-islamic-state-in-syria and http://thekurdishproject.org/history-and-culture/kurdish-nationalism/pkk-kurdistan-workers-party accessed 30 March

hand, sees the YPG/YPJ as simply PKK factions and therefore classes them as terrorist organisations. However, the YPG/YPJ are not a proscribed group in the UK, therefore fighting with them is not deemed to be terrorist action, despite Turkey's position on this subject.

Concerns regarding the lack of a provision allowing a freedom fighter style defence were actually raised during the debating stages of the Terrorism Act 2000, whereby Parliamentarians focused on the proposed vagueness surrounding the terms used, and whether such a provision would have unfairly criminalised modern equivalents of the Suffragettes or the South African opponents of apartheid.[180] Sir Igor Judge in *R v F* appeared to have proffered caution in not permitting some defence typology:

> The call of resistance to tyranny and invasion evokes an echoing response down the ages. We note, as a matter of historical knowledge, that many of those whose violent activities in support of national independence or freedom from oppression, who were once described as terrorists, are now honoured as 'freedom fighters'.[181]

Although acknowledging this, the Court held 'terrorism is terrorism, whatever the motives of the perpetrators'.[182] Igor Judge's statement was unsurprisingly rejected by the Government, which led Lord Carlile, the then independent reviewer of anti-terrorism legislation in 2007, to advocate a form of statutory obligation that required the executive to look into the nature and target of the action, and towards international legal obligations, prior to the instigation of criminal charges.[183] Walker proffers a rather scathing view for not creating or allowing a type of freedom fighter defence or exception where he states that this is 'an antidote to the trend that the UK Government values friendship with oil-owning despots much more highly that the political freedom exercised by refugee underdogs'.[184]

Despite the international conventions, the UK Court of Appeal drew attention to the fact that no internationally agreed definition of terrorism exists. Although re-visited in 2002 and 2004 by the Member States of the UN, the impasse in the

2018. See also M. Blake (2017) Blackburn Activisty Becomes First British Woman to Join Fight against ISIS in Syria, *Guardian*, 9 February 2017, available at https://www.theguardian.com/uk-news/2017/feb/09/blackburn-activist-kimberly-taylor-becomes-first-british-woman-join-fight-isis-syria accessed 30 March 2018.

180 A. W. Bradley and K. D. Ewing (2011) *Constitutional and Administrative Law* (15th Edition, Pearson Education Ltd) p.590. See also C. Walker (2008c) Terrorism: Terrorism Act 2000 ss. 1 and 58 – Possession of Terrorist Documents, Case Comment, *Criminal Law Review* [2008], 160–165, 162. Suffragettes were members of women's organisations in the late 19th and early 20th century that advocated the extension of the 'franchise', or the right to vote in public elections, to women.

181 *R v F* [2007] EWCA Crim 243, [9].

182 *Ibid*, [9] and [27].

183 *Supra* as per Lord Carlile of Berriew QC (2007) paragraph 58.

184 *Supra* as per C. Walker (2008c) p.165.

negotiations surrounded whether such a definition would be applicable to the armed forces of a state (state terrorism) and to liberation movements (freedom fighters).[185] Focusing on the latter point, domestically this provides a problem as expressed by the UK judiciary above, because should violent action or the threat of action by persons engaged in armed conflict overseas be distinguished, it would no longer constitute terrorism.[186] The UK judiciary have shown that although deliberate targeting of civilians is prohibited by International Humanitarian Law and could constitute a war crime, such prosecutions are highly unusual.[187] The UK Court of Appeals' decision follows such concern, where it was held that the conflicts in Afghanistan and Iraq were both regarded as non-international armed conflicts, thereby removing the possibility of a claim for combatant immunity for legitimate insurgency.

UK discretionary power to prosecute

Perhaps providing some reprieve from the over broad definition of terrorism, the executive functions are able to offer some moderation, prior to formal charges being brought. Under section 117 of the Terrorism Act 2000, prior to the instigation of proceedings the consent of the Director of Public Prosecutions (DPP) is required.[188] However, allowing discretionary power to the DPP was criticised by the UK Supreme Court in *R v Gul* as 'intrinsically unattractive', amounting to the legislature abdicating prosecutorial powers to an unelected, albeit respected and independent lawyer.[189] The Court focused on the risk of undermining the rule of law given that although the DPP is accountable to Parliament, open and democratically accountable decisions are not made in the same manner and form as those in Parliament.[190] It is worth mentioning that other areas of UK criminal law have wide definitions that are moderated by the DPP. In fact, this appears to work reasonably well.[191]

The Sexual Offences Act 2003 serves to provide such an example whereby consent to sexual activity for persons under 16 was removed by way of section 4.[192] Therefore, two persons both under the age of 16 would effectively be guilty of committing an offence given they are unable to legally consent.[193] Following a similar trend in reassuring Parliamentarians that the term 'ideological' would not

185 T. Deen, (2005) U.N. Member States Struggle to Define Terrorism, *Inter Press Service*, see http://www.ipsnews.net/2005/07/politics-un-member-states-struggle-to-define-terrorism/ accessed 30 March 2018.

186 *R v Gul* [2012] EWCA Crim 280, [23], and *R v Gul* [2013] UKSC 64, [42].

187 *Supra* as per D. Anderson (2014) p.26.

188 Terrorism Act 2000, s 117(2)(a).

189 *R v Gul* [2013] UKSC 64, [35]-[36].

190 *Ibid.*

191 Such as the Sexual Offences Act 2003.

192 See http://www.cps.gov.uk/legal/p_to_r/rape_and_sexual_offences/consent/ accessed 30 March 2018.

193 D. Ormerod (2008) *Smith and Hogan Criminal Law* (12th Edition, Oxford University Press) pp.706–708.

extend to industrial action under the 2000 Act, the then Home Secretary made it clear that charges would not be brought against children under 16 who engaged in consensual sexual activity.[194] This statement is laced with ambiguity – but such criticism is beyond the scope of the current discussion. The Crown Prosecution Service (CPS) has since provided guidance to emphasise, 'it was not Parliament's intention to punish children unnecessarily'.[195] This type of safeguarding power could also be utilised to narrow the denotation of 'Government' within the definition of terrorism, to allow, at least at some level, a freedom fighter exclusion. Given the extremely broad nature of the Terrorism Act 2000, it is argued that without this safeguard the law could potentially be used inappropriately. It is further contended that although the DPP safeguard is useful, it does not replace legislative certainty.

Political value of terrorism

The impact of this lack of legislative certainty is realised where political influence and the political value of the terrorism currently prevails over its legal one, making its use difficult in legal discourse.[196] Internationally, and arguably domestically, left to its political meaning terrorism can change substantially to suit the interests of a particular state and government at a particular time.[197] For this reason it is argued the law should prevail and provide a clear and precise legal position, denying terrorism its political currency built upon historical attachments.[198] According to Gale, the lack of precision mitigates against due process of law, whereby the law should be as precise and foreseeable as possible as held in *Steel and others v United Kingdom*, and *Hashman and Harrup v United Kingdom.* [199] This is perhaps more prevalent within the international arena where the issue of an objective legal definition is compounded by the fact there are two terms of terrorism, that of the state and that of freedom fighters.[200] State terrorism and issues surrounding

194 *Ibid.*

195 *Supra* as per http://www.cps.gov.uk/legal/p_to_r/rape_and_sexual_offences/consent accessed 30 March 2018.

196 S. Zeidan (2004) Desperately Seeking Definition: The International Community's Quest for Identifying the Specter of Terrorism, *Cornell International Law Journal*, 36 (3), Article 5, 491–496, 491–492. See also *supra* as per B. Saul (2006) p.3.

197 *Ibid.*

198 The political value can be seen historically during the Peninsula Wars of 1809–1813, evidenced more recently where the Taliban and Osama bin Laden represented the US in Afghanistan, seen as President Regan's freedom fighters (Mujahideen) and supported by the US Central Intelligence Agency (CIA), where they were resisting the Soviet occupation. They changed, however, to President Bush Jnr's terrorists particularly after 2001. See G. Chaliand (1987) *Terrorism: From Popular Struggle to Media Spectacle* (Saqi Books) p.37. See also *supra* as per C. Walker (2009) p.1. See also *supra* as per S. Zeidan (2004) p.492.

199 *Supra* as per C. J. S. Gale, (2006). *Steel and others v United Kingdom* [1999] 28 EHRR 603 [54] and *Hashman and Harrup v United Kingdom* [2000] EHRR 241 [31].

200 *Supra* as per S. Zeidan (2004) pp.494–495.

counter-insurgency are both beyond the ambit of this book, however, in the interests of fullness, Marian Price, a convicted IRA terrorist, draws on this particular issue:

> I don't see any distinction between al-Qaeda and what George [W] Bush's pilots did in Afghanistan. I would equate those two as terror, because that's what they are designed to do … to terrorise a population into surrender. That's the real terrorism.[201]

The difference in opinion evidences further the associated subjectivity of the label and shows that the politically loaded term can be used beyond its legal meaning.[202] It also shows that the term can be abused extensively thereby confusing the concept.[203]

Conclusion

There are two main problems concerning the UK's legal definition of terrorism under the Terrorism Act 2000. The first is a definitional problem whereby the phrases used remain relatively undefined by Parliament. This has resulted in a display of difficulty when deciding which phrase to apply to a particular case, thereby affecting, at least to some degree, judicial application. The second, related problem concerns the political currency of the term's use. To ameliorate this, the UK could re-define terrorism so as to remove the various political references. In concert with this is the suggestion to introduce exclusion clauses for actions taken by way of protest and industrial action and dissent or during an international armed conflict in accordance with customary international law. Although it has been demonstrated that the UK legal definition of terrorism works reasonably well in practice, the lack of definitional certainty increases the political value and fuels criticisms based on the rule of law. For this to change, the UK must harmonise the definition of an act of terrorism with international law and comparatives. As an example, it could read as follows:

> Terrorism is the use or threat of serious violence, designed to unduly compel a government or an international organisation, or to seriously intimidate the

201 *Supra* as per R. English (2010) p.20.

202 *Supra* as per C. Walker (2009) p.3, See also *supra* as per B. Saul (2006) p.3.

203 *Ibid* as per B. Saul (2006) p.3. See also W. Laqueur (1987) *The Age of Terrorism* (Little, Brown and Company) p.143. See also M. Freeman (2005) *Order, Rights and Threats: Terrorism and Global Justice*, in R. M. A. Wilson (ed.) *Human Rights in the War on Terror* (Cambridge University Press). For example, see UN ComHR preambles in 1998/47, 1999/27, 2000/30, 2001/31, 2002/35. It has also been made clear that terrorist activity cannot be used as a means to protect human rights. See A. Byrnes (2002) Apocalyptic Visions and the Law: The Legacy of September 11, a professorial address by Byrnes at the ANU Law School for the Faculty's Inaugural and Valedictory Lecture Series, 30 May, available at https://law.anu.edu.au/CIPL/StaffPapersTalks&Submissions/Byrnes30May02.pdf accessed 30 March 2018.

public, or section thereof, and is made for the purposes of advancing a political, religious, ideological, or racial cause.

Protest, dissent or industrial action is omitted from this definition. Action taken during an armed conflict as part of a legitimate struggle of peoples fighting in the exercise of their right to self-determination is not terrorism, unless such action is directed towards non-combatants and/or civilians.

2 The 21st Century terrorist threat: how terrorist groups and terrorists communicate and the unknown threat

Introduction

This chapter outlines the way in which terrorist groups and individual terrorists communicate in the 21st Century. Concentrating on the terrorist group Islamic State (IS) as a case study, this chapter will highlight the interdisciplinary relationships formed between the group and its individual supporters and cells, by utilising digital means. The chapter will explore the vertical effect of the group's propaganda and communication through the Internet, and how this impacts upon the current risk posed to UK security by terrorists. The rationale for focusing on the IS terrorist group is their efficient and prolific use of 21st Century digital technology. The vertical effect of IS's successful and expert use of electronic communications data will be assessed, illustrating the need for new legislative measures. The horizontal effect of terrorist communication will then be analysed, which will demonstrate the difficulties faced by UK lawmakers and UK policing and security agencies, specifically with regards to encryption technology in the 21st Century, and the growth of the darknet.

Following on from discussing the problems faced, the chapter will then place emphasis on the legal efforts made by the UK to combat the collection of terrorist materials, the dissemination of such and efforts to prohibit direct and indirect encouragement to commit a terrorist act. The effects of terrorist communication in radicalising citizens to commit acts of terrorism will then be discussed, showing a worrying trend in jihadi tourism and increased individual operational abilities.

Terrorist group: Islamic State

For the media and the world the IS terrorist group appeared to come from nowhere and spread across Syria and Iraq at incredible speed.[1] According to news reports, IS was founded by Abu Musab al-Zarqawi in 2004. Originally the group was called Islamic State in Iraq and the group became an umbrella organisation under al-Qaeda in Iraq in 2006.[2] In 2010 the leadership was transferred to

1 D. Byman (2015) *Al Qaeda, The Islamic State and the Global Jihadist Movement* (Oxford University Press) pp.166–167. See also M. W. Nance (2015) *The Terrorists of Iraq: Inside the Strategy and Tactics of the Iraqi Insurgency 2003–2014* (CRC Press) pp.297–300.

2 See http://www.bbc.co.uk/news/world-middle-east-29052144 accessed 30 March 2018.

Awwad Ibrahim Ali al-Badri al-Samarrai, also known as al-Baghdadi, who started to rebuild its military capabilities and within three years the group was carrying out terrorist attacks in the local region.[3] In an attempt to draw more support to IS, al-Samarrai took the name Abu Bakr al-Baghdadi, and in April announced the merger of IS with other groups to create the Islamic State in Iraq and the Levant/al-Sham (ISIL/ISIS).[4] Taking advantage of political unrest in the region ISIL/ISIS grew exponentially taking control of various villages, towns and cities, finally resulting in the group's proclamation of a caliphate, becoming known thereafter simply as Islamic State (IS). Abu Mosa was appointed as the head press officer, and in June 2014 he made it clear that the caliphate had been established, stating:

> the Islamic State has been established. And we will not stop. Don't be cowards and attack us with drones. Instead send your soldiers, the ones we humiliated in Iraq. We will humiliate them everywhere, God willing, and we will raise the flag of Allah in the White House.[5]

Building from this statement and in order for the group to expand and fill the shortfall of fighters, a press office was developed launching an advertising and marketing campaign. As a result of the statement and the swift gains of territory in the Anbar area of Iraq and North Syria the UK proscribed the terrorist group in July 2014.[6] Since then IS has perhaps become one of the most notorious and influential groups within the Middle East and North Africa, posing a direct terrorist threat not only to those regions, but also to the nation states around the world. The level of violence directed towards all those that oppose its own religious interpretation and political doctrine has been merciless, with beheadings of UK, US and Japanese citizens and Syrian opposition forces, and total destruction of Sunni Muslim cities such as Tikrit in Iraq.[7] Attacks inspired by IS were committed in 2015 in Paris and in a Tunisian holiday resort resulting in the

3 *Supra* as per Byman (2015) pp.306–308.
4 Abu Bakr is an infamous name within the Islamic religion, being the name of the prophet Muhammad's father-in-law and chief adviser, who became a caliph. This name resonates with Muslims and deep within the Muslim psychology, and was therefore chosen very carefully. For further information see P. Mosendz (2014) How the Head of ISIS Got His Name: Abu Bakr al-Baghdadi Chose a Name with Historic Resonance in the Muslim World, *Europe Newsweek*, available at http://europe.newsweek.com/abu-bakr-al-baghdadi-abu-dua-invisible-sheikh-awwad-ibrahim-ali-al-badri-al-282939?rm=eu accessed 30 March 2018.
5 Seehttp://www.counterextremism.com/content/abu-moussa-isis-press-officer-june-2014. See also http://www.theatlantic.com/international/archive/2014/08/isil-press-officer-abu-mosa-killed-by-syrian-army/378994 accessed 30 March 2018.
6 House of Commons Library (2014) The Terrorism Act 2000: Proscribed Organisations, Standard Note SN/HA/00815, 25 July 2014, available at researchbriefings.files.parliament.uk/documents/SN00815/SN00815.pdf accessed 30 March 2018 p.8.
7 N. Khomami (2015) Mohammad Emwazi: Who Were His Victims? *Guardian*, 13 November 2015, available at http://www.theguardian.com/uk-news/2015/nov/13/mohammed-emwazi-who-were-his-victims accessed 30 March 2018

death of 38 UK citizens. In Nice on Bastille Day, a lone actor inspired by IS killed 86 civilians and injured 303, by driving a 17-ton heavy goods vehicle through a crowd. This type of attack has since been emulated on Westminster Bridge and in Finsbury Park, London in 2017. Atrocities such as these have been witnessed by the world at large due to the group's efficient use of electronic communications technology.

21st Century methods of communication: how terrorist groups use the Internet in the digital age

Utilising the Internet to market the IS brand, which is now available in over 40 languages, the group has been able to infiltrate citizens' homes and effectively persuade them to join the fight in Syria and Iraq, or to commit lone Islamist attacks in their home nation states.[8] For Klausen, the Internet and social media outlets have been a gift to terrorist groups such as IS, allowing them to meet their strategic aims in recruitment, financing and publicising their cause.[9]

Glorifying images and IS's propaganda are spread through the Internet by largely utilising social media outlets. Such outlets consist of Twitter, Facebook and YouTube, in addition to dedicated websites that publish online Islamist magazines translated into various languages, such as the *Dar al-Islam* and *Dabiq*, both created by IS, and *Inspire* created by al-Qaeda, found on the dedicated website Jihadology.[10] IS has created a media ministry and effectively decentralised social media use. In forming part of this ministry, IS has shown awareness of the potential to increase its capacity through mass Internet media attracting others to their cause. One of its tactics included the holding of a hostage John Cantlie, who read out messages from IS explaining the group had been misrepresented by Western media and it would be presenting the truth in future videos.[11] These videos, as with all IS's propaganda, are skilfully produced to a high quality, with great care taken in terms of presentation. For Milton, the mixing of fear and reason makes a potent combination.[12]

In creating and maintaining the centrally controlled Ministry of Media, IS have managed to spread its multilingual propaganda effectively. Outlets of the Ministry

8 J. Klausen (2015) Tweeting the Jihad: Social Media Networks of Western Foreign Fighters in Syria and Iraq, *Studies in Conflict & Terrorism,* 39(1), 1–22, 3.

9 *Ibid.* For an example image see https://www.reddit.com/r/jihadpropaganda accessed 30 March 2018.

10 See http://jihadology.net/category/dar-al-islam-magazine and https://azelin.files.wordpress.com/2016/07/al-qacc84_idah-in-the-arabian-peninsula-e2809cinspire-guide-2-nice-operatione2809d.pdf accessed 30 March 2018.

11 BBC News (2014) Video of British Hostage John Cantlie Released, 18 September 2014, available at http://www.bbc.co.uk/news/uk-29258201 accessed 30 March 2018.

12 D. Milton (2014) The Islamic State: An Adaptive Organisation Facing Increasing Challenges. In M. al-Ubaydi, N. Lahoud, D. Milton and B. Price (eds), *The Group That Calls Itself a State: Understanding the Evolution and Challenges of the Islamic State*, The Combating Terrorism Center at West Point, p.53, available at www.ctc.usma.edu accessed 30 March 2018.

include the al-Furqan Institute, the I'tisaam Media Foundation, the Anjad Media Foundations and the English based outlet the al-Hayat Media Centre.[13] The al-Furqan manufactures DVDs, posters and brochures that the al'tisaam then disseminate through the Internet in various languages, including English, French, German and Russian.[14] IS's high-quality glossy magazine *Dabiq* is also printed in several different languages and contains a large number of articles and presentations that seek to legitimise IS's actions and the idea of the caliphate, all aimed at recruitment.[15] IS's 15th issue of *Dabiq* starts with the comment: 'The spark has been lit here in Iraq, and its heat will continue to intensify – by Allah's permission – until it burns the Crusader armies ...'[16]

Along with various links to videos, all of which represent high-quality filming, there are many articles dedicated to legitimising IS's struggle against the West, and what they call the Crusaders.[17] The articles themselves are extremely biased and clearly aim to spread IS's rather cynical take on Christianity, Judaism and all other forms of religion and non-religion that do not follow its own interpretation of Islam.[18] With one photo showing a jihadi fighter holding a kitten and then one showing children playing, the magazine is clearly attempting to show a caring side of the IS.[19] One particular story glamorises an individual Islamist fighter story and illustrates the terrorist attack that took place in Nice:

> Between the release of this issue of *Dabiq* and the next slaughter to be executed against them [the West] by the hidden soldiers of the Caliphate – who are ordered to attack without delay – the Crusaders can read into why Muslims hate and fight them, why pagan Christians should break their crosses, why liberalist secularists should return to the fitrah (natural human disposition), and why sceptical atheists should recognize their Creator and submit to Him. In essence, we explain why they must abandon their infidelity and accept Islam, the religion of sincerity and submission ...[20]

In attempting to give a rationale IS's terrorist actions one section of the magazine is titled, 'Why We Hate You and Why We Fight You'.[21] As one would expect, the

13 *Ibid.*
14 A. Khan (2014) What ISIL's English-language Propaganda Tells Us about Its Goals, *Aljazeera*, 20 June, available at http://america.aljazeera.com/watch/shows/america-tonight/articles/2014/6/19/how-isil-is-remakingitsbrandontheinternet.html accessed 30 March 2018. See also H. J. Ingram (2015a) The Strategic Logic of Islamic State Information Operations, *Australian Journal of International Affairs*, 69(6), 729–752, 732.
15 H. J. Ingram (2015b) Three Traits of the Islamic State's Information Warfare, T*he Rusi Journal*, 159(6), 4–11, 5.
16 *Dabiq* (2016) Breaking the Cross, 15, 1437 Shawwal, p.1, available at http://jihadology.net accessed 30 March 2018.
17 *Ibid.*
18 *Ibid* p.67.
19 *Ibid* p.10.
20 *Ibid* p.4.
21 *Ibid.*

hatred starts with the fact Christians are in fact Christian, then the article moves on to describe how Western views are far too liberal. What must be remembered is that these messages may perhaps resonate with many people and simply seek to radicalise others in their call for support.

Social media: Twitter, Facebook and YouTube

Social media is open source and essentially available for all citizens to use worldwide. IS has used this rather cynically to its advantage to disseminate its message. In 2015 the Director of Europol confirmed the IS terrorist group is believed to directly control 50,000 different Twitter accounts and coupled with individual Islamists was sending up to 100,000 Twitter messages per day in an attempt to market its propaganda, radicalise others and plan an attack.[22]

Berger and Morgan further this claim, arguing IS may actually have direct control of over 90,000 Twitter accounts, thereby doubling the amount of daily messages sent.[23] In August 2016, Twitter announced it had closed over 235,000 accounts with links to IS over a six-month period.[24] Such IS messages read:

> You can sit at home and play call of duty or you can come here and respond to the real call of duty … Kill the police and soldiers … carry out lone wolf operations … smash his head with a rock, or slaughter him with a knife, or run him over with your car, or throw him down from a high place, or choke him, or poison him … Muslims stand by [their] black brothers and sisters. Your [You're] all welcome to Islamic State we will embrace you and love you.[25]

For Ingram, although these messages and the dissemination of information regarding IS actions overseas have proved effective through social media.[26]

22 See http://www.dailymail.co.uk/sciencetech/article-3747501/Twitter-s-terror-crackdown-Social-network-says-shut-235-000-accounts-linked-Islamic-State-groups-six-months.html accessed 30 March 2018.

23 J. M. Berger and J. Morgan (2015) The ISIS Twitter Census: Defining and Describing the Population of ISIS Supporters on Twitter, 20 March, Center for Middle East Policy at Brooking, available at http://webcache.googleusercontent.com/search?q=cache:nUpiATbv50wJ:www.brookings.edu/~/media/research/files/papers/2015/03/isis-twitter-census-berger-morgan/isis_twitter_census_berger_morgan.pdf+&cd=1&hl=en&ct=clnk&gl=uk accessed 30 March 2018.

24 See http://www.dailymail.co.uk/sciencetech/article-3747501/Twitter-s-terror-crackdown-Social-network-says-shut-235-000-accounts-linked-Islamic-State-groups-six-months.html accessed 30 March 2018.

25 See http://www.memrijttm.org/jihadi-reactions-to-nice-terror-attack-we-want-paris-before-rome.html. See also http://www.independent.co.uk/news/world/middle-east/isis-urges-more-attacks-on-western-disbelievers-9749512.html accessed 30 March 2018.

26 H. J. Ingram (2016) An Analysis of *Inspire* and *Dabiq*: Lessons from AQAP and Islamic State's Propaganda War, *Studies in Conflict & Terrorism*, 40(5), 357–375

According to Ingram, the group has simply mimicked the way in which international businesses and companies have used social media to improve their position.[27] This has resulted in its success at spreading its message, thereby gaining support and financial donations.

IS has posted many videos on YouTube, which are often graphic and horrifying, showing the beheading and killing of its so-called enemies. It has also used YouTube to spread its message and show recent adherents to their cause sitting happily holding a firearm, knives and grenades. These videos often also have a message of their own, encouraging others to join IS in the fighting in Syria and Iraq.[28] As with Twitter, supporters use this format to continue IS's message and add their own comments, often creating their own specific channel.[29] Anjem Choudary represents one such example in the UK, where his YouTube channel remains live despite his criminal conviction for terrorist offences.[30]

In order to combat terrorist use of social media, Internet companies have started using new software originally designed to remove copyrighted material. Looking for 'hashes' that is a unique digital fingerprint assigned to specific videos posted online, the Internet companies' software is now able to automatically target terrorist material. Due to the advancing capabilities highlighted here, it is possible that such groups will increase their usage of other means of dissemination. First they could increase their use of specific Internet webpages allowing for anonymity of postings. Second they could simply increase the use of the 'darknet', which UK law enforcement agencies are currently struggling to effectively police. With all of these formats, the aim is to bring people round to their way of thinking.

Regardless of this action, along with Facebook's, Keith Vaz MP, former Chair of the Home Affairs Select Committee said:

> Huge corporations like Google, Facebook and Twitter ... are consciously failing to tackle this threat and passing the buck by hiding behind their supranational legal status, despite knowing that their sites are being used by the instigators of terror. The companies' failure to tackle this threat has left some parts of the Internet ungoverned, unregulated and lawless.[31]

27 *Ibid.*

28 See https://www.youtube.com/watch?v=lFlsv0xpBKc at 19:50, for mass killing see 32:00, and see https://www.youtube.com/watch?v=WS2bX8X7eZk accessed 30 March 2018.

29 See https://www.youtube.com/channel/UCOr3TFdnT1yyrQIVQV007gw accessed 30 March 2018.

30 See http://www.dailymail.co.uk/news/article-3750223/Outrage-extremist-hate-videos-starring-hate-preacher-Anjem-Choudary-s-followers-available-online-despite-jailing.html accessed 30 March 2018.

31 See http://www.independent.co.uk/life-style/gadgets-and-tech/news/facebook-twitter-google-isis-daesh-internet-youtube-social-media-home-affairs-a7208131.html accessed 30 March 2018.

Katz highlights the difficulty faced by policing and security agencies as they endeavour to monitor social media.[32] She explains how, with the benefit of encryption, IS is circumventing the blocking of its Twitter feeds by having multiple backup accounts.[33] Furthermore, a point that seems to be overlooked is that IS's social media campaign is networked, rather than having a centralised person in control. Many of IS's recruits have an average age of 24, meaning many have grown up with social media as part of their lives, which in turn means tools such as Twitter and Instagram come easy to them.[34] For Katz this represents the real threat of IS as these young people use Twitter to launch recruitment and calls for lone jihad.[35] Supporting citizens simply re-post or quote what they see from those they follow.[36] This particular aspect forms IS's unofficial communications strategy whereby the number of followers can be increased with the use of hashtags.[37]

The Internet and application protocols, smartphones and encryption

It must be remembered that citizens born in the early 1990s have not known life without the Internet. Due to the growth in technology the use of written letters and telephone landlines was the first to decline. Research shows that in 1989 the main types of communication were by letters and landline.[38] Since 2014 less than three in ten 16–24 year-olds continue to use these methods. In fact less than 16 per cent of UK households still have a landline and the UK Communications Infrastructure Report suggests this will decrease further bringing an end to its use as citizens prefer Internet telephony.[39] Now, electronic mailing (emails) and text messaging are becoming a thing of the past. Utilising smartphones, instant direct messaging applications more commonly known as chat apps, such as Apples iMessage and Facebook Messenger, appears to be the current favourite.[40] To this end, the ownership of smartphones dramatically increased between 2000 and

32 R. Katz (2015) How Islamic State Is Still Thriving on Twitter, 11 April, InSite Blog on Terrorism & Extremism, available at http://news.siteintelgroup.com/blog/index.php/entry/377-how-the-islamic-state-is-still-thriving-on-twitter accessed 30 March 2018.

33 *Ibid.*

34 See http://www.popsci.com/terror-on-twitter-how-isis-is-taking-war-to-social-media accessed 30 March 2018.

35 *Supra* as per Katz (2015).

36 See https://www.theguardian.com/uk-news/2016/aug/16/anjem-choudary-convicted-of-supporting-islamic-state accessed 30 March 2018.

37 *Supra* as per J. M. Berger and J. Morgan (2015).

38 *Supra* as per D. Anderson QC (2015) pp.49–50.

39 *Ibid.*

40 *Ibid*, 'Instant messaging apps have overtaken traditional SMS services. In 2012, 19 billion messages were sent per day on instant messaging apps, compared to 17.6 billion text messages. Since 2012 the number of instant messaging apps has grown considerably.' See also https://www.whatsapp.com, and http://en.people.cn/102774/8568312.html accessed 30 March 2018.

2014, which effectively allows for many different types of electronic communication methods.[41]

The Internet

Internet technology and the growth in its use have been extensive, as people tend to favour making a call via the smartphone or tablet over the Internet. The number of citizens making an Internet call tripled between 2009 and 2014.[42] In addition to this vast increase in volume of information sent and received, it is estimated that by 2021 3.3 zettabytes of data will travel over the Internet annually.[43] It is important to note that in addition to this growth in use, the Internet is not territorially bound making it difficult for law enforcement to trace information sent on it. Emails, for example, are not confined to the country of origin or receipt, rather they move freely across borders utilising the quickest path possible. This means an email between two people in the UK may actually travel via another country. The servers of email services for many companies, such as Hotmail and Gmail, are based outside the UK.[44] Therefore, although UK legislation may require Internet and service providers to hold data for a certain length of time, the transnational nature of the medium means external agreements must be drafted.

The Internet structure is made up of three categories.[45] The 'surface web' represents webpages that can be found using standard search engines such as Bing and Google.[46] This is what the majority of users see and can find. The 'deep web', or 'invisible web', represents parts of the open web that are simply not indexed by standard search engines.[47] Although sinister sounding, this part of the web has many legitimate uses such as, web email, online banking and PayPal, and videos on demand such as those available through Amazon.[48] It makes up almost 90 per cent of Internet usage figures.[49] The 'dark web' or 'darknet' is a small proportion

41 *Ibid.*
42 OFCOM, The Communications Market (2016), Telecoms and Networks, available at https://www.ofcom.org.uk/__data/assets/pdf_file/0026/26648/uk_telecoms.pdf accessed 30 March 2018.
43 See https://www.cisco.com/c/en/us/solutions/collateral/service-provider/visual-networking-index-vni/complete-white-paper-c11-481360.html accessed 12 March 2018.
44 *Supra* as per D. Anderson QC (2015) p.51.
45 See https://www.reference.com/technology/basic-structure-internet-91e2893b49bd7bbd accessed 30 March 2018.
46 *Ibid.*
47 *Ibid.*
48 P. Paganini (2012) The Good and the Bad of the Deep Web, *The Hacker New Magazine*, 17 September 2012, available at http://securityaffairs.co/wordpress/8719/deep-web/the-good-and-the-bad-of-the-deep-web.html accessed 30 March 2018.
49 *Ibid.*

of the invisible web that consists of tens of thousands of websites.[50] To clarify the current acronyms and types of Internet companies are listed below:

- Communications Service Providers (CSPs) provide services that transport information electronically. Examples of CSPs include companies such as British Telecom, TalkTalk, Facebook and Twitter. They may be based anywhere in the world, and offer communications services and Internet access;
- Companies that simply provide Internet access are referred to as Internet Service Providers (ISPs) such as Plusnet, Virgin Media and Sky;
- Companies that provide applications or services, over the physical networks provided by CSPs and ISPs are called Applications Service Providers (ASPs). Examples of ASPs include Google, Whatsapp, Snapchat, Facebook, Yahoo, Skype and Apple.

Attributing the communication

Aggravating the current problem surrounding terrorist communication is the difficulty in attributing Internet communication to a specific user of a device. Devices, such as computers, laptops and smartphones, when utilising a network, use an IP address. There is only one IP address assigned to an Internet router, which can of course accommodate many devices. It has been noted by Brown that this infrastructure of the Internet makes it difficult for the policing and security agencies to attribute a particular communication to the sender, and thereby offers a 'cloak of anonymity'.[51] First, many family members and friends effectively share the same IP address and also share devices. Secondly, IP addresses change depending upon where the person is accessing the Internet from, such as from the home, the coffee shop or the place of work. More serious is the fact that thirdly a person can utilise software that purposefully creates ghost or proxy IP addresses that are then untraceable.[52] It is therefore sometime impossible for the agencies to discover which device was used and by whom.[53]

In an attempt to remedy this problem, the Counter Terrorism and Security Act 2015 (CTSA) was enacted, partly to 'address the difficulty that arises when IP addresses are shared by a number of users simultaneously, by requiring the retention of "relevant internet data" in addition to the shared IP address'.[54] However,

50 *Ibid.*
51 C. S. D. Brown (2015) Investigating and Prosecuting Cyber Crime: Forensic Dependencies and Barriers to Justice, *International Journal of Cyber Criminology*, 9(1), January–June, p.58, available at http://www.cybercrimejournal.com/Brown2015vol9issue1.pdf accessed 30 March 2018.
52 *Ibid* p.68.
53 *Ibid.*
54 *The Home Office Counter-Terrorism and Security Bill Factsheet*, Part 3 Internet Protocol (IP) Address Resolution, available at https://www.gov.uk/government/uploads/system/uploads/attachment_data/file/540538/CTS_Bill_-_Factsheet_5_-_IP_Resolution_v2.pdf accessed 30 March 2018.

this attempt appears to have failed because the CSP can only provide the data of the subscribed person, usually the bill payer, not the details of the person using a particular device at a particular time.[55] This represents what has been termed a 'capability gap in communications data' that has 'a serious impact on the ability of law enforcement to carry out their functions'.[56] Intensifying this gap further is the fact there is now a fragmentation of telecommunications and communications data service providers. This is built in to their respective business models highlighting the difference between a UK landline call and a Voice Over Internet Protocol (VOIP). Landline calls are much more traceable with the provider knowing the endpoints of both parties to the call, whereas, the majority of VOIP services, such as Skype, operate through an Internet connection.[57] Many Internet and Over-The-Top (OTT) providers are based overseas, which makes it more difficult for the UK policing and security agencies to obtain data from them .[58] OTT providers in particular are free at the point of access and require little to none subscriber data, and additionally 'communications data relating to a single communication may not be in a single location due to the collaboration of companies'.[59]

Application protocols and encryption

When terrorist groups such as al-Qaeda in the Arabian Peninsula (AQAP) first started using encryption technology it was in its infancy. During the investigation into Rajib Karim communications to Anwar al-Awlaki, it became clear to the policing and security agencies that Karim used a multi-layered approach to encrypting his messages. This whole process was vastly time-consuming, as Karim would first write the message into a Microsoft Excel document using macros to encrypt it, then copy and paste that into a Microsoft Word document. This document would then be saved using the 'password protect' feature that is unbreakable should the password used be long and complex. The document was then compressed and encrypted using another piece of software called RAR, again unbreakable, and then posted online through a URL shortened to render the metadata anonymous.[60] It took UK law enforcement nine months to decrypt Karim's computer.[61] For Graham, things have now moved on whereby the 'ubiquity of encryption in commercially available messaging

55 *Ibid.*
56 *Ibid.*
57 *Supra* as per D. Anderson QC (2015) p.52.
58 For OTT see http://digiday.com/platforms/what-is-over-the-top-ott accessed 30 March 2018.
59 *Supra* as per D. Anderson QC (2015) p.52.
60 R. Graham (2016) How Terrorists Use Encryption, Combating Terrorism Center, available at https://www.ctc.usma.edu/posts/how-terrorists-use-encryption accessed 30 March 2018.
61 V. Dodd (2011a) British Airways Worker Rajib Karim Convicted of Terrorist Plot, *Guardian*, 28 February 2011, available at https://www.theguardian.com/uk/2011/feb/28/british-airways-bomb-guilty-karim accessed 30 March 2018.

tools and devices has made it increasingly easy for terrorists to communicate securely'.[62]

Encryption has now legitimately developed as a commercial communication technology and commodity, and is readily available, provided two main forms exist:

1 Encryption in transit: this provides security during the transmission;
2 End-to-end encryption: this renders the message unreadable to all but the sender and the intended recipient.

The first example represents technology used by the banking industry to make communication safe and secure for customers. The second type, in addition to device encryption, seems to follow a similar rationale having been developed for smartphone and tablet device usage. End-to-end encryption is when the contents of a message are converted into an unreadable form, whereby only the person with the correct decryption key can read it. Both communication and device encryption is legitimately important in securing an individual's privacy, given it is perhaps safe to say the majority of smartphone users, for example, store private information, photos and notes in their phone's memory, which can then be stored on an iCloud server.[63] It is also important to mention that particularly since the introduction of applications such as Apple Pay, smartphone and server encryption forms an essential part of providing the customer with a high level of safety.[64]

In order to ensure this high level of security, the network provider or company overseeing the communication exchange is often unable to decrypt a message, or gain entry into an individual's data stored on their smartphone.[65] Whilst these represent genuine uses for encryption and introduces an increased level of customer security, what often follows such legitimate technological advances is criminal exploitation.[66] Criminal and terrorist use of commercially available encryption pinpoints exactly the point where UK law enforcement suffer its capabilities gap. Apple's security on the iPhone, for example, is extremely high, whereby the device and the internal memory disk are individually encrypted. Remaining with Apple for the moment, since 2014 it has provided data encryption built in to its software, and accordingly it has stated that:

> Apple has no way to decrypt iMessage and Face Time data when it's in transit between devices. So unlike other companies' messaging services, Apple does not scan your communications, and we wouldn't be able to comply with a wiretap order even if we wanted to.[67]

62 *Supra* as per R. Graham (2016).
63 See https://support.apple.com/en-gb/HT202303 accessed 30 March 2018.
64 See https://support.apple.com/en-gb/HT203027 accessed 30 March 2018.
65 *Ibid.*
66 R. Smith (1998) Criminal Exploitation of New Technologies, Australian Institute of Criminology, *Trends & Issues in Crime and Criminal Justice*, (1), 1-6, 1.
67 *Supra* as per D. Anderson QC (2015) p.206. See also Apple's website http://www.apple.com/uk/privacy/approach-to-privacy accessed 30 March 2018.

Messaging applications

21st Century messaging application technology follows a similar format to Apple's iMessage service. More commonly known as 'chat apps', when they were first developed the encryption technology used stopped at the service provider's server, meaning that policing and security agencies could obtain the electronic communications data. This also meant, of course, that cyber criminals could also hack into the service provider's server and obtain the same data. This led to one of the first chat apps to employ end-to-end encryption called Telegram. Al-Qaeda operatives were very quick to start using this technology illustrating terrorist exploitation of this legitimate development.[68] Currently there are many direct messaging applications, in addition to Apples iMessage, all offering end-to-end encryption protocols, such as Whatsapp, Facebook Messenger, Instagram, Wickr, Line, Signal and Google.[69]

The technology used is similar to that used by the military on personal computers, rendering it near impossible to break into. In addition, most chat apps now automatically delete messages after an hour or a day, depending upon the user's settings. The growing user trend in this type of software has caused concern for UK law enforcement. The encryption allows terrorists to communicate freely and if caught, evidential problems may ensue because the messages are no longer available, or traceable. According to the UK's Government Communication Headquarters (GCHQ), such devices and applications have become the 'command and control network' of terrorists.[70] The terrorists who attacked Paris, for example, utilised messaging apps in addition to using disposable 'burner' phones to congregate in safe houses in Belgium.[71] This allowed them to plan and carry out their attack on 15 November 2015 resulting in 130 deaths with hundreds more injured.[72]

It is worth mentioning that it would not be difficult for the would-be-terrorist to quickly learn about all the available encryption techniques. In April 2016, the IS French online magazine *Dar al-Islam* demonstrated the importance of securing communications.[73] This further illustrates how the Internet

68 See http://gizmodo.com/the-best-and-worst-encrypted-messaging-apps-1782424449 accessed 30 March 2018.

69 See http://gizmodo.com/the-best-and-worst-encrypted-messaging-apps-1782424449 and http://www.techtimes.com/articles/169154/20160709/9-messaging-apps-with-end-to-end-encryption-facebook-messenger-whatsapp-imessage-and-more.htm accessed 30 March 2018.

70 B. Quinn and D. Rushe (2014) GCHQ Chief Accuses US Tech Giants of Becoming Terrorists' Networks of Choice, *Guardian*, 3 November 2014, available at https://www.theguardian.com/uk-news/2014/nov/03/privacy-gchq-spying-robert-hannigan accessed 30 March 2018.

71 J. Stone (2016) ISIS Terrorists Used Disposable Burner Phones, Activated Just Hours Before, to Carry Out Paris Attacks, *International Business Times*, 21 March 2016, available at http://www.ibtimes.com/isis-terrorists-used-disposable-burner-phones-activated-just-hours-carry-out-paris-2340265 accessed 30 March 2018.

72 *Ibid.*

73 *Supra* as per R. Graham (2016).

assists terrorists in creating and maintaining an international presence, and according to Ban Ki-moon, Secretary-General of the United Nations, 'the Internet is a prime example of how terrorists can behave in a truly transnational way'.[74] These issues have led Wainwright, Director of Europol, to comment:

> as the communications of terrorist networks and criminal groups have moved increasingly [online], it's opened up a whole new wave of problems for us even in the open internet, let alone the Darknet.[75]

The darknet

Utilising specific software and Internet configurations, the darknet allows for a 'world of complete freedom and anonymity, where users say and do what they like, uncensored, unregulated, and outside of society's norms'.[76] An illegal marketplace exists, such as the well-known 'Silk Road', where people can buy and sell illegal items such as drugs, counterfeit goods, child pornography, books and firearms. Europol in its 2016 TE-SAT report, which illustrates the development of a 'professional, service-based underground economy', has identified the proliferation of cybercrime and terrorism.[77] IS is also known to operate through this medium to raise funds and sell books on how to carry out jihad and how to make bombs and create homemade firearms.[78] The darknet works by sending and receiving messages through a network that involves a process known as 'onion rooting'.[79] This process protects the identity of the people involved in the electronic communication by wrapping layers around it. According to Lakhani this renders the communication impenetrable and therefore untraceable.[80] A software program called Tor is one of the most popular networks, and is used by IS because this permits them to hide their location and identity. Encrypted jihadi forums exist, along with chat rooms where terrorists and supporters can communicate freely, without fear of detection.[81] Parts of this network allow the transfer of unique funds, the purchase of explosives and firearms (of a type that are illegal in the

74 *Ibid.*

75 See http://www.dailymail.co.uk/sciencetech/article-3747501/Twitter-s-terror-crackdown-Social-network-says-shut-235-000-accounts-linked-Islamic-State-groups-six-months.html#ixzz4OIUlFVVU accessed 30 March 2018.

76 *Ibid.*

77 Europol (2016) *EU Terrorism Situation and Trend Report TE-SAT 2016*, (Europol) pp.8–9.

78 See http://uk.businessinsider.com/isis-is-using-the-dark-web-2015-7 accessed 30 March 2018.

79 See http://uk.businessinsider.com/isis-is-using-the-dark-web-2015-7. See also http://www.pri.org/stories/2016-05-13/how-isis-recruits-online-using-encryption-chat-rooms-and-even-dating-sites accessed 30 March 2018.

80 *Ibid.*

81 *Ibid.*

UK) and the acquisition of fraudulent passports along with other items to go undetected.[82]

Using a 'normal' search engine, such as Google, it is not very difficult to find the Tor software program nor is it difficult to download.[83] Tor has been in operation since October 2003 and is described as providing an open network 'that helps you defend against traffic analysis, a form of network surveillance that threatens personal freedom and privacy, confidential business activities and relationships, and State security'.[84] But in actual fact Tor allows a person to access the deeper realms of the darknet, called 'Onionland'.[85] Utilising Tor, 'Onionland' allows criminals a free space to work and effectively 'cloak themselves in obscurity with specialised software that guarantees encryption and anonymity between users, as well as protocols or domains that the average person will never stumble across'.[86]

The main concern is that terrorists may be able to launch more advanced attacks, and by utilising Tor make it harder for policing and security agencies to detect and prevent such attacks. Europol's 2016 TE-SAT Report confirms that IS has an advanced level of encryption knowledge. Coupled with Anders Breivik's step-by-step guide on how to use Tor, Onionland and the darknet, it is clear that the 'likelihood of future attacks being based on new modus operandi with a stronger cyber dimension' is an increasing reality.[87] 'Terrorists have certainly demonstrated their flexibility and willingness to learn and further develop their technical skills'.[88] To this end policing the darknet represents a very real challenge for policing and security services. For Brown law enforcement agencies 'face a serious capabilities gap', both in terms of expertise and budget.[89] To tackle the latter, the UK's former Treasury Minister George Osborne MP committed an extra £1.9 billion to be invested in cybercrime in November 2015.[90] This investment will partially be used to overcome the lacking expertise; according to news

82 See http://www.huffingtonpost.com/kevin-goodman/internet-black-markets_b_4111000.html. See: http://www.foxnews.com/tech/2015/04/23/darknet-danger-organs-murder-credit-card-info-all-for-sale-on-internet.html accessed 30 March 2018. See also N. Bertrand (2015) ISIS is Taking Full Advantage of the Darkest Corners of the Internet, Business Insider UK, available at http://uk.businessinsider.com/isis-is-using-the-dark-web-2015-7?r=US&IR=T accessed 30 March 2018, and Semtex Explosive, taken from J. Patrice (2016) Bombs Used by ISIS in Brussels Terror Attacks are for Sale Online, *NewsGrio*, available at http://www.newsgrio.com/articles/world/uk/244032-bombs-used-by-isis-in-brussels-terror-attacks-are-for-sale-online.html accessed 30 March 2018.

83 See https://www.google.co.uk/#q=Tor accessed 30 March 2018.

84 See https://www.torproject.org accessed 30 March 2018.

85 See http://www.pcworld.com/article/2046227/meet-darknet-the-hidden-anonymous-underbelly-of-the-searchable-web.html accessed 30 March 2018.

86 *Ibid.*

87 *Supra* as per Europol (2016).

88 *Ibid.*

89 *Supra* as per C. S. D. Brown (2015).

90 See https://www.gov.uk/government/speeches/chancellors-speech-to-gchq-on-cyber-security accessed 30 March 2018.

reports, GCHQ is planning to share its cryptography and intelligence analysis knowledge with other private companies in in an attempt to collaborate on an effective approach to cybercrime.[91] In addition GCHQ and the National Crime Agency (NCA) have co-located a Joint Operations Cell (JOC) in order to increase their abilities.[92]

It is clear that from propaganda spread through open sources such as social media, through to mainstream Internet providing dedicated websites, to the darknet allowing the purchase of illegal weapons and information useful to a terrorist, overall IS's digital communicational strategy has proved first class. Such propaganda has led directly to the radicalisation of citizens resulting in terrorist attacks being committed, or thwarted. Such radicalisation was seen in the UK in 2015, when a 15-year-old boy from Blackburn used Internet communication to plot with Australian counterparts to behead Australian police officers at the ANZAC Day celebrations. Having received a life sentence, the UK now has the youngest convicted terrorist.[93] In the UK in 2015 seven major planned IS attacks were prevented by the policing and security services, with intelligence suggesting more were being planned.[94]

Conclusion

Terrorist groups and self-starters have embraced modern communication technology, using it from marketing up to coordinating an attack. Given these technological advancements have brought about economic and societal change, it is of little surprise that it has had a similar effect of terrorism and criminality.[95] It is interesting to note that in response the then UK Prime Minister David Cameron announced that if he was leading the next government, he would introduce legislation in 2016 to eliminate 'safe spaces' for terrorists to communicate.[96] Clearly this has failed to come to fruition.

It is estimated that technology doubles every two years.[97] Although beyond the ambit of this book, this figure is now vehemently contested with some recent debates suggesting technological advancements are slowing down. However, for

91 R. Perez (2016) GCHQ to Fund Startups to Fight Cyber-Crime, *SC Magazine*, available at http://www.scmagazineuk.com/gchq-to-fund-startups-to-fight-cyber-crime/article/524540/ accessed 30 March 2018.

92 See http://www.nationalcrimeagency.gov.uk/news/736-gchq-and-nca-join-forces-to-ensure-no-hiding-place-online-for-criminals accessed 21 November 2016.

93 BBC News (2015) Anzac Day Terror Plot: Blackburn Teenager Admits Inciting Attack, 23 July 2015, available at http://www.bbc.co.uk/news/uk-england-manchester-33633915 accessed 30 March 2018.

94 S. Coates (2015) PM: Seven Terror Attacks in UK Stopped in Last Year, *The Times*, 16 November 2015, available at http://www.thetimes.co.uk/tto/news/uk/article4615198.ece accessed 30 March 2018.

95 See https://www.gov.uk/government/uploads/system/uploads/attachment_data/file/504187/Operational_Case_for_Bulk_Powers.pdf accessed 30 March 2018.

96 *Ibid.*

97 See https://www.extremetech.com/extreme/210872-extremetech-explains-what-is-moores-law accessed 30 March 2018.

Tim Simonite the growth in mobile telephonic smartphone applications, the figure of two years could prove to be a little low.[98] It is reasonably well known the legislature is slow in keeping up with the growth in technology, and it is surmised this would continue for the foreseeable future. A unique threat has been created, whereby the vertical effects of terrorist groups' communication radicalise others, then the horizontal effect that allows people to operate under an anonymity cloak, who have advanced independent operational abilities with potential access to explosives and firearms purchased on the darknet.

Considering this predicament, legislation, namely the Investigatory Power Act (IPA), has been created aimed at policing the Internet. A cooperative approach with ISPs is essential to this aim, ensuring the dark sides of the web are monitored and then removed should they be deemed illegal. It is also essential the Government collaborate with smartphone application providers to allow targeted decryption of messages.

98 See https://www.technologyreview.com/s/601441/moores-law-is-dead-now-what/ accessed 30 March 2018.

3 The necessity of bulk communications data surveillance

Introduction

This chapter will look at the legislative measures the UK Government has introduced in its attempt to deal with terrorist electronic communication and the resulting terrorist threat. The technological advances have been described in the previous chapter, now the emphasis will change to assess the tasks of the UK policing and security agencies in carrying out efficient and effective surveillance on terrorist activity and terrorism communications. Starting with the legal surveillance powers in the UK and focusing on those aimed at dealing with counterterrorism, the chapter will focus on the main contentious issues in the 21st Century which are the bulk interception and retention of electronic communications data powers and bulk equipment interference.

The UK's legal surveillance framework changed on 29 November 2016 with the enactment of the Investigatory Powers Act 2016 (IPA). This Act does not entirely replace the existing foundations stone to the surveillance framework provided by the Regulation and Investigatory Powers Act 2000 (RIPA). IPA does, however, replace the bulk powers found under RIPA and introduces a new decryption power. This chapter will show that the surveillance structure consists largely of RIPA and IPA, which provides the required structural integrity. The chapter will start with an in-depth analysis of IPA, focusing on the extent of the powers of bulk data surveillance, which reveals legislative definitional difficulties within the UK's approach. The analysis then examines the broadness of the powers, albeit with restricted access to the data collated, illustrating the minimum protection afforded to citizens, especially when dealing with open source data that is considered to be private. Case examples will be used to demonstrate how complicated and difficult terrorist communications can be to locate, and whether the materials communicated cross the legal definition of terrorism threshold.

The need for IPA will become clear once the chapter has highlighted the difficulty faced by the UK's law enforcement agencies in deciphering friend from foe, particularly in light of the extensive technological advances made in electronic communications. Chapter 4 will then focus on other counterterrorism-focused measures, illustrating the apparent ineffectiveness of pre-emptive measures, which may change as a result of IPA.

The Investigatory Powers Act 2016

IPA was enacted on 29 November 2016. In amalgamating other surveillance powers contained in various statutes into one piece of legislation, it contains nine parts with 272 sections. This makes IPA a substantial statute designed to make it easier for the relevant agencies to apply for authorities and warrants as well as making it easier for the courts to determine under which statute the authority or warrant was issued. In the preamble of the Act it states:

> An Act to make provision about the interception of communications, equipment interference and the acquisition and retention of communications data, bulk personal datasets and other information; to make provision about the treatment of material held as a result of such interception, equipment interference or acquisition or retention; to establish the Investigatory Powers Commissioner and other Judicial Commissioners and make provision about them and other oversight arrangements; to make further provision about investigatory powers and national security; to amend sections 3 and 5 of the Intelligence Services Act 1994; and for connected purposes.

Forming a significant part of the UK's legal surveillance framework, it provides structural support to already existing powers located under RIPA, the Intelligence Services Act 1994 (ISA) and the Security Services Act 1985 (SSA).[1] Although RIPA continues to provide the foundation stone to this legal framework, IPA is significantly larger amending parts of RIPA, the ISA and additionally the Wireless Telegraphy Act 2006. Bringing them within its ambit, IPA focuses more on electronic communications data surveillance and bulk powers, in line with 21st Century technology, and to combat terrorist communication discussed in the previous chapter.[2] RIPA, however, still governs the different types of surveillance, such as random or overt (i.e. the use of CCTV), and directed or covert, where the targets are monitored from static observation points and followed, and intrusive surveillance where premises and property are interfered with.

Prior to IPA, RIPA also governed the interception of communications and electronic communications data, whereby communications were monitored either under a direct-targeted authority or a bulk data warrant. RIPA also governs the use of covert human intelligence sources (CHIS) more commonly known as informants. However, both Houses of Parliament and the various committee stages gave careful consideration to IPA, and seemingly decided that it was unnecessary for the Act to merge all the various powers into one. IPA appears to be focused entirely on powers related to the surveillance of electronic communications data, and is arguably already adequately large.

1 Investigatory Powers Act 2016, s 251.
2 Investigatory Powers Act 2016, s 259.

This particular point was emphasised by the Rt. Hon. Dominic Grieve QC in the Intelligence and Security Committee's report on IPA.[3] Grieve's report found that although IPA, makes 'some attempt to improve transparency', the Intelligence and Security Committee were rather disappointed to note that it does not cover all the agencies' intrusive capabilities.[4] As a general overview, Part One of the Act proffers a new human rights approach from the UK Government, dealing specifically with privacy protections including offences and penalties for the misuse of electronic communications data surveillance.[5] It appears the UK Government has learnt from previous human rights related case decisions and critiques, and ensured there is a form of judicial scrutiny and wider safeguards to protect personal data and privacy rights. to the Government has also removed certain powers to obtain communications data previously authorised under RIPA, such as some local authorities and those listed under Schedule 2 of IPA.[6] Part Two of IPA introduces the use of targeted interception, which needs to be considered alongside Part Five dealing with the use of targeted equipment interference. Part Two also introduces two further types of interception warrant: targeted examination and mutual assistance.[7] The list of persons able to request an interception warrant are the same as those listed in section 6 of RIPA, albeit with the introduction of some language simplification.[8]

Parts Three and Four of IPA deal with the obtaining and retention of, and access to electronic communications data. Parts Six and Seven introduce new bulk powers, the retention of such and the use of personal datasets, with Part Eight providing a new oversight regime, and Part Nine providing the Secretary of State with the powers to review the operation of IPA, initially within the first six months and then subsequently five years later, and obliging him to report to Parliament with the findings.[9] The authorisation processes are similar in nature to those already provided for under RIPA, requiring the Secretary of State to sanction the warrant. However, as will be discussed later, the Act does introduce a 'double lock' system whereby an independent judicial commissioner must review the authorisation prior to any police action, and the authorisation of the warrant is to be reviewed at a later stage by a new Independent Investigatory Powers Commissioner.[10]

I intend to concentrate on the new legalised bulk powers of interception, acquisition and equipment interference, and their impact on privacy, whilst discussing the new oversight regime and safeguards, with particular reverence to judicial review principles.

3 The Rt. Hon. Dominic Grieve QC MP (2016) *Intelligence and Security Committee of Parliament, Report on the Draft Investigatory Powers Bill*, 9 February, HC 795, p.1.
4 *Ibid.*
5 Investigatory Powers Act 2016, s 11.
6 Investigatory Powers Act 2016, s 12.
7 Investigatory Powers Act 2016, s 15(1).
8 Investigatory Powers Act 2016, s 18(1).
9 Investigatory Powers Act 2016, s 260. See also House of Lords Second Reading 27 June 2016, Volume 773, Column 1361–1362, available at https://hansard.parliament.uk/lords/2016-06-27/debates/1606278000466/InvestigatoryPowersBill accessed 30 March 2018.
10 Investigatory Powers Act 2016, ss 19 and 23.

The bulk powers: the general rationale

The bulk powers of surveillance are perhaps the most important parts of IPA. They are aimed at closing the UK's law enforcement agencies' technological capabilities gap covered in Chapter 2. They are not entirely uncontroversial, because they have the potential to affect the whole population, or at least a large section thereof (although it will be evidenced in practice this is unlikely), and are aimed at identifying potential terrorists who remain unknown to the policing and security agencies. It is quite simply about finding potential investigative leads, perhaps better explained as allowing law enforcement an opportunity to 'find the needle in the haystack', as highlighted in Chapter 2, and developed further below when looking at issues surrounding the traceability and typecasting of terrorists. The bulk powers contained in IPA are split into four sections:

- Section 136 Bulk interception warrants;
- Section 158 Power to issue bulk acquisition warrants;
- Section 176 Bulk equipment interference warrants;
- Section 199 Bulk personal datasets.

The former Director General of the Security Service (MI5) Lord Evans evidenced the essential part they play in countering the terrorist threat, using an example of how the agency might use the bulk powers provided during the First Sitting Committee Debate on IPA in March 2016.[11] He suggests that using these powers allows law enforcement to find people who 'might' be members of IS and thereby 'may' pose a threat by 'look[ing] at *all individuals* from the UK who are known to have travelled into or out of the Middle East and the area around Syria over the past six months'.[12] Once this task is complete, law enforcement can then narrow the field of search by looking for electronic communications data on individuals who have been in Molenbeek, for example, because 'it looks as though quite a lot of the problems have emerged from that particular part of Brussels'.[13] The next steps continue to narrow the field, as Evans explains:

> Put all those elements of data together and you will end up with perhaps a few dozen ... You might then say, "Let's take all those phones and see which of those telephones has been in first or second-order contact with known extremists" ... That might refine it down from 150 to half a dozen. Then you might start to think, "Actually, there's quite a high likelihood, although one cannot be certain, that these half a dozen might be people of security interest" ... At that point, having gone through those various layers of putting different sorts of data together, comparing, contrasting and seeing what

11 *Supra* as per First Sitting Committee Debate Session 2015–16, Column 23, available at http://www.publications.parliament.uk/pa/cm201516/cmpublic/investigatorypowers/160324/am/160324s01.htm accessed 30 March 2018.

12 *Ibid.*

13 *Ibid.*

> comes out, you might say, "Perhaps for those half a dozen, some more targeted form of surveillance is justified" … Once you have done that [subject to authorisations], you might then find that some of them are self-evidently not, because they are BBC journalists who have been following the story or similar … But you might find that you have one or two who look as though they might be IS activists … so you put some resource into establishing what they are doing and who they are associating with.[14] [My emphasis]

This represents the 'sort of process in which MI5 have used these sorts of capability over the last 10 years or so', and, according to Evans, it has been 'absolutely central' to law enforcement agencies in identifying individuals involved in terrorist planning.[15] The information attained is then fed through into more intensive investigations, enabling policing and security agencies to prevent terrorist attacks.[16] Regardless of the centrality, these powers form part of the agencies' capabilities and it is quite clear from this statement that UK law enforcement have been using bulk collection powers for more than the last ten years, with little or no legal regulation. According to Evans, IPA merely includes legal regulation in an attempt to remedy the lacking provisions, transparency and accountability.[17]

Bulk interception of electronic communications data and content: the legal definitions

The entire framework provides extraordinarily vast surveillance powers to state agencies, particularly law enforcement agencies, when acting in the interests of national security. One of those powers allows for the bulk interception and acquisition and retention of electronic communications data. In order to understand the extent of these powers, the legal definition of electronic communications data and what is meant by interception must first be elaborated on.

Electronic communications data is data in the course of transmission. This does not include the content of the communication, merely the record of a transmission that has taken place, and the interception of communications is the action of procuring data in transition.[18] Electronic communications data remains defined in RIPA as:

> the times while a communication is being transmitted by means of a telecommunication system shall be taken to include any time when the system by means of which the communication *is being*, or *has been*, transmitted is used

14 *Ibid.*
15 *Ibid.*
16 *Supra* as per First Sitting Committee Debate Session 2015–16, Column 23.
17 *Ibid*, Column 23.
18 Regulation of Investigatory Powers Act 2000, s 2(7).

> for *storing* it in a manner that enables the intended recipient to collect it or otherwise to have access to it [My emphasis].[19]

However, due to the inclusion of the word 'storing', the interception may ultimately lead the policing and security agencies to look at some, if not all of the content, as per the general understanding of the word 'content'.[20] Confusingly, should law enforcement require access to data that is not in the course of transmission, then this is known legally as 'content', which has not been defined in RIPA. This has now been addressed and under section 261(6) of IPA, content is defined as follows:

> "Content", in relation to a communication and a telecommunications operator, telecommunications service or telecommunication system, means *any element* of the communication, or *any data attached* to or *logically associated* with the communication, which *reveals* anything of what might reasonably be considered to be the meaning (if any) of the communication, but –
>
> (a) any meaning arising from the fact of the communication or from any data relating to the transmission of the communication is to be *disregarded*; and
> (b) anything which is systems data is not content. [My emphasis]

This appears to mean that should the content be inadvertently obtained as part of the electronic communications data, for example, the content of a text message or email in transmission, it is to be disregarded. However, IPA has not taken the opportunity to redefine 'communications data'. It is therefore difficult to assess if this definition of 'content' has remedied the confusion surrounding the word 'storing' under RIPA. In 2013, the UK's Court of Appeal in *R v Coulson* ultimately held that electronic communications data is to be classed as being in the course of transmission when it is stored on an Internet server.[21] This in turn means that what may at first be generally considered to be content, such as an email, is in fact communications data, whilst it is being, or has been sent, or is in fact stored on an Internet server.

The impact of *Coulson* cannot be understated, as it permits UK law enforcement agencies access to the contents stored on an Internet server. Storing information by this method has increased exponentially in the 21st Century, particularly since the introduction of the online 'cloud' systems. These 'clouds' allow vast amounts of data to be stored, as covered in Chapter 2, such as that saved on smartphones or other smart devices, or word documents and research

19 Regulation of Investigatory Powers Act 2000, s 2(7). See Investigatory Powers Act 2016, s 261(5).
20 Regulation of Investigatory Powers Act 2000, ss 1(1) and 1(A)(3) and Wireless Telegraphy Act 2006, s 48(1)(4), Intelligence Services Act 1994, s 3(1)(a) and Security Service Act 1989, s 1(2)(3).
21 *R v Coulson* [2013] EWCA Crim 1026.

papers. It is debatable whether or not the definition of 'content' under IPA has remedied this problem given it remains untested by the courts.

Bulk communications data: interception, collection and retention

Bulk interception of electronic communications data was provided for under section 8(4) of RIPA. Section 136 of IPA has now replaced these provisions, maintaining law enforcement capabilities and introducing further safeguards. The idea behind this power is to allow law enforcement agencies to effectively monitor the Internet traffic and for the interception of large volumes of electronic communications in order to acquire the communications of terrorists and serious criminals that would not otherwise be available.[22] Should the warrant be authorised it could potentially establish links between known suspects, and also serve to increase the understanding of their behaviour. It could also assist law enforcement to understand new technologies, and how connections and multiple methods of electronic communications are made.[23]

It was argued during IPA's passage through Parliament that the initial collection and retention of bulk data lacked the requisite necessity and proportionality, despite a warrant having been granted.[24] Anderson so much as agreed with this point, confirming that the 'bulk powers are extraordinarily broad in scope'.[25] Eric King, the Director of 'Don't Spy On Us', voiced concerns with regard to the level of interception, practised disproportionately by GCHQ in particular, that permits the collection of '50 billion pieces of communication every single day'.[26] For King, it is this initial collection stage that lacks safeguards and accountability, and is deployed as a phishing exercise at the will of the security agencies.[27] He provided an example whereby GCHQ intercepted, '50 million pieces of webcam traffic', with 3–11 per cent of material containing undesirable nudity, under a computer program named Optic Nerve.[28] Once collected, GCHQ 'deployed facial recognition on it' without any further warrants being required.[29] A computer program completes this process, with little or no input from a human source.[30] With the processing complete, it is the next stage that requires authorisation via a targeted warrant.[31] However, in admitting that the security agencies require the power to collect data and analyse it, King confirmed that

22 Operational Case for Bulk Powers, p.26, available at https://www.gov.uk/government/uploads/system/uploads/attachment_data/file/504187/Operational_Case_for_Bulk_Powers.pdf accessed 12 March 2018.
23 Draft Codes of Practice: Investigatory Powers Act 2016, Paragraph 6.3, available at https://www.gov.uk/government/uploads/system/uploads/attachment_data/file/561091/16-10-18_Interception_code_of_practice_draft.pdf accessed 30 March 2018.
24 *Supra* as per First Sitting Committee Debate Session 2015–16, Column 13.
25 *Ibid*, Column 7.
26 *Ibid*, Column 13.
27 *Ibid*.
28 *Ibid*.
29 *Ibid*.
30 *Ibid*, Column 14.
31 *Ibid*, Column 13.

the more one knows and understands about the inner workings of the security agencies the 'more reassured' one becomes.[32] There certainly exists within the political establishment a clear difference of opinion between those that know and understand this work and those that do not in offering support for IPA and increased state powers. Considering the sheer amount of terrorism-related electronic communications data traffic and the successful expert use by IS as covered in Chapter 2, such powers are essential in reducing and combatting the threat posed.

In procedural terms, a bulk interception warrant can be issued under section 136 of IPA, should conditions A and B be met. Condition A represents the main purpose of the warrant, which must be one or both of the following:

(a) the interception of overseas-related communications;
(b) the obtaining of secondary data from such communications.[33]

Condition B is that the warrant authorises the person to whom it is addressed to secure any of the following activities:

(a) the interception, in the course of their transmission by means of a telecommunication system, of communications described in the warrant;
(b) the obtaining of secondary data from communications transmitted by means of such a system and described in the warrant;
(c) the selection for examination, in any manner described in the warrant, of intercepted content or secondary data obtained under the warrant;
(d) the disclosure, in any manner described in the warrant, of anything obtained under the warrant to the person to whom the warrant is addressed or to any person acting on that person's behalf.[34]

Importantly IPA defines secondary data in relation to communications, which could include: messages sent between items of network infrastructure to enable the system to manage the flow of communications; router configurations or firewall configurations; software operating systems; the period of time a router had been active in a network; the location of a meeting in a calendar appointment; photograph information.[35]

Interestingly, section 136(5) permits under the warrant the interception of communications that are not specifically described in the warrant. This means that law enforcement agencies are able to use unconstrained methods not reliant upon the type of surveillance device being used or the type of communication being

32 *Ibid*, Column 20.
33 Investigatory Powers Act 2016, s 136(2).
34 Investigatory Powers Act 2016, s 136(4).
35 Investigatory Powers Act 2016, s 137. See also Investigatory Powers Bill Explanatory Notes, p.50, 8 June 2016, available at http://www.publications.parliament.uk/pa/bills/lbill/2016-2017/0040/17040en.pdf accessed 30 March 2018.

intercepted. Surveillance legislation has been somewhat hindered in the past, focused on the types of devices and surveillance techniques used. For example, as evidenced in *Khan v UK*, the Interception of Communications Act 1985 (ICA) failed at the time to offer a progressive surveillance framework, instead being limited by surveillance technology such as cordless telephones and private networks.[36]

Bulk acquisition

The same procedural authorisation process is followed in section 158, which deals with the power to issue bulk acquisition warrants. According to the *Bulk Acquisition Draft Code of Practice*, this type of warrant authorises the obtainment of electronic communications data from a communication service provider (CSP).[37] This may comprise of the systems data and the communications content.[38] Here the UK Government has introduced a two-stage process, first obtaining the bulk electronic communications data from a CSP, and secondly selecting from that data communications to be examined.[39] This type of warrant is not targeted and thereby not constrained to a specific operation. It is therefore limitless in terms of the amount of electronic communications data that can be obtained. This is a seriously invasive power and as such only members of the security agencies can apply for the warrant, such as the Secret Intelligence Service and GCHQ.

The type of data: access and procedure

Two issues arise from both the bulk powers of interception and acquisition of electronic communications data. First, once the electronic communications data is intercepted and then stored, law enforcement such as the Secret Intelligence Service can acquire the communications data under IPA.[40] With similar provisions present to those governing interception, it must be evidenced that obtaining such electronic communications data is necessary for one of the purposes set out in IPA, and that it is necessary and proportionate to do so.[41] Additional safeguards are provided currently by independent judicial commissioners, and are reviewable by the Independent Investigatory Powers Commissioner who

36 *Khan v UK* [2000] 31 EHRR 1016, ECHR 195. See I. Leigh (1986) A Tapper's Charter? *Public Law*, Spring, 8–18. See also *Effick* [1994] 99 Cr. App. R. 312, and *Halford v UK* [1997] EHRLR 540.

37 Bulk Acquisition Draft Code of Practice, Published for consultation alongside the Investigatory Powers Bill, Home Office, Spring 2016, at 1.2, available at https://www.gov.uk/government/uploads/system/uploads/attachment_data/file/505412/Bulk_Acquisition_draft_code_of_practice.PDF accessed 13 March 2018.

38 *Ibid* 2.8.

39 *Ibid* 3.1.

40 Investigatory Powers Act 2016, s 158(1).

41 Investigatory Powers Act 2016, s 158(1)(b). See also Regulation of Investigatory Powers Act 2000, s (7).

oversees the security agencies' arrangements for access to the data.[42] This 'double lock' system provides a new proactively pervaded human rights agenda.

Procedurally, in accessing the collected communications data, it is important to note at this point that the level of authorisation required depends on the level of information requested, and by whom. Public authorities, for example, can only request service use information and subscriber information. Policing and security agencies, however, may additionally be able to access raffic data, dependent upon the specific agency. Although a designated police inspector may request and authorise subscriber information, only a superintendent may authorise a request for traffic data and service use information. In order to understand further, RIPA divides communications data into three categories:

> *Traffic data* that identifies the person or suspect, the apparatus used, and the location or address of where a communication is transmitted including the information about a computer file or a program, which has been accessed or run in the course of sending or receiving a communication.[43] Traffic data includes location software used by mobile telephones (geodata) when either stationary or moving, and private Wi-Fi networks. According to the Acquisition Code, website addresses beyond the uniform resource locator (url) first slash are not traffic data, but classed as contents. IP addresses remain classed as traffic data;[44] *Service use information* relates to the use of a specific telecommunications service. The service provider records and holds the usage frequency and specific details of the service used by the citizen, such as the amount of data downloaded;[45] *Subscriber information* includes data such as their postal address, telephone numbers and email address. It can also cover their bank account data and personal information divulged at the time the citizen requested an account with the service provider.[46] [My emphasis]

However, providing the interception of electronic communications is necessary and proportionate, the law enforcement agencies can use their powers of interception through RIPA and IPA, which is issued under any international mutual assistance agreement.[47]

42 See https://www.gov.uk/government/uploads/system/uploads/attachment_data/file/473744/Factsheet-Investigatory_Powers_Commission.pdf accessed 13 March 2018.
43 Regulation of Investigatory Powers Act 2000, s 21(4)(a), 21(6).
44 Acquisition Code, paragraph 2.20 states 'traffic data may identify a server or domain name (i.e. a web site) but not a web page'. As pointed out by the Interception of Communications Commissioners Office, there is a degree of ambiguity arising out of the absence of any definition of 'content' within RIPA. See the Interception of Communications Commissioner's submission to D. Anderson QC (2015). Also note the Acquisition Code provides at 2.26 and at 42 that IP addresses can be stored by a service provider in conjunction with subscriber information, in which case it would need to be treated as subscriber information, not traffic data.
45 Regulation of Investigatory Powers Act 2000, ss 21(4)(b) and 22(4).
46 Regulation of Investigatory Powers Act 2000, s 21(4)(c).
47 Regulation of Investigatory Powers Act 2000, ss 4, 6. See also Investigatory Powers Act 2016, ss 10, 15, 18, 20, 40, 56 and Schedule 9, 1.

Internet Connection Records: the definition and controversy

Internet Connection Records (ICRs) have caused some controversy and are covered specifically by section 62 of IPA. According to the UK's Prime Minister Theresa May they are the modern day equivalent of an itemised telephone bill, a fact others uncompromisingly dispute.[48] The then Shadow Home Secretary Andy Burnham, for example, has argued they are much more enlightening than an itemised bill, revealing an itinerary style that includes location data.[49] Regardless, May laboured the point that 'Internet connection records *do not* provide access to a person's *full web browsing* history. An Internet connection record is a record of what *Internet services a device* or person has *connected* to, not every web page they have visited'[50] . ICRs, however, are not a real record *per se*, or indeed similar to that of a call data record held by telephone service operators. At best they may be a collection of, or a subset of, retained electronic communications data. The problem here is that 'an operator subject to a retention order will have to decide on a case-by-case basis what data the operator shall retain, and it will not be the same for all operators and could be very different indeed'.[51] The next issue concerns the definition of ICRs under IPA, whereby section 62(7) states that ICRs means communications data that:

> may be used to identify, or assist in identifying, a telecommunications service to which a communication is transmitted by means of a telecommunication system for the purpose of obtaining access to, or running, a computer file or computer program, and, comprises data generated or processed by a telecommunications operator in the process of supplying the telecommunications service to the sender of the communication (whether or not a person).[52]

Clearly, as indicated in earlier text provided by the UK Government, ICRs will be used by law enforcement to identify the communications service to which a device is connected; in an attempt to close the capabilities gap as discussed in Chapter 2.[53] According to the Government an ICR does not represent a citizen's full Internet browsing history, only a record of the services connected to. Therefore, following this statement, an ICR would only show the url up to the first slash, as in www.bla

48 House of Commons Second Reading, 15 March 2016, Column 830, available at http://www.publications.parliament.uk/pa/cm201516/cmhansrd/cm160315/debtext/160315-0001.htm#16031546000001.accessed 30 March 2018

49 *Ibid.*

50 *Ibid* Column 820.

51 Andrews and Arnold Ltd. (2015) Written evidence (DIP0001) submitted to the Joint Committee on the Draft Investigatory Powers Bill, available at https://www.parliament.uk/documents/joint-committees/draft-investigatory-powers-bill/written-evidence-draft-investigatory-powers-committee.pdf accessed 13 March 2018.

52 Investigatory Powers Act 2016, s 62(7).

53 Draft Investigatory Powers Bill: Guide to Powers and Safeguards, November 2015, Cm9152.

rblarblar.co.uk, as opposed to www.blarblarblar.co.uk/isis/mosul. On this basis, 'it seems reasonable to assume that in relation to app-based access to the Internet via smartphones or tablets the ICR would include the activation of the app, but nothing further'.[54]

The definition of ICRs does not seem to be satisfactory in terms of precision and clarity, and the accompanying codes of practice offer no real practicable assistance as such. IPA describes the functions of ICRs are to identify which 'person or apparatus is using an internet service where, the service and time of use are already known, but the identity of the person or apparatus using the service is not known'.[55] According to IPA, ICRs can be used to identify which Internet communications service is being used, when and how it is being used and by whom.[56] Finding out who the specific person was who used the particular device is only possible, however, by performing some sort of profiling. Additionally, the ICR could also be utilised to confirm the identity of the person who is obtaining access to, or running a computer file or computer program, which involves making available, or acquiring, material the possession of which is a crime.[57] For Bernal, all three examples of how ICRs can be used are 'poorly suited to performing these functions'.[58] ICRs can potentially carry more communications data than required, hence be more intrusive on the individual's privacy, and at the same time provide inadequate information to enable law enforcement to make a decision as to whether or not target surveillance be initiated.[59]

Prime Minister Theresa May's statement is misleading, therefore, because ICRs cannot simply be equated to an itemised telephone bill because they do not record with whom a citizen has been communicating.[60] Instead they show a record of websites visited which has the potential to reveal innocent intimate, personal and sensitive data.[61] The amount of information that can be attained from this Internet history is much greater than an itemised telephone bill, with the potential to reveal the citizens' political interests, general health and sexuality. According to Bernal this 'makes ICRs ideal for profiling and potentially subject to function-creep/mission-creep'.[62] It would appear that using ICRs in this fashion is the only way of accurately assessing the identity of the user. As covered in Chapter 2, IP addresses are useless in this regard. Because of the amount of information that an ICR can yield, it is not surprising that the Government would want potential access to it in preventing serious crime, and pre-empting a terrorist attack.

54 P. Bernal (2015), Supplementary Written Evidence (IPB0018) Submitted to the Joint Committee on the Draft Investigatory Powers Bill, available at https://www.parliament.uk/documents/joint-committees/draft-investigatory-powers-bill/written-evidence-draft-investigatory-powers-committee.pdf accessed 30 March 2018.
55 Investigatory Powers Act 2016, s 62(3).
56 Investigatory Powers Act 2016, s 62(3).
57 Investigatory Powers Act 2016, s 62(3).
58 *Supra* as per P. Bernal (2015).
59 *Ibid.*
60 *Ibid.*
61 *Ibid.*
62 *Ibid.*

These powers are not only aimed at terrorism, however, given that ICRs are often used to combat online child sexual exploitation.[63] Ministers Simon Hoare and Lucy Frazer noted that ICRs had led to the identification by police of at least 600 child abusers in the UK, where it was shown that '92% of the communications data requested proved helpful'.[64] Anderson's 2015 report further highlights this fact, where only 1 per cent of communications data was used in investigating terrorism, against 15 per cent used for sexual offences and vulnerable or missing persons.[65]

Internet Connection Records: vulnerabilities

The problem with operators holding ICR data is the linked risk to criminality, meaning that the potential for new vulnerabilities is fashioned by the gathering and retaining of ICRs. In terms of cybercrime and cyber terrorism, the databases of ICRs could potentially be interfered with, or hacked into, and used maliciously. The recent hacking of TalkTalk provides an example of this vulnerability to data privacy. According to news reports, as opposed to being carried out by professional criminals, it was in fact a bored 17-year-old who wanted to 'show off'.[66] Cyber security is becoming increasingly important in the 21st Century, and it is concerning to note that some service providers do not have adequately high levels of security built in to their frameworks.[67] It is clear from news reports that even those that do have high levels of security, companies such as Apple and Sony and some banking corporations, have all been vulnerable to hacking.[68] It therefore follows that ICR databases may be attractive for cyber criminals. Additionally, the vulnerabilities are intensified by the potential for human error or internal corruption.[69]

63 House of Commons Second Reading, 15 March 2016, Column 830, available at http://www.publications.parliament.uk/pa/cm201516/cmhansrd/cm160315/debtext/160315-0001.htm#16031546000001 accessed 27 March 2018

64 First Sitting Committee Debate Session 2015–16, Investigatory Powers Bill, Publications on the Internet, Columns 13 and 20, 24 March 2016, available at http://www.publications.parliament.uk/pa/cm201516/cmpublic/investigatorypowers/160324/am/160324s01.htm accessed 30 March 2018.

65 D. Anderson QC, Independent Reviewer of Terrorism Legislation (2015) *A Question of Trust: Report of the Investigatory Powers Review*, June, (The Stationary Office) p.135, see Table.

66 See http://www.bbc.co.uk/news/uk-37990246 accessed 30 March 2018.

67 See http://www.bbc.co.uk/news/technology-38223805 accessed 30 March 2018. See also http://www.ispreview.co.uk/index.php/2016/06/uk-inquiry-threatens-fine-isps-internet-data-security-fails.html accessed 30 March 2018.

68 See, for example, L. Bell (2016) Millions of Apple Devices at Risk of Attack due to a Security Bug, Wired Cyber Security, 22 July 2016, available at http://www.wired.co.uk/article/apple-security-bug-hackers-steal-your-password accessed 30 March 2018. See https://www.ft.com/content/f6c1c0b3-af81-3ac8-812c-d26a66e5ba8a accessed 30 March 2018. See also https://hakin9.org/hacking-social-media-threats-vulnerabilities-threats-anti-threats-strategies-for-social-networking-websites accessed 30 March 2018.

69 *Ibid.*

Internet Connection Records and Open Source Intelligence: the privacy conundrum

Although the necessity of these bulk powers to attain ICRs have proved useful, it remains the case that electronic communications data surveillance represents the new contemporary method of collecting information about an individual. This is understandable given the growth and use of technology, which continually increases as highlighted in Chapter 2. For Clarke, this has resulted in this type of surveillance becoming the guiding principle for 'social control, particularly by managing populations through collection, sorting, management and risk assessment of data'.[70] Further evidence of this move is located in the 2008 Home Affairs Select Committee's report titled 'A Surveillance Society', where it was concluded that the 'foundation for all new surveillance is the database'.[71] According to Haggerty, data surveillance has moved from the traditional top-down or panoptic state approach to more of an informational gathering exercise carried out by retailers, employers, insurers, Her Majesty's Revenue and Customs (HMRC) and information intermediaries such as social networks and online gaming companies.[72]

In a rather surprising twist law enforcement agencies have copied the approach taken by private companies and incorporated this use in their own procedures. Following the changes in technology, as Trottier proffers, data surveillance in terms of social media policing forms part of this new contemporary framework.[73] This move, however, is essential in dealing with the issues raised in Chapter 2, concerning how terrorist groups communicate by exploiting social media and electronic communications. Considering private companies and private individuals use Open Source Intelligence (OSINT) and Social Media Intelligence (SMI or SOCMINT) to monitor other people in way that might assist in private civil litigation matters, it is not a tall ask to permit the same ability for law enforcement in assisting them to prevent a terrorist attack.

OSINT is defined as the collection, analysis and use of data from openly available sources for intelligence purposes.[74] Although there is some overlap, SOCMINT involves the analysis of social media, Facebook and YouTube, for example, in order

70 R. Clarke (1991) Information Technology and Dataveillance. In C. Dunlop and R. Kling (eds), *Computerization and Controversy: Value Conflicts and Social Choices* (Academic Press, Inc.).

71 Home Affairs Select Committee, *A Surveillance Society? Fifth Report of Session 2007–2008* (HC 2008–2009 58-I, 8 June 2008).

72 K. Haggerty (2006) Tearing Down the Walls: On Demolishing the Panopticon. In D. Lyon (ed.), *Theorizing Surveillance: The Panopticon and Beyond* (Willan). See R. Jones (2000) Digital Rule: Punishment, Control and Technology, *Punishment and Society,* 2 (5), 5–22. See also R. Boyne (2000) Post Panopticism, *Economy and Society,* 29, 285–307. See also W. Bogard (2006) Welcome to the Society of Control. In K. D. Haggerty and R.V. Ericson (eds) *The New Politics of Surveillance Visibility* (University of Toronto Press) p.10.

73 D. Trottier (2012) *Social Media as Surveillance: Rethinking Visibility in a Converging World* (Ashgate Publishing).

74 B. J. Koops, J. Hoepman and R. Leenes (2013) Open Source Intelligence and Privacy by Design, *Computer Law and Security Review,* 29, 676–688, 676.

to measure and arguably monitor the 'millions of people digitally arguing, talking, joking, condemning and applauding online' in order to facilitate the identification of criminal activity, 'indicate early warning of outbreaks of disorder, provide information and intelligence about groups and individuals, and help understand and respond to public concerns'.[75] Considering IS's decentralised electronic communications strategy raised in Chapter 2, monitoring individuals that like or re-tweet, for example, an IS message is essential. They both represent the new 21st Century categories of intelligence used by the UK policing security agencies.[76] As above, private companies and individuals, for example a solicitor, also use this type of intelligence in identifying fraudulent civil claims for personal injury. Considering the extensive use of the Internet and open sources data, it is not surprising to see an increase in the utilisation for intelligence.

The Intelligence and Security Committee's report of 2015 highlighted the fact that the Internet carries the communications of 2.4 billion Internet users. In one minute, those 2.4 billion transfer 1,572,877 gigabytes of data, including 204 million emails, 4.1 million Google searches, 6.9 million messages sent via Facebook, 347,222 posts to Twitter and 138,889 hours of video watched on YouTube.[77] This highlights the point that increasingly people are living their lives online. Having the ability to tap into this mass of information has proved essential for law enforcement agencies. To this end, the potential value of OSINT and SOCMINT available to law enforcement agencies was first realised during the investigation into the London 2011 riots.[78] This allows for intelligence-led policing, where predictive analytical software is used to anticipate and predict crime.[79] According to the RUSI report of 2015, up to 95% of the intelligence that was collected by UK policing and security agencies , originated from OSINT, not closed sources.[80] It could be argued that this is a much more cost-effective method of conducting electronic communication data surveillance.[81] In 2014 James Clapper of the US Office of the Director of National Intelligence described social media as being 'huge for intelligence purposes'.[82]

75 *Ibid.*

76 D. Omand, J. Bartlett and C. Miller (2012) Introducing Social Media Intelligence, *Intelligence and National Security Review*, 27(6), 801–823, 801.

77 Intelligence and Security Committee (2015) *Privacy and Security: A Modern and Transparent Legal Framework*, HC 1075 2014/15, 12 March, paragraph 55.

78 P. Lewis *et al.* (2012) Reading the Riots: Investigating England's Summer of Disorder, *Guardian shorts* and *Guardian*, Chapter 8.

79 C. Miller and S. Ginnis *et al.* (2015) The Road to Representivity (Centre for the Analysis of Social Media at Demos/IPSOS Mori, September) available at http://www.demos.co.uk/project/the-road-to-representivity accessed 13 March 2018.

80 Royal United Services Institute (RUSI) (2015) *A Democratic Licence to Operate: Report of the Independent Surveillance Review Panel of the Independent Surveillance Review*, Whitehall Reports, 13 July 2015, available at https://rusi.org/publication/whitehall-reports/democratic-licence-operate-report-independent-surveillance-review, paragraph 3.16, accessed 13 March 2018.

81 *Ibid.*

82 See https://www.dni.gov/index.php/about/leadership/director-of-national-intelli gence Accessed 27 March 2018.

Anderson also refers to the increasing use and central reliance on OSINT and SOCMINT in his 2015 report.[83]

This type of electronic communications data surveillance fits with the understanding of intelligence-led policing.[84] For Tilley, this represents the most practical way for the police to do business, 'more smartly, incorporating modern information technology and modern methods', involving 'developing and maintaining a detailed and up-to-date picture of patterns of crime and criminality in order to intervene most effectively'.[85] Fitting in further with the risk-management style of counter-terrorism measures, intelligence-led policing has shifted from reactive to proactive in nature.[86] Examples of the operational and procedural side to OSINT and SOCMINT systems include the EU's Virtuoso OSINT software. This allows law enforcement agencies to gather together OSINT and Raytheon's Rapid Information Overlay Technology (RIOT) in one place, allowing assessments to be carried out quickly, by tracking an individual or group over different social networking sites.[87]

This area of surveillance lacks legal regulation and legal analysis. The acquisition of OSINT and SOCMINT is carried out without the consent or perhaps knowledge of the user. Perhaps this is simply down to the assumption that such open source information is accessible to the world, and therefore 'fair-game' for law enforcement surveillance. However, considering the amount of private, personal and intimate information disclosed via social media, coupled with the increase in police surveillance, often used to profile and target individuals autonomously, it presents a serious concern in terms of privacy. Current surveillance laws do not regulate OSINT or SOCMINT, so they remain vague and underexplored. In assessing this issue, for Gillespie OSINT and SOCMINT do not require legal regulation because

> when postings are public and available for all to see it unlikely that it could be concluded that the viewing of the information is covert in that there must be an awareness that those in authority could look at the postings.[88]

83 *Supra* as per D. Anderson QC (2015) p.55.
84 N. Tilley (2008) Modern Approaches to Policing: Community, Problem Orientated and Intelligence Led. In T. Newburn (ed.) *Handbook of Policing* (Willan) pp.373–383.
85 *Ibid.*
86 T. Newburn, T. Williamson and A. Wright (2008) *Handbook of Criminal Investigation* (2nd edition, Willan) p.653.
87 B. J. Koops (2013) Police Investigations in Internet Open Sources: Procedural Law Issues, *Computer Law and Security Review,* 29(6), 654–655, 654. See also S. Vaughan-Nicols (2013) Raytheon Riot: Defence Spying is Coming to Social Networks, ZDNet, 12 February 2013, available at http://www.zdnet.com/raytheon-riot-defense-spying-is-coming-to-social-networks 7000011191 accessed 13 March 2018. See also R. Gallagher (2013) Software that Tracks People on Social Media Created by Defence Firm, *Guardian,* 10 February 2013, available at http://www.theguardian.com/world/2013/feb/10/software-trackssocial-media-defence accessed 13 March 2018.
88 A. Gillespie (2009) Regulation of Internet Surveillance, *European Human Rights Law Review,* 4, 552–565, 552.

However, receiving little public attention or legal analysis, private information shared on a public format such as social media remains private if one were to follow the framework of the EU's 2002 e-Privacy Directive, discussed at length in Chapter 4. Accordingly, Omand *et al.* concluded that the use of OSINT and SOCMINT must be 'grounded in respect for human rights and the associated principles of accountability, proportionality and necessity'.[89]

The US has led the key developments in this area, where a 2012 survey of 1,221 federal, state and local law enforcement agencies highlighted four out of five enforcement professionals admitted to using SOCMINT in the course of their investigations.[90] Of the many stories provided, one in particular was emphasised whereby the law enforcement official stated that:

> Further investigation (utilising Facebook) revealed the threats were credible and we conducted follow-up investigations, which revealed a student intent on harming others (detailed emails and notebooks). The student was in the process of attempting to acquire weapons. It's my belief we avoided a 'Columbine' type scenario.[91]

For Trottier, the EU Member States and UK have been slow to utilise OSINT and SOCMINT in comparison to the US, describing them both as still in a 'formative stage'.[92] It did, however, prove pivotal during the police investigation into the London Riots in 2011, where encrypted Blackberry instant messages and Twitter were used.[93] It was also interesting to see the police using social media to enhance the chances of identifying suspects; by creating a Flickr account and

89 *Supra* as per D. Omand *et al.* (2012). See also D. Omand, J. Bartlett and C. Miller (for UK Cabinet Office) (2010) *A Strong Britain in an Age of Uncertainty: The National Security Strategy,* October (HMSO) p.5. See also G. Deleuze (1992) Postscripts on the Societies of Control, *The MIT Press*, October Winter edition, 59, 3–7, 3.

90 LexisNexis® Risk Solutions (2012) Survey of Law Enforcement Personnel and Their Use of Social Media in Investigations. , Lexis Nexis, available at https://www.lexisnexis.com/risk/downloads/whitepaper/Infographic-Social-Media-Use-in-Law-Enforcement.pdf accessed 30 March 2018.

91 *Ibid.*

92 D. Trottier (2015) Open Source Intelligence, Social Media and Law Enforcement: Visions, Constraints and Critiques, *European Journal of Cultural Studies,* 18(4–5), 530–547. 542.

93 V. Dodd (2011b) Police Accessed Blackberry Messages to Thwart Planned Riots, *Guardian*, 16 August 2011, available at https://www.theguardian.com/uk/2011/aug/16/police-accessed-blackberry-messages-thwart-riots accessed 30 March 2018, see also K. Wynn and K. Blyth (2011) Predicting a Riot: At What Price Privacy? Practical Law Company, available at http://uk.practicallaw.com/9-507-6354 accessed 30 March 2018, see also C. Williams (2011) London Riots: BlackBerry Manufacturer Offers to Help Police, *Telegraph*, 8 August 2011, available at http://www.telegraph.co.uk/technology/blackberry/8689313/London-riots-BlackBerry-manufacturer-offers-to-help-police-in-any-way-we-can.html accessed 30 March 2018. See also J. Ball and P. Lewis (2011) Twitter and the Riots: How the News Spread, *Guardian*, 7 December 2011, available at http://www.theguardian.com/uk/2011/dec/07/twitter-riots-how-news-spread accessed 30 March 2018.

by posting pictures they effectively conscripted the public to assist in the identification of individuals.[94] Conversely police forces across the UK have recently created Facebook accounts and often post pictures of wanted suspects.[95] Exact figures are difficult to attain, as is the actual effectiveness. However, in 2012 a news report suggested that there were 4,908 reports in which Facebook and Twitter were factored.[96]

Similar to the US, as part of OSINT and SOCMINT, the UK has started to use predictive profiling technological systems such as the IBM Predictive system.[97] In 2013, the UK launched the EMOTIVE project using an OSINT approach whereby the experimental automated software scanned up to 2000 tweets per second.[98] In response to the potential growth in utilising open sources as part of law enforcement intelligence, the UK College of Policing in 2015 issued guidance on its use.[99] It notes that 'open sources of information are widely available but may not be accurate, reliable or valid'.[100] Despite this, when used in conjunction with other intelligence sources, it has been proved to be useful in seeking a prosecution for terrorist offences.[101] This was seen with the prosecution of Anjem Choudary and Mohammed Rahman in 2016, following their online posts on YouTube, Twitter and on an extremist website encouraging support for the IS terrorist group.[102] Although this is an important point, Choudary was a key figure in al-Muhajiroun, a group that is proscribed by the UK. Choudary was prolific in his quest, constantly re-inventing the group using different names following

94 J. Bartlett, C. Miller, J. Crump and L. Middleton (2013) Policing in an Information Age, Centre for Analysis of Social Media, Demos, March, available at http://www.demos.co.uk/files/DEMOS_Policing_in_an_Information_Age_v1.pdf?1364295365 accessed 30 March 2018.

95 See https://www.facebook.com/cheshirepolice/?fref=ts&ref=br_tf accessed 30 December 2016. See also http://www.digitaltrends.com/social-media/the-new-inside-source-for-police-forces-social-networks accessed 30 March 2018.

96 See https://www.theguardian.com/media/2012/dec/27/social-media-crime-facebook-twitter and https://smallbiztrends.com/2015/12/police-using-facebook-to-solve-crimes.html accessed 30 March 2018.

97 T. Thomson (2010) Crime Software May Help Police Predict Violent Offences, *Guardian*, 25 July 2010, available at http://www.guardian.co.uk/uk/2010/jul/25/police-software-crime-prediction accessed 13 March 2018. See also IBM (2010) Ministry of Justice Chooses IBM Predictive Analytics to Make Streets Safe, IBM Press Release, 16 March 2010.

98 BBC News (2013) Computer Program Uses Twitter to Map Mood of Nation, 7 September 2013, available at http://www.bbc.co.uk/news/technology-24001692 accessed 13 March 2018.

99 College of Policing (2015) Intelligence Collection, Development and Dissemination, available at https://www.app.college.police.uk/app-content/intelligence-management/intelligence-cycle accessed 30 March 2018.

100 *Ibid.*

101 *Ibid.*

102 J. Grierson, V. Dodd and J. Rodrigues (2016) Anjem Choudary Convicted of Supporting Islamic State, *Guardian*, 16 August 2016, available at https://www.theguardian.com/uk-news/2016/aug/16/anjem-choudary-convicted-of-supporting-islamic-state accessed 30 March 2018.

continuous proscription. Some of the names used were Ghurabaa, Isman4UK and Muslims Against Crusades. In investigating IS law enforcement assessed 20 years' worth of material, held on 333 electronic devices containing 12.1TB of data.[103]

The law enforcement agencies' use of OSINT and SOCMINT has yielded some positive results. However, concerns turn on two specific points: they potentially lack legal regulation and privacy safeguards. In terms of legal regulation, it is not as simple to merely stating the information in the public domain is fair-game for authorities to use as part of their data mining or profiling exercises, as this should almost be expected. Rules exist through RIPA, IPA and the other Acts of Parliament, as per above, controlling access to electronic communications data, and equipment interference is discussed below. Bartlow, drawing on Semitsu's words, confirms that 'Facebook is a giant surveillance tool, no warrant required, which the government can use in a mind boggling creative range of ways with almost no practical constraints from existing laws'.[104]

Although there may be some obviousness to the fact that SOCMINT should not require privacy protection, Edwards and Urquhart note three rebutted points.[105] First is the potential it has to greatly advance intelligence in terms of data mining and profiling. This is because, in addition to pictures, videos and interest links, the authorities peruse the individual's friends list, or follows and followers, in order to draw up a type of social graph.[106] Another important point to mention is the fact some social media sites automatically post an individual's location upon posting.[107] This type of profiling could lead authorities to draw a 'guilty by association' conclusion. Inferences can also be drawn from this type of data, utilising software such as EMOTIVE, whereby the analysis is done through automated algorithmic means targeting online behaviours, rather than involving human scrutiny at that early stage. It has been evidenced that an analysis of Facebook 'Likes' can be used to indicate the most sensitive of data including sexuality, for example. According to a recent study carried out at Cambridge University, 'by mining Facebook Likes, the computer

103 V. Dodd (2016) Anjem Choudary Jailed for Five-and-a-Half Years for Urging Support for ISIS, *Guardian*, 6 September 2016, available at https://www.theguardian.com/uk-news/2016/sep/06/anjem-choudary-jailed-for-five-years-and-six-months-for-urging-support-of-isis accessed 30 March 2018.

104 J. Semitsu (2011) From Facebook to Mug Shot: How the Death of Social Networking Privacy Rights Revolutionized Online Government Surveillance, *Pace Law Review* 31(1), 291–381. See also A. Bartow (2011) Facebook and the Fourth Amendment: Expecting Any Privacy May be Unreasonable, *Jotwell*, 18 April 2011, available at http://cyber.jotwell.com/2011/04 accessed 30 March 2018.

105 L. Edwards and L. Urquhart (2015) Privacy in Public Spaces: What Expectations of Privacy Do We Have in Social Media Intelligence? *International Journal of Law and Information Technology*, 24(3), 279–310.

106 *Ibid.*

107 *Ibid.*

model was able to predict a person's personality more accurately than most of their friends and family'.[108]

The second point concerns the reliability of the content posted on social media. One may find oneself 'tagged' in a picture that is either not of you, or has been doctored to a great extent.[109] One can also be added to groups and pages without actually accepting the invitation.[110] The third and final observation point involves the constant changes in social media platforms that require the user to update their privacy settings regularly. As highlighted by Edwards and Urquhart, 'different privacy settings and different changes, apply to different types of content, such as posts, comments, groups, photos and friends lists'.[111] It is well known that some users are deluded both in their belief that all the information on social media is private, and that they have protected themselves adequately by updating their security settings.[112] For these reasons, it is argued this, 'contributes strongly to an argument that material placed on social media can still carry with it reasonable expectations of privacy'.[113] This is continually highlighted through Facebook,'s for example, whereby despite reassurances that information added to Facebook will remain safe and secure, some users post a meaningless notice re-affirming their privacy.[114]

Despite the UK Government's recent ability to provide legal regulation, there remains no specific guidance, or indeed a mention in the UK surveillance legislation, regarding the acquisition of OSINT and SOCMINT data. There is furthermore little evidence to suggest the policing authorities consider themselves constrained by RIPA, or now, by extension, IPA.[115] This is not surprising given that open sources can be used by anyone, such as an employer who can Google search a prospective employee and access their social media, without a warrant or authority. Therefore, one might argue why should law enforcement state agencies be handicapped by having to obtain an authority, not forgetting that access to such communications data could save citizens' lives.

Considering the reality of social media's use it could be argued such data collection should fall within the meaning of RIPA and IPA, meaning that it is treated the same way as covert and intrusive, and thereby within the remit of interception of communications data.[116] This would create a safeguarding level of protection for an individual's privacy, requiring the same authorisations and internal and external controlling mechanisms. O'Floinn and Ormerod purpose an interception

108 See http://www.cam.ac.uk/research/news/computers-using-digital-footprints-a re-better-judges-of-personality-than- friends-and-family#sthash.OSQ8dqdr.dpuf accessed 30 March 2018.

109 *Ibid* p.15.

110 *Ibid.*

111 *Ibid.*

112 *Ibid.*

113 *Ibid* p.16.

114 See https://blog.malwarebytes.com/cybercrime/2016/10/facebook-will-make-all-p osts-public-not accessed 30 March 2018.

115 *Ibid.*

116 M. O'Floinn and D. Ormerod (2011) Social Networking Sites, RIPA and Criminal Investigations, *Criminal Law Review*, 10, 766–789, 766.

warrant be necessary, especially when policing authorities utilise 'backdoor' methods, by means of equipment interference, in order to acquire direct messages sent through social media.[117] Although one could assume such messages are no longer within the definition of communications data, section 2(7) of RIPA extends the period of transmission to 'anytime when the system is used for storing it in a manner that enables the intended recipient to collect it or otherwise have access to it'.[118] This would fit with the earlier mentioned case *R v Coulson* where it was held voicemail messages stored for future use remained in transmission.[119] The impact of IPA on this legal authority is as yet unknown.

What is clear from RIPA and IPA is the fact that the main aim is to intercept communications data in 'real time'. This is essential for law enforcement to keep up with the potential terrorists, and allows it to pre-empt the next step, as the terrorists progress with their plans. It remains unclear if an interception warrant would be appropriate, given it would have to remain in place for an indefinite period. For Edwards and Urquhart it 'remains an open problem if an interception warrant could appropriately be issued after a social media post has been read and perhaps replied to'.[120] This could have further impact on an individual's right to privacy and data protection, particularly for anyone not suspected of criminal activity. Access to this type of data is invaluable to UK policing and security agencies. It has been shown that the intrusive power of communication interception is one of the most important techniques that can be used, by only a small number of policing agencies for specific purposes, in the investigation of terrorism.[121] It is in this sense that interception of communications data, OSINT and SOCMINT supports criminal investigations by providing pivotal intelligence.[122] The Director-General of the Office of Security and Counter-Terrorism (OSCT) pointed out the importance of this power:

> Intelligence [from interception] has led *directly* to the prevention of terrorist attacks and serious crime, the success of operations aimed at countering the proliferation of weapons of mass destruction and the saving of lives. Overall, RIPA interception is a *critical tool* in investigations into the full range of threats to national security.[123] [My emphasis]

In Anderson's 2015 report, policing and security agencies in the UK laboured the point that inception was vital to the success of their work. Of this MI5 said that interception powers were crucial where intelligence gained is unique to electronic

117 *Ibid.*
118 Regulation of Investigatory Powers Act 2000, s 2(7).
119 *R v Coulson* [2013] EWCA Crim 1026.
120 *Supra* as per L. Edwards and L. Urquhart (2015) p.18.
121 *Intercept as Evidence*, The Office for Security and Counter-Terrorism (Cm8989, December 2014), a report by a committee of Privy Counsellors led by the Rt. Hon. Sir John Chilcott, p.4.
122 *Ibid.*
123 *Supra* as per D. Anderson QC (2015) p.126.

communications data.[124] Accordingly this would be hard to replicate.[125] The National Crime Agency (NCA) went further and confirmed that the intelligence gathered from interceptions of electronic communications data assisted them in prioritising their work. They continued:

> For some areas of NCA activity ... there are *no practical alternatives* to using ... interception ... In 2013–14, interception played a *critical role* in investigations that resulted in: Over 2,200 arrests; Over 750kg of heroin and 2,000kg of cocaine seized; Over 140 firearms seized; and Over £20,000,000 seized. Police impressed upon [Anderson] that intercepted material may be useful in other types of cases, ranging from corruption investigations to domestic murder.[126] [My emphasis]

In response to Rifkind's 2013 report into access to communications data the Director General of MI5 stated:

> access to communications data of one sort or another is very important indeed. It's part of the backbone of the way in which we would approach investigations. I think I would be accurate in saying there are no significant investigations that we undertake across the service that don't use communications data because of its ability to tell you the who and the when and the where of your target's activities. It tends to be relatively reliable. It's relatively accessible at the moment in a number of areas, and from our point of view it's a very, very important capability ...[127]

Whilst it is accepted there are issues and concerns over citizens' data protection and privacy rights, the key points raised here and in Chapter 2 highlight the fact that in today's communications culture and issues related to law enforcement having to carry out surveillance these powers are essential. Safeguarding a citizen's right to life must be law enforcement's primary concern. Data protection and privacy rights must at these times take a back seat. In order to access some types of communications data, such as emails that have not been sent but simply saved on the server, or on a note-taking application on the smartphone device, law enforcement argue they need the power to interfere, or otherwise hack into the equipment.

124 *Ibid* p.127.
125 *Ibid.*
126 *Ibid* p.127.
127 The Rt. Hon. Sir Malcolm Rifkind MP (2013), Intelligence and Security Committee, Access to Communications Data by the Intelligence and Security Agencies, February 2013, Cm8514, p.9.

Bulk equipment interference: computer network exploitation

Bulk equipment interference is currently provided for under section 176 of IPA and sections 5 and 7 of ISA. According to the UK Government, equipment interference is used increasingly by law enforcement to mitigate the inability to acquire intelligence through conventional bulk interception, and to access data directly from computers and other devices, which may never have been obtainable otherwise. Alongside the proposed power comes another draft code of practice made pursuant to IPA.[128] These types of warrants are only available for operations overseas, whereby an example put forward illustrating the use states:

> Intelligence suggests that a [Islamic State]-inspired cell in a particular location in the Middle East is plotting an imminent bomb attack against UK interests in the region. Little is known about the individual members of the terrorist cell. However, it is known that a particular software package is commonly – but not exclusively – used by some terrorist groups. After using equipment interference to obtain equipment data from a large number of devices in the specified location, analysts apply analytical techniques to the data, starting with a search term ('selector') related to the known software package, to find common factors that indicate a terrorist connection. A series of refined searches of this kind, using evolving factors that are uncovered during the course of the analytical process, gradually identify devices within the original 'pot' of data collected that belong to the terrorist cell. Their communications (including content) can then be retrieved and examined. As the cell members can only be identified through a series of refined searches that cannot all be assessed in advance at the time the warrant is issued, second stage access controls are required to govern all of the data selection within the operation. Accordingly, a bulk equipment interference warrant is suitable.[129]

For Anderson, however, the UK Government has failed in this instance to make its case evidencing the need for this bulk power.[130] He goes on to emphasise the differences between the targeted equipment interference power and the bulk, where he notes his concerns lie 'particularly in relation to equipment interference, in that, if one looks at the so-called targeted power and, in particular, at its potential thematic use, it is quite extraordinarily broad'.[131] 'The code of practice indicates that the power is very broad indeed and that matters because the

128 Equipment Interference Draft Code of Practice, Home Office, Spring 2016, available at https://www.gov.uk/government/uploads/system/uploads/attachment_data/file/504238/Equipment_interference_draft_code_of_practice.PDF accessed 30 March 2018.

129 *Ibid.*

130 First Sitting Committee Debate Session 2015–2016, Investigatory Powers Bill, Publications on the Internet, Column 6, 24 March 2016, available at http://www.publications.parliament.uk/pa/cm201516/cmpublic/investigatorypowers/160324/am/160324s01.htm accessed 30 March 2018.

131 *Ibid.*

safeguards on the targeted power are less than those on bulk. For a start, you do not need to be aiming only at a person or persons outside the UK. You can quite properly target it at people inside the UK'.[132]

Bulk equipment interference: 'legalised hacking'

Following the *R v Coulson* authority, procedurally utilising Computer Network Exploitation (CNE), the UK policing and security agencies can legitimately hack into Internet servers, such as cloud storage systems, and view the content without the person affected knowing.[133] Martin raises two complaints that were made by Privacy International and a global coalition of ISPs claiming GCHQ lacked clear lawful authority to conduct specifically CNE operations.[134] Since Martin's assessment, the enactment of IPA and the *Coulson* case, the Government has introduced the Equipment Interference Code of Practice 2016, which confirms that an application must be made under section 5 or section 7 of the Intelligence Services Act 1994:

> a warrant under section 5 of the [ISA] should be sought wherever members of the Intelligence Services, or persons acting on their behalf or in their support, conduct equipment interference in relation to equipment located in the British Islands that would be otherwise unlawful ... If the equipment is located outside the British Islands, and the interference would be otherwise unlawful, the Security Service should seek a warrant under section 5 of the 1994 Act. In the case of SIS [Secret Intelligence Service/MI6] and GCHQ, an authorisation under section 7 may be obtained instead of a warrant under section 5.[135]

In essence bulk equipment interference introduces legalised hacking and is perhaps one of the most intrusive powers available to law enforcement. The fact these powers can be used en masse potentially places a camera in people's homes by hacking into their personal computers and smartphones, and activating them. The 21st Century citizen, for the main part at least, is totally reliant on their use of technology. The amount of sensitive data people store on their smartphones and other devices continually increases, and at the same time the sophistication and

132 *Ibid.*
133 *R v Coulson* [2013] EWCA Crim 1026. CNE is also known as Equipment Interference.
134 A. J. Martin (2105) GCHQ v Privacy International: Computer Hacking Tribunal Showdown Begins, *The Register*, 1 December 2015, available at http://www.theregister.co.uk/2015/12/01/gchq_privacy_international_investigatory_powers_tribunal accessed 30 March 2018.
135 Equipment Interference Code of Practice, Pursuant to Section 71 of the Regulation of Investigatory Powers Act 2000, January 2016, Home Office (The Stationary Office) paragraphs 4.1 and 4.2, https://www.gov.uk/government/uploads/system/uploads/attachment_data/file/496069/53693_CoP_Equipment_Interference_Accessible.pdf accessed 30 March 2018.

fortitude of cyber criminals has increased. In order to facilitate access to people's smartphones and other devices, IPA sets the scene introducing two new powers, the national security notice and the technical capabilities notice. Both these elements target applications providers and encryption. In contrast, two points are prevalent. First it would be logistically impossible in terms of law enforcement resources to hack into every citizen's pieces of digital equipment, and secondly, as pointed out in Chapter 2, terrorists are using encryption to hide their electronic communications data.[136] This means that smartphones and other smart devices, once decrypted, may hold vast quantities of quality intelligence essential to law enforcement.

The Equipment Interference Code of Practice has been introduced to also assist those working in counterterrorism to understand the procedure.[137] This code is one of many newly introduced by the Government that clearly show the authorisation processes that must be taken by the policing and security agencies. It worth mentioning here that the MI5 is governed by the Security Service Act 1989 and is primary concerned with internal threats to UK national security. The Secret Intelligence Service (more commonly referred to as MI6) is governed by the Intelligence Services Act 1994, and is primarily concerned with preventing external threats by obtaining and providing information relating to the actions or intentions of persons outside the British Islands, and to perform other tasks relating to the actions or intentions of such persons in the interests of national security.[138] Under the same authority, GCHQ's functions are to monitor or interfere with electromagnetic, acoustic and other emissions, and to obtain and provide information derived from or related to such emissions or equipment and from encrypted material in the interests of national security, or in support of the prevention or detection of serious crime.[139] The service's role here is essential in finding the ever elusive terrorist in the many technological haystacks.

Broad powers with restricted use and access: evidence of necessity

Within this broad yet restricted framework, according to the security agencies, accessing communications data or other information saved on computers or other devices plays a pivotal role in gaining valuable information, allowing them to build an accurate picture of the suspect, and serves to make up for the loss of intelligence that may otherwise be unobtainable through other surveillance techniques, such as end-to-end encryption.[140] Therefore 'it can sometimes be the only method available by which the security services can acquire the data'.[141] The Rt.

136 See http://www.telegraph.co.uk/news/uknews/1494190/MI5-we-did-no t-receive-a-warning.html accessed 30 March 2018.
137 *R v Coulson* [2013] EWCA Crim 1026, see also *supra* as per Equipment Interference Code of Practice.
138 *Ibid.*
139 *Ibid.*
140 *Ibid.*
141 *Ibid.*

Hon. Sir Malcolm Rifkind's research into the murder of Fusilier Lee Rigby on 22 May 2013 found that such bulk powers allow the security services to see what the suspect has been looking at and downloading from the Internet.[142] One of the terrorists, Adebowale, in fact came under the security services' gaze following his interest in online extremist material.[143] Although parts of Rifkind's report have been sanitised, it appears clear that in addition to the many extremist publications available online, Adebowale had been looking at *Inspire* magazine, created by al-Qaeda in the Arabian Peninsula (AQAP) to disseminate extremist information on the Internet in English.[144] According to MI5 in 2012–213:

> Inspire seeks to promote home-grown *lone actor* attacks, providing the ideological backing and *practical* instruction for users to commit attacks … [It] presents a variety of risks to the UK, including providing *** [sanitized text] instruction for violent attacks … we can now say that Inspire has been read by those involved in at least *seven out of the ten attacks* planned within the UK since its first issue [in 2010]. We judge that it significantly enhanced the capability of individuals in four of these ten attack plots …[145] [My emphasis]

Despite these findings, it is interesting to note that MI5 would not carry out any intrusive surveillance on an individual if they had only read the *Inspire* or *Dabiq* magazine. This is where we see the term proportionality added to necessity, as MI5 confirms that criterion alone would not be sufficient to qualify for intrusion.[146] Some individuals may well simply look at the material to satisfy their curiosity or perhaps have extremist views and enjoy reading it. However, there is no precise way at that stage of knowing if they are using the material in an instructive way to plan and carry out an attack. MI5 confirmed '[t]hat whilst there is a potential risk posed by those who access extremist media, they also caution that it does not follow that everyone who does so then engages with violent extremism'.[147]

Through IPA authorities, law enforcement must evidence that the action required is necessary and proportionate.[148] Both are international human rights principles that must be applied to electronic communications data surveillance. Representing an ECHR mechanism, any interference with a qualified right, in this case Article 8 the right to privacy, must be 'necessary in a democratic society'. This means that law enforcement must show a 'pressing social need', in addition to showing that the action required is proportionate. When reviewing these essential elements it becomes quite clear that the threshold is reasonably high, in terms of authorising state action. The disparity between those who merely read a terrorist

142 *Supra* as per The Rt. Hon. Sir Malcolm Rifkind MP (2014) p.59.
143 *Ibid* p.59.
144 *Ibid* pp.59–60.
145 *Ibid* p.60.
146 *Ibid* pp.60–61.
147 *Ibid* p.61.
148 Investigatory Powers Act 2016, s 227.

publication and intend no violent action, and those that intend to carry out violence is limitless. It is therefore questionable as to whether merely engaging with online extremist material such as *Inspire* or *Dabiq*, should be considered sufficient grounds to justify intrusive action.[149]

The end of encryption: national security and technical capabilities notices

Towards the end of IPA lies perhaps one of the most intrusive powers ever placed on the statute book. The 'national security notice' places an operator under an obligation to carry out any conduct, including the provision of services or amenities, facilitating anything to be done by the intelligence service.[150] Comparable to the provision of bulk powers, the Secretary of State must make the order based on proportionality, which then must be approved by an independent Judicial Commissioner.[151] Should the action be proportionate and necessary, there is in essence no time limit applicable within IPA, simply what the Secretary of State feels is reasonable.[152] This means that any notice could last three days, or three months, or three years. However, judicial authority will be required, which should safeguard this power from any type of abuse. Likewise, under section 252 of IPA, the Secretary of State can give any relevant service operator a 'technical capability notice'. Following a Judicial Commissioner's approval, should the Secretary of State consider the notice required to be necessary and proportionate, he or she may impose an obligation on the operator to remove any electronic protection applied.[153] Otherwise known as encryption, this power places the operator under an obligation to decrypt the communication or device, permitting law enforcement agencies unrestricted access as per the conditions of the notice. This power can be imposed extra-jurisdictionally, which places many operators in a difficult position in terms of privacy protection requirements.[154] It also has the potential to weaken the security model of many device and applications providers.

Dealing with the latter point, as discussed in Chapter 2, encryption is as ubiquitous as computing itself, and many people and companies rely on it for security. Apple in particular noted its concern that removing encryption will put law-abiding citizens at risk from cyber criminals, rather than actually affect the cyber criminals who can continue to access other means of encryption.[155] As with ICR, equipment interference could also impede the operation of smartphones and other

149 *Supra* as per The Rt. Hon. Sir Malcolm Rifkind MP (2014) p.61.
150 Investigatory Powers Act 2016, s 252(3).
151 Investigatory Powers Act 2016, s 252(1).
152 Investigatory Powers Act 2016, s 252(7).
153 Investigatory Powers Act 2016, ss 253(5)(c) and 254.
154 Investigatory Powers Act 2016, s 253(8).
155 Apple Inc. and Apple Distribution International – written evidence (IPB0093) submitted to the Joint Committee on the Draft Investigatory Powers Bill, available at https://www.parliament.uk/documents/joint-committees/draft-investigatory-powers-bill/written-evidence-draft-investigatory-powers-committee.pdf accessed 30 March 2018.

devices, rendering that particular device or server easier for criminals to access. Apple states that 'surely such an intrusive power, if allowed at all, should only be targeted at the most serious of criminal suspects', rather than en masse, which overwhelmingly and inevitably includes innocent people.[156] Apple in fact made a formal submission to the UK Joint Committee saying:

> We believe it would be wrong to weaken security for hundreds of millions of law-abiding customers so that it will also be weaker for the very few who pose a threat. In this rapidly evolving cyber-threat environment, companies should remain free to implement strong encryption to protect customers.[157]

It could also affect their position in the international sense given many Internet service providers are located overseas, meaning they are put in the impossible position of choosing which law and which authority to follow, and which to disregard. Apple, for example, has offices registered in Ireland, meaning they are subject to EU data protection laws, and the US where US law controls access to that data by law enforcement. Any failure to follow requirements under Title III of the US Omnibus Crime Control and Safe Streets Act would subject Apple to criminal sanctions for any unauthorised interception of content in transit.[158] What must be remembered here, of course, is that the EU has been instrumental in forming UK data protection law since 1995, so it may be likely that IPA powers are compatible.[159] These issues will be returned to when assessing IPA's legitimacy with EU law.

Bulk personal datasets

For now it is important to discuss the issue of bulk personal datasets facilitated by section 199 of IPA, that have created quite a lot of criticism surrounding the authorisation and safeguards, and the storage of such information, along with the legitimate security risks of illegal hacking. The datasets represent information that includes personal data relating to a number of individuals. As with all proposed bulk powers, initially an automated computer programme processes the data,

156 *Ibid.*

157 Joint Committee on the Draft Investigatory Powers Bill (2016) Report of Session 2015–2016, 11 February, HL Paper 93 and HC 651, available at http://www.publications.parliament.uk/pa/jt201516/jtselect/jtinvpowers/93/9302.htm. See also http://www.computerworlduk.com/security/draft-investigatory-powers-bill-what-you-need-know-3629116 accessed 13 March 2018

158 Apple Inc. and Apple Distribution International – written evidence (IPB0093) submitted to the Joint Committee on the Draft Investigatory Powers Bill, available at https://www.parliament.uk/documents/joint-committees/draft-investigatory-powers-bill/written-evidence-draft-investigatory-powers-committee.pdf accessed 13 March 2018.

159 *R (on the application of David Davis MP, Tom Watson MP, Peter Brice and Geoffrey Lewis) v The Secretary of State for the Home Department* [2015] EWHC 2092, [6]–[8], [11].

filters out the unnecessary and unwanted information, and effectively serves to profile individuals.[160] Lynskey contends that this may be abused if adequate safeguards are not placed correctly, and 'that decisions based on processing such datasets may profoundly affect individuals without their knowledge or consent' falling within the data protection scope.[161] Accordingly IPA is antithetical towards data protection, conflicting with an individual's autonomy and personality-enhancing aspects, by facilitating profiling.[162] IPA distinguishes between 'specific' and 'class' bulk data sets.[163] For Lynskey, 'specific' could mean, for instance, the national insurance number database, and the 'class' could be 'all information held by football clubs about their season ticketholders, or CCTV data held by local borough councils'.[164] The proposed introduction of these powers caused political concern with regard to access to health records. Section 206 of IPA introduces additional safeguards for such information, where an explicit reason for such collection and access has to be made by a statement from the head of the intelligence service.

Additionally, this type of surveillance profiling sits uneasily with rights such as the presumption of innocence and freedom from discrimination.[165] This is simply because the profiling computer program used to screen the bulk data, authorised by the initial warrant, effectively singles out an individual based on the fact they are part of a group or has particular characteristics, 'that correlate to suspects or persons of interest to the security and intelligence agencies, and cannot therefore have negative freedom'.[166] According to Lynskey, the individual

> may not know they are part of a group, or why this group is set apart from others, and he also may not know what future impact this categorisation might have on him. This Kafkaesque scenario shall become a reality for some UK residents under IPA.[167]

According to MI5, the personal datasets are held for analysis whereby analysts will 'only look at the data relating to the minority who are of intelligence interest'.[168] Therefore, although a large number of individuals may have personal information stored, for the majority of cases this will never actually be looked at. They form an essential element in the identification of subjects of interest, or other individuals

160 O. Lynskey (2015) Beyond Privacy: The Data Protection Implications of the IP Bill, LSE Law Department Briefings on the Investigatory Powers Bill, *LSE Law Policy Briefings*, 15, Social Science Research Network, available at http://ssrn.com/abstract=2704299 accessed 13 March 2018.
161 *Ibid.*
162 *Ibid.*
163 Investigatory Powers Act 2016, s 204 Class BPD warrants, and s 205 Specific BPD warrants.
164 *Supra* as per O. Lynskey (2015).
165 *Ibid.*
166 *Ibid.*
167 *Ibid.*
168 See https://www.mi5.gov.uk/bulk-data accessed 12 December 2016.

who 'surface during the course of an investigation'.[169] This assists MI5 in establishing communicational links between terrorist groups and potential terrorists, allowing them to filter out innocent citizens as quickly as possible, focusing instead on those that pose a threat. Accordingly MI5 confirms 'The analysis of BPD is a critical part of our response to the increasingly complicated and challenging task of defending the UK's interests and protecting its citizens' in a digital age.[170]

The main aim is to protect citizens' lives and, ultimately, this is what the bulk powers are trying to achieve. This is not a new power and MI5 has been carrying out this function since the enactment of the SSA 1989. At this point it is perhaps relevant to discuss positive case studies illustrating the practical application of these powers in the practical sense.

Bulk powers: the case studies

Financially, these powers have made an impact on the amount of fraud committed in the UK, whereby the 'HMRC started using interception to support investigations into MTIC fraud. As a result the level of attempted fraud has reduced substantially from an estimated high of £5 billion in 2005/2006 to an estimated current figure of £750 million'.[171] Moving back to the terrorist threat in the late 2000s, bulk data enabled GCHQ to trigger a manhunt for a known terrorist linked to previous attacks on UK citizens. At a time when other intelligence sources had gone cold, GCHQ was able to pick up the trail by identifying patterns of activity online believed to be unique to the suspect. Follow-up searches of bulk data provided further leads for the investigation. This work in turn highlighted links to extremists in the UK. Through a series of arrests, the network was successfully disrupted before any attack could take place.[172] Similarly in 2010 a UK 'intelligence operation identified a plot, which came from the top of al-Qaida's leadership structure, to send out waves of operatives to Europe to act as sleeper cells and prepare waves of attacks' using a unique communications method.[173] Working with international partners, GCHQ was able to identify operatives by requesting bulk data collection for these distinctive communicative patterns.[174]

It has been said by the UK's intelligence community that the nature of the international Islamist terror threat means that bulk data is the 'first and last line of defence'.[175] The same has been said for the retention of such data collected where the studies have shown it can be put to great use in preventing and detecting serious crime.[176] One particular case study highlighted that:

169 *Ibid.*
170 *Ibid.*
171 D. Anderson QC (2015) *A Question of Trust: Report of the Investigatory Powers Review* (The Stationary Office) p.337.
172 *Ibid.*
173 *Ibid.*
174 *Ibid.*
175 *Ibid.*
176 *Ibid.*

> UK authorities received intelligence from US authorities that an individual using email had sent a movie file of a woman sexually abusing a four-month-old girl. The log-on IP address for this account was registered to a male from Northampton. Further enquiries established that a girlfriend of the individual had three children all less than four years old. After investigation both were convicted of serious sexual abuse of the children.[177]

This shows the necessity for bulk powers in terms of pre-empting crime and terrorist activity.

Terrorist communication: the rationale for bulk powers

The terrorist group IS's propaganda and marketing campaign coupled with the encryption capabilities has led to a situation whereby it has become difficult to distinguish friend from foe. Determining who is and who is not a potential terrorist has become increasingly difficult in the 21st Century. Porous borders within the EU and terrorist attacks committed within the EU and the UK by EU and UK citizens, also known as 'home-grown' or 'lone jihad', mean it has become increasingly difficult for the law enforcement agencies to make this determination.[178] The question of friend or foe conjoined with the fact terrorists lack a specific typecast has led to the EU and UK adopting risk management strategies to pre-empt and thereby prevent a terrorist attack.[179] This is because this type of threat is posed by individuals outside any terrorist organisational structure or franchise, and they could be almost anyone within the UK and EU population, and could attack at any given moment. In identifying potential terrorists, MI5 highlighted this difficulty in their explanation to Sir Malcolm Rifkind:

> In order to maximise our chances of detecting such individuals, we use a set of factors identified as being common, but not unique, to many lone actors: an inability to cope with stress and anxiety; a pre-existing history of violence; mental health issues; blaming others for (personal or group) grievances; an immediate need to act to rectify grievances; social isolation; and significant interest in extremist material encouraging lone actor attacks. We use the factors, drawing on psychologists in our Behavioural Science Unit (BSU) where appropriate, in conjunction with other intelligence to inform risk assessments.[180]

177 *Ibid* pp.339–340.
178 C. Walker (2008b) Know Thine Enemy as Thyself: Discerning Friend from Foe under Anti-Terrorism Laws, *Melbourne University Law Review*, 32, 275–301, 276. See also https://azelin.files.wordpress.com/2016/07/al-qacc84_idah-in-the-arabian-peninsula-e2809cinspire-guide-2-nice-operatione2809d.pdf accessed 13 March 2018.
179 *Ibid.*
180 The Rt. Hon. Sir Malcolm Rifkind MP (2014) *Report on the Intelligence Relating to the Murder of Fusilier Lee Rigby*, Intelligence and Security Committee of Parliament, HC 795, p.81.

Traceability and typecasting

The key problem facing the UK is the traceability and typecasting of potential terrorists. This threat is not exclusive to the UK and is reflective of a larger international problem. Moeckli and King suggest that the main problem facing policing and security agencies is the overall lack of traceability of the terrorist threat to a clearly defined group, such as ETA, or the many factions of the Irish Republican Army (IRA) based in Northern Ireland and the Republic of Ireland.[181] The 21st Century international terrorist threat emanates from stateless organs, ubiquitous in nature, aimed at threatening the value systems of the Western world, rather than showing a particular grievance aimed at a specific state.[182] Carter moves the analysis away from stateless groups and traces a new evolution of tactics, and subsequent growth in prevalence of the 'self-radicalised' terrorist, which commenced following al-Qaeda's successful attack on the US on 11 September 2001.[183] Following this analytical line, Carter goes on to postulate that the current terrorist threat comes from individuals who lack formal ties to international terrorist groups, such as al-Qaeda and al-Shabaab.[184]

Although terrorism emanating from foreign citizens tasked by a stateless international terrorist organisation remains a threat, it is UK and EU citizens who have been influenced or otherwise radicalised, who then go on to commit acts of terrorism within their home country, more commonly known as home-grown terrorists, or lone-wolves, or lone Islamists, that pose the most tangible menace. As above, it is important to note that the UK and EU are not the only Western countries facing this type of threat. Carter and Carter furnish evidence of the transnational nature of this home-grown threat when they conclude that the same risks are posed in the US.[185] Although beyond the ambit of this book to better understand the nature of the home-grown terror threat it is important to briefly note the radicalisation process achieved by terrorist communication. According to Gartenstein-Ross and Gossman *et al.*, it is believed to involve four stages:

1 *Pre-radicalisation*: an individual alters their lifestyle prior to radicalisation, such as relationships, employment and social life;
2 *Self-identification*: an individual is influenced by internal and external push/pull factors, attributing to the exploration of extremist philosophies, ideologies and values;
3 *Indoctrination*: an individual intensifies their beliefs and adopts extreme philosophies, ideologies and values with no exceptions;

181 D. Moeckli & T. King (2010) Human Rights and Non-discrimination on the "War on Terror", Publication Review, *European Journal of International Law*, 21(4), 1109–1111, 1109. For ETA see https://theblureview.org/rise-fall-eta and for the IRA see http://terrorism.about.com/od/groupsleader1/p/IRA.htm accessed 30 March 2018.
182 *Ibid.*
183 G. Carter and D. L. Carter (2012) Law Enforcement Intelligence: Implications for Self-radicalized Terrorism, *Police Practice and Research*, 13(2), 138–154, 139.
184 *Ibid.*
185 *Ibid.*

4 *Soldier*: accepting their duty to participate in the struggle as a warrior fighting those who oppose the ideology in an attempt to achieve realisation of the ideology.[186]

State powers of surveillance can lead to those individuals within this process, at almost any stage, coming to the attention of the security services. However, this does depend on a number of factors. It is proposed the home-grown terrorist threat be broken down into two subdivisions.[187]

The self-starting terrorist

First, there are the self-starting terrorists who are in contact with other like-minded extremists and seek inspiration and encouragement from them, but who have not been tasked by a stateless terrorist organisation to commit a violent act (such as IS or al-Qaeda).[188] These types of start-ups are made fairly effortlessly, and ensure a decent level of safety from electronic communications data surveillance capture for the would-be-terrorist, due to the amount of commercial encryption available on the open market, and the darknet. They are, however, more likely to come to the attention of the policing and security agencies, partl because of their online presence, but more so because they may be socialising and meeting other persons whom are already known to the agencies, and may already be a 'Subject of Interest'.[189] Sir Malcolm Rifkind MP, former Chairman of the UK's Intelligence and Security Committee (ISC) highlighted this in the 2013 Committee report into the killing of Fusilier Lee Rigby.[190] This report highlights further how MI5 in particular works in practice, when identification of the would-be terrorist is essential. The issue of finite resources faced by the UK agencies is also highlighted in this report, which results in MI5 having to prioritise their investigations, enabling the allocation of resources. They do this by ascribing a priority level determined on the available evidence at the given time:

- Priority 1 (P1a and P1b) is the highest, meaning there is intelligence to suggest attack planning;
- Priority 2 (P2H and P2M) is used when there is intelligence to suggest a high or medium risk such as terrorist training;
- Priority 3 (P3) is used when intelligence is uncorroborated;
- Priority 4 (P4) is assigned to those individuals where there is a risk of re-engagement with extremist activity.[191]

186 D. Gartenstein-Ross and L. Grossman (2009) *Homegrown Terrorists in the U.S. and U.K. An Empirical Examination of the Radicalization Process* (Foundation for Defense of Democracies Press). See also M. D. Silber and A. Bhatt (2007) *Radicalisation in the West: The Homegrown Threat* (Police Department, Intelligence Division).
187 *Supra* as per the Rt. Hon. Sir Malcolm Rifkind MP (2014) p.80.
188 *Ibid.*
189 *Ibid.*
190 *Ibid.*
191 *Ibid* p.13.

The importance of this priority system cannot be overlooked, given that P3 and P4 cases are often paused or suspended in favour of concentrating on the higher levels. This is emphasised by the Rifkind findings when questioning MI5 about the delay in identifying the terrorist Adebowale, which took the Digital Intelligence Team (DIGINT) five months.[192] The average length of time for P3 cases is 69 days, but the Director General of MI5 confirmed:

> If there was a P1 case that meant that we had significant urgency behind it, then we could do it much, much quicker. We have a finite amount of resource and we need to focus it on the highest priority work. No delay is desirable, but it is the reality of what we do that we carry delays in lower priority casework.[193]

It is accepted that P1 cases must take priority; after all they bear a more significant immediate risk. However, as evidenced the timescales surrounding the lower level cases must be improved.

In addition to the priority of the overall investigation, Subjects of Interest are identified and placed in a tier system dependent upon their level of engagement.[194] As per the written evidence submitted to Rifkind's report, as of October 2014 MI5 was investigating several thousand individual Subjects of Interest with links to Islamist extremist activity in the UK:

- Tier 1: Main targets of an investigation, likely to be involved in all aspects of the investigated activities;
- Tier 2: Key contacts of the main targets, likely to be involved in a significant portion of the investigated activities;
- Tier 3: Contact with other Tier targets and likely to be only marginally involved with the investigated activities.[195]

This is where the importance of the intelligence-led policing framework and philosophy for preventing acts of terrorism come to fruition. The idea here is to allow for the collection and analysis of electronic communications data and other information related to terrorism, which results in actionable intelligence aiding law enforcement to develop tactical responses to the threats, or emerging threats.[196]

The lone-actor terrorist

The second type of home-grown terrorist is the 'self-radicalising lone-actors', sometimes referred to as 'lone-wolves' or 'lone Islamists'. They have often been influenced and thereby radicalised at home via the Internet and terrorist

192 *Ibid* pp.63–64.
193 *Ibid* p.64 and p.88.
194 A Subject of Interest is an individual who is being investigated because they are suspected of being a threat to national security.
195 *Supra* as per the Rt. Hon. Sir Malcolm Rifkind MP (2014) pp.13–14.
196 *Supra* as per D. L. Carter and J. G. Carter (2009) p.317.

communication, indirectly in some circumstances, and consequently inspired to commit an act of terror, doing so outside any command type stateless structure, and without direct material assistance from any group.[197] The differences between the subdivisions become important when looking through the UK security agencies' lens. Simply put, the lone-actor subdivision allows the individual to remain under the security services' radar, entirely in some cases, whereby the person's identity poses a real challenge for the UK's law enforcement agencies.[198] Examples of lone-actors are:

- Anders Behring Breivik on 22 July 2011, Norway, killed 77 people in two consecutive terrorist attacks. First, he killed eight people with a car-bomb placed at the Norwegian Government headquarters in Oslo. Then, an hour later, he went to the summer camp of the Worker's Youth League (the youth organisation of the Labour Party) where he shot and killed 69 people;[199]
- In Nice on Bastille Day 2016, Mohamed Lahouaiej Bouhlel drove an articulated lorry into a crowd killing 84 people. Although IS claimed responsibility it has been suggested he was in fact a lone-actor, with no known direct association to the group;[200]
- Omar Mateen in June 2016 entered a homosexual club in Orlando, Florida, and killed 50 people by shooting them. Shortly before the attack he pledged allegiance to IS;[201]
- In September 2016 Ahmad Khan Rahami carried out four bombings or bombing attempts in the US. As law enforcement personnel were apprehending him he shot and injured three police officers. According to the US policing agencies, Rahami was not part of any terrorist group or cell, but was simply motivated and inspired by the communications of al-Qaeda's Osama bin Laden and Anwar al-Awlaki;[202]

197 C. Bockstette (2010) Terrorists Exploit Information Technologies: Use of Strategic Communication Calls for United Response, *Pre Concordiam, Journal of European Security and Defense Issues*, 1(3), 1–70, 11.

198 *Supra* as per The Rt. Hon. Sir Malcolm Rifkind MP (2014) p.5.

199 See http://www.telegraph.co.uk/news/2016/07/22/anders-breivik-inside-the-warped-mind-of-a-mass-killer accessed 30 March 2018.

200 B. Henderson and R. Sabur (2016) Nice Terrorist Attack on Bastille Day: Everything We Know So Far, *Telegraph*, 18 July 2016, available at http://www.telegraph.co.uk/news/2016/07/15/nice-terror-attack-on-bastille-day-everything-we-know-so-far-on accessed 30 March 2018.

201 H. Tsukayama, M. Berman and J. Markon (2016) Terror in Orlando: 50 killed in Shooting Rampage at Gay Club, Gunman Pledged Allegiance to ISIS, *Washington Post*, 13 June 2016, available at https://www.washingtonpost.com/news/post-nation/wp/2016/06/12/orlando-nightclub-shooting-about-20-dead-in-domestic-terror-incident-at-gay-club/?hpid=hp_hp-top-table-high_orlando-banner%3Ahomepage%2Fstory&utm_term=.8adec967a5ff. See also http://www.reuters.com/article/us-florida-shooting-mateen-idUSKCN0YY0SY accessed 30 March 2018.

202 M. Santora, W. K. Rashbaum, A. Baker and A. Goldman (2016) Ahmad Khan Rahami is Arrested in Manhattan and New Jersey Bombings, *New York Times*, 19 September,

- In 2016 Adel Kermiche and Abdel Malik Petitjean went into a Roman Catholic church in Rouen, France, and killed the priest. The two terrorists had only met in person a few days before the attack but had communicated through the encrypted messaging application 'Telegram'.[203]

It is clear from this list that it is not only Islamist terrorism that poses a risk to UK security. In the UK there has been an increase in far-right extremism, with new groups being created such as National Action, and Britain First.[204] Although such right-wing groups have not been defined by the UK as terrorist, the threat posed has been assessed as more harmful and dangerous than that posed by Islamist lone- actors.[205] In 2016 Thomas Mair, who according to evidence presented had some connection to far right groups, killed Jo Cox MP utilising a knife and an illegally held firearm, and reportedly repeatedly shouted 'Britain First' repeatedly during his attack. Despite claims to the contrary, it has been dealt with as a terrorist incident and Mair was sentenced accordingly.[206] As with Fusilier Lee Rigby's killing, the defendants were tried for murder contrary to UK Common Law, and terrorism was a sentencing factor in both trials. Moreover in Mair's trial a substantial quantity of evidence was produced showing his links to far right extremism.[207] As covered in Chapter 1, the UK's definition of terrorism changes when a firearm is used: 'the use or threat of action, involving firearms or explosives, made for the purpose of advancing a political, religious, racial or ideological cause'.[208]

Clearly from Rifkind's report findings in 2014, both types of home-grown Islamist terrorists pose a significant challenge for the UK law enforcement agencies. Another issue that must be considered is the fact that both self-starters and

available at http://www.nytimes.com/2016/09/20/nyregion/nyc-nj-explosions-ahmad-khan-rahami.html?_r=0. See also M. Santora and A. Goldman (2016) Ahmad Khan Rahami Was Inspired by Bin Laden, Charges Say, *New York Times*, 21 September, available at http://www.nytimes.com/2016/09/21/nyregion/ahmad-khan-rahami-suspect.html accessed 30 March 2018.

203 See http://www.bbc.co.uk/news/world-europe-36892785. See also K. Willsher (2016) Powerful Tributes at Funeral of Priest Killed in France Terrorist Attack, *Guardian*, 2 August 2016, available at https://www.theguardian.com/world/2016/aug/02/thousands-expected-funeral-priest-killed-in-france-terror-attack accessed 30 March 2018.

204 See https://www.rt.com/uk/347581-far-right-extremism-cox. See also http://national-action.info accessed 30 March 2018.

205 M. Bentham (2016) Lone Right Wing Extremists 'Kill and Harm More People than Lone Islamist Terrorists', *Evening Standard*, 21 June, available at http://www.standard.co.uk/news/uk/lone-right-wing-extremists-kill-and-harm-more-people-than-islamist-terrorists-a3276876.html accessed 30 March 2018.

206 G. Greenwald (2016) Why is the Killer of British MP Jo Cox not Being Called a 'Terrorist'? *The Intercept*, 17 June 2016, available at https://theintercept.com/2016/06/17/why-is-the-killer-of-british-mp-jo-cox-not-being-called-a-terrorist accessed 30 March 2018.

207 See http://www.bbc.co.uk/news/uk-38076755 accessed 30 December 2016.

208 Terrorism Act 2000, s 1(3).

lone-actors show an increase in independent operational abilities, which simply compounds this issue further.[209] This sudden increase in independent operational abilities, along with the issue of finite resources, has led Rob Wainwright, head of Europol, to assert that the EU currently faces the highest terror threat since the US attack by al-Qaeda in 2001.[210]

Conclusion

In the digital age most people do virtually everything online, including research, banking, shopping, finding new relationships, holiday planning and self-diagnosing health concerns. In conjunction with social media use, it has become almost impossible to separate people's lives in the real world from their lives online. Likewise, people are increasingly becoming reliant on smartphones and other similar devices, storing private pictures and other personal data on them, such as calendars and reminders. This means that bulk interception of communications data and bulk equipment interference are extraordinarily powerful tools to be wielded, having a much bigger impact upon individual privacy than traditional communications interception and surveillance might have had. Intercepting electronic communications data and content is not the same as intercepting a landline call as evidenced in this chapter. Additionally it is unhelpful and disappointing to note that IPA does not expressly cover OSINT and SOCMINT collection, although the Government had plenty of time to implement such measures.

It has been argued that electronic communications data, by nature of its digital form, is ideal for analysis and profiling individuals. Data mining, or perhaps better-termed filtering arrangements as per section 62 of IPA, will increasingly become autonomous as automated computer programs carry out the first bulk interception step. Aimed at the population, who as a whole are not suspected of being involved in any criminal or terrorist activity, these bulk powers have the potential to effectively destroy the privacy rights of millions of people in order to find the elusive terrorist in the haystack. It has been substantiated that monitoring the whole population of the UK would be logistically impossible. However, in contrast it has been shown that due to the issues raised in Chapter 2, these powers are necessary. The balance between collective security and individual data privacy rights in the UK is fairly stable because of the role and importance of judicial review, judicial independence and the overarching scrutiny provided by commissioners and parliamentary committees.

209 V. Dodd (2015), Europe Faces Highest Terror Threat Since 9/11, MPs Told, *Guardian*, 13 January 2015, http://www.theguardian.com/uk-news/2015/jan/13/europe-highest-terror-threat-911-europol-fighting-overseas accessed 30 March 2018. For Paris terrorist attack see http://www.bbc.co.uk/news/world-europe-30708237 accessed 30 March 2018. For Copenhagen terrorism attack see http://www.theguardian.com/world/2015/feb/14/copenhagen-blasphemy-lars-vilks-prophet-muhammad-krudttonden-cafe accessed 30 March 2018. For Belgium terrorist attack see http://www.theguardian.com/world/2014/may/24/brussels-jewish-museum-attack-three-dead accessed 30 March 2018.

210 *Ibid* as per V. Dodd (2015.

4 The necessity of pre-emptive legal counterterrorism measures

Introduction

Adding more contention to the arguably unquantifiable threat posed is the sudden increase in independent operational abilities. These are gained through information obtained on the Internet, or through the terrorist travelling to areas of conflict to receive the equivalent of military training.

Building upon the issues raised in Chapter 3, this chapter will highlight further the requirement for mass data collection and pre-emptive legislative measures aimed at reducing the terrorist threat. The pre-emptive measures that will be focused on include temporary travel restrictions and the criminalisation of neutral behaviour, such as the collection of data deemed to be useful to a terrorist. Although the chapter will highlight the connection between the risk society theory and predictive policing, it will remain within the legal research framework, discrediting terms used such as 'mass data surveillance' and 'pre-crime'. It will show that data retention is not the same as mass surveillance and that 'pre-crime' is a fabricated term used misleadingly, given that pre-emptive measures are in fact criminal offences.

The need for pre-emptive measures will be evidenced, highlighting that currently counterterrorism legislation has failed to eradicate terrorist groups' propaganda and infiltrate terrorist encrypted electronic communications data.

Operational abilities: Islamist terrorist training

The sudden increase in independent operational abilities as alluded to in the previous chapter can be attributed to the amount of extremist material readily available on the Internet, or the fct that an individual can travel to another country to receive terrorist training, known within the UK's law enforcement services as 'Jihadi tourism'.[1] Reports from 2015 suggest approximately 5000 EU citizens have been and/or are currently engaged in terrorist-related activities in conflict zones such as Somalia, Syria, Iraq, Libya and Yemen. According to the Soufan

1 The Rt. Hon. Sir Malcolm Rifkind MP (2014) *Report on the Intelligence Relating to the Murder of Fusilier Lee Rigby*, Intelligence and Security Committee of Parliament, HC 795,

Centre, which informed the European Parliament Committee, estimates suggest that 1 in 15 of those returning from conflict zones suspected of involvement in terrorist activities potentially pose a threat to their respective nation states upon return.[2] In October 2017 the Soufan Centre confirmed the number of EU citizens leaving to fight with IS froze in 2015, as the group began to lose territorial control.[3] The methodology used to calculate these figures is unknown, mainly due to the difficulty in gathering such accurate data, and given they come from the UK security services and are deemed classified. It is argued therefore that these estimates could in actual fact be much higher, or indeed lower, rendering the terror threat unquantifiable. Add to this the issue of finite resources, and the extraordinarily difficult if not impossible task of monitoring potential terrorists and suspects presents itself.

Islamist or Jihadi tourism brings with it its own danger, serving to not only increase independent operational abilities but also provide extensive hands-on military training in the use of firearms and explosives.[4] Although travelling to conflict zones increases the likelihood of the individual becoming known to the law enforcement agencies, the risk still remains somewhat unquantifiable. What is clear from Rifkind's 2014 report is that the independent operational abilities in conjunction with the methods used by lone actors and self-starting terrorists offer fewer opportunities for the security services to detect their activity.[5] Because of the changes in the nature of the threats, 'the practices and policies necessary for prevention must change to reflect the threats'.[6] In recognising the type of threats, which according to the Director General of the Security Service, is mounting, 'diversifying and is increasingly complex', what can be seen is a sudden growth in risk management styles being employed by the police and security services when assessing intelligence.[7]

A point that must be made due to the successful marketing and promotion of IS is that this has led to many foreign fighters travelling to Syria and Iraq. According to the National Counterterrorism Centre Director Nicholas Rasmussen, in October 2015 IS had 'attracted more than 28,000 foreign fighters, including at least 5000 westerners'.[8]

2 G. Buttarelli (2015) Counter-Terrorism, De-Radicalisation and Foreign Fighters, Joint debate during the extraordinary meeting of the LIBE Committee. European Parliament, Brussels, 27 January 2015.

3 R. Barrett (2017) Beyond the Caliphate: Foreign Fighters and the Threat of Returnees, October, The Soufan Center, http://thesoufancenter.org/wp-content/uploads/2017/11/Beyond-the-Caliphate-Foreign-Fighters-and-the-Threat-of-Returnees-TSC-Report-October-2017-v3.pdf accessed 20 March 2018.

4 *Supra* as per G. Buttarelli (2015).

5 *Supra* as per The Rt. Hon. Sir Malcolm Rifkind MP (2014) p.82.

6 J. G. Carter and D. L. Carter (2012) Law Enforcement Intelligence: Implications for Self-Radicalized Terrorism, *Police Practice and Research*, 13(2), 138–154, 138.

7 *Supra* as per the Rt. Hon. Sir Malcolm Rifkind MP (2014) pp.81–82.

8 See http://www.bbc.co.uk/news/world-middle-east-29052144 accessed 30 March 2018.

Jihadi tourism: seizure of passports and travel documents

In order to deal with and ultimately stop UK citizens leaving the UK to engage in terrorist-related activity, the Counter-Terrorism and Security Act 2015 (CTSA) introduced further pre-emptive measures. The CTSA also had to address and implement measures to halt the return of those citizens returning to the UK after training and fighting with terrorist groups. The main pre-emptive power is found under Part 1 Chapter 1 of the CTSA, which allows law enforcement agencies to seize passports and travel documents from persons suspected of involvement in terrorism. To this end Schedule One of the CTSA makes provision for citizens to be retained for up to 14 days from the day after the initial seizure.[9] Although a short-term measure, this time allowance can be extended with judicial approval to 30 days from the day after the initial seizure. Judicial approval is required whereby the Secretary of State must show that the relevant persons have been acting diligently and expeditiously in relation to the matters.[10] These provision were debated heavily during the enactment stages which led Lord Carlile to state:

> We heard some criticism of Clause 1, but I say… [Lordships] have got to get real about what Clause 1 is dealing with. Let me give you [a hypothetical] example … Suppose a suspicious travel agent who is public spirited telephones the police and says, 'I have just sold an air ticket in suspicious circumstances', and the authorities decide it is worth following the person who has bought the air ticket. That kind of incident can occur within an hour, and it does not leave the time to go off to a judge to get permission to seize that passport. We have to allow the authorities to deal with the urgent provisions made in Clause 1 and Schedule 1.[11]

According to Rowley, the Metropolitan Police Assistant Commissioner, at the very least a total of 700 UK citizens have travelled to Syria, with apparently more than half having returned to the UK, where they now pose a significant threat. The urgency and requirement for such emergency power can therefore be appreciated.[12] Although the time limitations are not too restrictive, there is still the issue of due process and the impact upon the individual's privacy, and in particular their right under Article 45 of the EU Charter of Fundamental Rights to freedom of movement and of residence.[13] Similar to that of the ECHR, any limitation on

9 Counter Terrorism and Security Act 2015, see paragraph 5(2) and (3)(a).
10 Counter Terrorism and Security Act 2015 see paragraph 8(4), (5), (6) and (7).
11 Lord Carlile of Berriew, Counter-Terrorism and Security Bill 2015, House of Lords Second Reading Stage, 13 January 2015, Column 722 7.27pm.
12 P. Wintour (2015) UK Parents to Get Power to Cancel Children's Passports over ISIS Fears, *Guardian*, 20 July 2015, available at https://www.theguardian.com/politics/2015/jul/20/uk-parents-power-cancel-childrens-passports-isis-fears accessed 30 March 2018.
13 Charter of Fundamental Rights of the European Union, see http://eur-lex.europa.eu/legal-content/EN/TXT/?uri=CELEX:12012P/TXT accessed 30 March 2018. 'The free movement of persons is a fundamental right guaranteed by the EU to its citizens'. It

the exercise of the rights and freedoms under the Charter must be provided for by law.[14] Proportionality is the ultimate test of course and any such limitation must be deemed necessary in meeting recognised Union objectives, or to protect the rights and freedom of others.[15] Ultimately these measures not only protect the public as a whole, they also protect vulnerable young adults and children from being further influenced and introduced to terrorist-related activity should they be permitted to leave the country.

The provisions under Schedule One are wide in nature and define involvement in terrorism related activity as:

> (a) the commission, preparation or instigation of acts of terrorism;
> (b) conduct that facilitates the commission, preparation or instigation of such acts, or is intended to do so;
> (c) conduct that gives encouragement to the commission, preparation or instigation of such acts, or is intended to do so;
> (d) conduct that gives support or assistance to individuals who are known or believed by the person concerned to be involved in conduct falling within paragraph (a).
>
> It is immaterial whether the acts of terrorism in question are specific acts of terrorism or acts of terrorism in general.[16]

Should a constable or qualified officer have reasonable grounds to suspect a person is leaving the UK for the purposes of involvement in terrorism-related activity, or has arrived and is about to leave the UK to do so, then a number of powers are made available under Schedule 1, paragraph 2(5):

> (a) to require the person to hand over all travel documents in his or her possession to the constable or (as the case may be) the qualified officer;
> (b) to search for travel documents relating to the person and to take possession of any that the constable or officer finds;

entitles every EU citizen to travel, work and live in any EU country without special formalities. [Although the UK is not a member of Schengen] … Schengen cooperation enhances this freedom by enabling citizens to cross-internal borders without being subjected to border checks. The border-free Schengen Area guarantees free movement to more than 400 million EU citizens, as well as to many non-EU nationals, businessmen, tourists or other persons legally present on the EU territory.' See http://ec.europa.eu/dgs/home-affairs/what-we-do/policies/borders-and-visas/schengen/index_en.htm accessed 30 March 2018. And see also 'Free movement of workers is a fundamental principle of the Treaty enshrined in Article 45 of the Treaty on the Functioning of the European Union and developed by EU secondary legislation and the Case law of the Court of Justice', available at http://ec.europa.eu/social/main.jsp?catId=457 accessed 30 March 2018.

14 Charter of Fundamental Rights of the European Union, Article 52(1).

15 *Ibid.*

16 Counter-Terrorism and Security Act 2015, Schedule 1, paragraph 1(10).

(c) to inspect any travel document relating to the person;
(d) to retain any travel document relating to the person that is lawfully in the possession of the constable or officer.

In order to retain the travel documents for the specified length of time, authorisation from a senior officer must be attained.[17] The documents can then be retained whilst the Secretary of State considers the case.[18] They can also be retained whilst the authorities consider whether to charge the citizen with an offence, or subject the person of interests to further measures.[19] A person who fails to hand over all travel documentation, or obstructs the process, if found guilty of the offence, may be liable to six months' imprisonment.[20] The issue here of course is that the citizen may request a judicial review of the decision to retain their passport, but the intelligence and evidence gathered may be withheld from the suspect,[21] thus making it almost impossible for a citizen to make a reviewable argument.

Temporary exclusion orders

The UK by way of Part 1 Chapter 2 of the CTSA fashions further intrusive pre-emptive measures aimed at preventing highly trained and militarily hardened terrorists from returning to the UK, who may then pose a direct or indirect threat to national security. Termed 'temporary exclusion orders' they state:

(1) A temporary exclusion order is an order which requires an individual not to return to the United Kingdom unless –
  (a) the return is in accordance with a permit to return issued by the Secretary of State before the individual began the return; or
  (b) the return is the result of the individual's deportation to the UK.

Five conditions must be met before an order by the Secretary of State can be made and the order lasts up to two years.[22] Importantly, they require the Secretary of State to reasonably suspect that the individual is, or has been, involved in terrorism-related activity outside the UK, and reasonably considers that it is necessary, for purposes connected with protecting members of the public in the UK from a risk of terrorism, for a temporary exclusion order to be imposed on the individual.[23] Either the UK court can grant the Secretary of State permission to make an order under section 3, or the Secretary of State can show they consider the

17 Counter-Terrorism and Security Act 2015, Schedule 1, paragraph 4(1)(a).
18 Counter-Terrorism and Security Act 2015, Schedule 1, paragraph 5(1)(a).
19 Counter-Terrorism and Security Act 2015, Schedule 1, paragraph 5(1)(b)(c).
20 Counter-Terrorism and Security Act 2015, Schedule 1, paragraph 15(1)(2)(3).
21 Counter-Terrorism and Security Act 2015, Schedule 1, paragraph 10(2), dealing with the extension period to 30 days.
22 Counter-Terrorism and Security Act 2015, s 4(3)(b) limits the temporary exclusion orders to two years inclusive.
23 Counter-Terrorism and Security Act 2015, Chapter 2.

urgency of the case requires a temporary exclusion order to be imposed without obtaining permission.[24] The Act provides exceptionally wide powers to the executive, however there is some protection afforded to the citizen by way of judicial supervision.

First, the Secretary of State must include a statement outlining the urgency of the case and the requirement that the order be imposed without obtaining the permission of the court.[25] Notice of the order must be provided to the court immediately after the temporary exclusion order is imposed, and the court must review the decision within seven days of the order being made.[26] If the urgency of the order satisfies the court it must affirm the imposition, however, should the court determine the order is flawed it can quash it.[27] Judicial supervision, somewhat similar to that found in IPA, is to be welcomed as a safeguarding development. Some other safeguarding clauses, such as the two-year limitation, were debated heavily during the enactment stages, leading Lord Carlile to state:

> I do not understand the two-year period contained in these amendments. The issue which we are dealing with and which is covered in this clause is, unfortunately, going to last for more than two years … having a two-year sunset clause … would send out a completely incorrect message to those who are minded to go abroad and participate in jihad … We have to show some enduring determination over this issue.[28]

Although the ECHR rights and the EU Charter rights appear to have lacked discussion, the Marquess of Lothian raised a valid concern, '[L]ooking at the time factor here, what is the legal and international status of someone who has been subjected to a temporary exclusion order?'[29]

International status

This question has relevance given the legal and practical implications for the citizen subjected to this type of order. The order is temporary, not indefinite. In essence, this is not rendering that person stateless. There are two UN Conventions to which the UK has long been a signatory, one of which serves to prevent a state from rendering a citizen stateless: the Convention relating to the Status of Stateless Persons 1954 and the 1961 Convention on the Reduction of Statelessness.[30] The 1961 Convention represents an international instrument safeguarding citizens

24 Counter-Terrorism and Security Act 2015, Chapter 2(7)(b).
25 Counter-Terrorism and Security Act 2015, Schedule 2, paragraph 2.
26 Counter-Terrorism and Security Act 2015, Schedule 2, paragraph 3.
27 Counter-Terrorism and Security Act 2015, Schedule 2, paragraph 4.
28 Lord Carlile of Berriew, Counter-Terrorism and Security Bill 2015, House of Lords First Committee Stage, 20 January 2015, Column 1212.
29 Marquess of Lothian, Counter-Terrorism and Security Bill 2015, House of Lords First Committee Stage, 20 January 2015, Column 1213.
30 See http://www.unhcr.org/pages/4a2535c3d.html accessed 30 March 2018.

from inappropriate and unfair threats of statelessness. What is interesting, however, is the Home Secretary, using Royal Prerogative power, can already revoke UK citizenship entitlement, so long as the person concerned holds a dual nationality.[31] Taken in conjunction with the current terrorist threat, the requirement for this genre of power to be on the statute book is clear. This is where the then Prime Minister David Cameron's dexterity could be seen in his use of words, describing the actions of UK citizens fighting for IS as disloyal.[32] Articles 8 and 9 of the 1961 Convention expressly forbid the deprivation of nationality on racial, ethnic, religious or political grounds. Although the religious beliefs and political aspirations shown by members of IS are abhorrent, they would appear to satisfy the above definition.[33]

However, under the Convention, if a citizen has committed acts inconsistent with the duty of loyalty to the state, the state retains the right to deprive that citizen of nationality, even if this leads to statelessness. One could argue the actions of IS terrorists are certainly inconsistent with loyalty to the UK. In addition, Article 19 of the EU Charter prohibits collective expulsion, or the expulsion of a person to a state where there is a risk of torture, the death penalty or other inhuman, degrading treatment. Although limited by law, it is argued this particular aspect of the UK's legislative measure will increasingly come under judicial scrutiny. The CJEU, for example, is not disinclined to strike down measures that are disproportionate in nature, particularly when such citizens could be permitted to return to the UK and subjected to other forms of pre-terrorism sanctions, in accordance with other existing legislative measures.[34] Lord Macdonald of River Glaven appears to have at least recognised the impact of these measures and the potential for such friction between the executive and the courts:

> we should not give away our freedoms in response to terrorism … [it] would be a good idea if [we] were to include a sunset clause … [because the] practicalities of this measure – how it will work in practice – … are most in doubt. Those practicalities will significantly impact on the rights of people on whom the orders are imposed … I support the idea of a sunset clause so that the House can thoroughly review how the legislation is working in practice.[35]

Mere suspicion that a citizen has engaged with terrorism-related activity is the required threshold for an exclusion order. Considering the length of time the

31 See http://www.findlaw.co.uk/law/government/constitutional_law/citizens_guide_to_government/500456.html accessed 30 March 2018.
32 See http://www.ibtimes.com/uk-cannot-strip-returning-islamic-state-fighters-british-citizenship-cameron-clegg-1675618 accessed 30 March 2018.
33 See http://www.independent.co.uk/news/world/middle-east/who-are-isis-the-rise-of-the-islamic-state-in-iraq-and-the-levant-9541421.html accessed 30 March 2018.
34 Terrorism Prevention and Investigation Measures Act 2011, s 2, and the extension to these measures brought about by the Counter-Terrorism and Security Act 2015, s 16.
35 Lord Macdonald of River Glaven, Counter-Terrorism and Security Bill 2015, House of Lords First Committee Stage, 20 January 2015, Column 1214.

temporary exclusion order may be in place and the intrusive nature of these orders, the threshold should be raised and the executive be satisfied the citizen would pose a serious threat upon return. The decision made is reviewable and can be appealed by the citizen, however, the same rules with regard to disclosure exist as per the removal of passports and travel documents.[36] The potential repercussions for a citizen returning to the UK following the making of a temporary exclusion order are severe, should they be found guilty of an offence, they can be sentenced for up to five years' imprisonment.[37]

Clearly the UK Government is trying to reduce the terrorist risk posed, as it is its duty to protect life and safeguard its citizens. These powers are relatively new and therefore data illustrating how they work in practice is short. In 2015 Germany took a similar approach to the UK in attempting to stop jihadi tourism.[38] According to the German Federal Ministry of the Interior, the number of people travelling to join IS had increased dramatically in early 2015, in comparison to 2013–2014, which posed a direct threat to their nation state.[39] In order to satisfy UN international norms, those persons who have been refused an identity card will instead be issued with a substitute identity document stating 'not valid for travel outside of Germany'. Forming part of the risk management strategy inherent in the international and national response to the terrorist threat, some members of Germany's opposition party provided argumentation similar to that raised by UK MPs during the enactment stages of the CTSA, in that the powers are unconstitutional as they criminalise neutral behaviour far in advance of the actual crime.[40] In introducing such measures, the state is simply trying to achieve good actionable intelligence, safeguarding citizens' lives.

Criminalising neutral behaviour: needles in haystacks, risk society and pre-emptive measures

Since the introduction of the various bulk powers and decryption under IPA, it is highly likely that the use of the legislative pre-emptive measures introduced will increase. In attempting to manage the potential terrorist threats posed, the retention of electronic communications data for a period of 12 months and the bulk powers allowing such data to be screened by an algorithm have proved essential in finding potential needles within the continually growing haystacks. As technology grows and the algorithms become more effective, the use of current pre-emptive measures will prove essential in the prevention of terrorist attacks. However, allowing the state to have such abilities has resulted in academic debates

36 Counter-Terrorism and Security Act 2015, Schedule 3, paragraph 4.

37 Counter-Terrorism and Security Act 2015, s 10.

38 See http://www.dw.com/en/german-cabinet-approves-bill-to-stop-radicals-traveling-to-middle-east/a-18233282 accessed 30 March 2018.

39 See https://www.loc.gov/law/foreign-news/article/germany-new-anti-terrorism-legislation-entered-into-force accessed 30 March 2018.

40 *Ibid.*

surrounding mass surveillance, risk society, predictive policing and so-called 'pre-crime' measures.

Mass data surveillance

According to Ratcliffe, Taniguchi and Taylor, in terms of CCTV camera use and its effects on crime reduction in the UK, citizens are subjected to mass surveillance.[41] However, in terms of electronic communications data and ICR records that are retained for 12 months, and under the legal definition of surveillance under RIPA, retention does not equate to mass surveillance. It would simply be impossible for UK law enforcement agencies to actively conduct surveillance on the entire data pool. The algorithmic screening of the electronic communications data stored means that the majority of UK citizens' data would not come under the remit.[42]

Risk society: the resulting increase in state powers

Collecting and storing vast amounts of data adds to the critical debate on the balancing of collective security with individual privacy, and essentially to the managing of risk. For Beck, the term 'risk' is a modern concept that 'inherently contains the concept of control ... presumes decision making [and involves] talking about calculating the incalculable'.[43] According to Beck's conceptualisation in 2002, citizens might increasingly become a paranoid 'risk society' as the international terror threat grows.[44] By linking prediction and risk, whereby fear of a potential terrorist attack leads to an increase in state law enforcement's capabilities, the result has arguably led to the development of computer algorithms to screen the vast amounts of data stored in order to search out the needles in the haystacks autonomously and quickly.[45] According to Furedi's analysis, 'fear plays a key role in twenty-first century consciousness', which has inevitably led to citizens' acceptance of increased state monitoring and thereby, for Garland at least, control.[46]

41 J. Ratcliffe, T. Taniguchi and R. B. Taylor (2009) The Crime Reduction Effects of Public CCTV Cameras: A Multi-Method Spatial Approach, *Justice Quarterly*, 26(4), 746–777.

42 I. Brown and D. Korff (2014) Foreign Surveillance: Law and Practice in a Global Digital Environment, *European Human Rights Law Review*, 3, 243–251. See also A. S. Reid and N. Ryder (2010) For Whose Eyes Only? A Critique of the United Kingdom's Regulation of Investigatory Powers Act 2000, *Information and Communications Technology Law*, 10 (2), 179–201.

43 U. Beck (2002) The Terrorist Threat: World Risk Society Revisited, *Theory, Culture and Society*, 19(4), 39–55, 40.

44 *Ibid.*

45 *Ibid.* See also I. Kerr and J. Earle (2013) Prediction, Preemption, Presumption: How Big Data Threatens Big Picture Privacy, *Stanford Law Review Online*, September, available at https://www.stanfordlawreview.org/online/privacy-and-big-data-prediction-preemption-presumption accessed 20 March 2018.

46 F. Furedi (2007) The Only Thing We Have to Fear is the 'Culture of Fear' Itself: How Human Thought and Action are being Stifled by a Regime of Uncertainty, available at http://frankfuredi.com/pdf/fearessay-20070404.pdf accessed 30 March 2018.

It is worth noting here that as citizens increasingly accept state monitoring of stored data due to the risk society theory, conjoined with technological advancets, the automated computer algorithms used may become progressively effective at screening the vast amounts of data for potential terrorists, in turn leading to intelligence-led policing evolving into a type of predictive-led policing.

Predictive policing and pre-emptive measures: pre-crime

Although the term predictive policing remains within the understanding of intelligence-led policing, it has nevertheless resulted in critics suggesting the UK is moving towards a 'pre-crime' scenario.[47] However, law enforcement cannot simply conduct surveillance or make an arrest without authorised legal powers, and a specific identifiable criminal offence being committed. As such, the term 'pre-crime' does not exist in legal terms. In fact it is simply a fabricated term used by Hollywood in the film *Minority Report.* As discussed further below, collecting or disseminating terrorist-related data through the Internet is a criminal offence.[48] The same can be said for encouraging another person to commit an act of terrorism. These are not pre-crime measures but pre-emptive criminal offences aimed at preventing the would-be-terrorist from committing the physical act. They are a crime.

Following Beck's conceptualisation above, pre-emptive measures are littered throughout the UK's legal counterterrorism structure, simply because of the extraordinary terror threat.[49] As with IPA, RIPA and the CTSA, there has been a growing tendency and common theme to address anticipatory risk.[50] For Walker, these measures have habitually been reactive to the politics of the last atrocity.[51] In response, the UK has enacted certain provisions aimed at criminalising the collection of terrorist material for terrorist purposes, and at criminalising the encouragement and dissemination of terrorist publications. Again for Walker, the process of the radicalisation of young Muslim men became a primary focus following the terrorist attack on London on 7 July 2005. In response to the gamut of ferociousness and the devastating nature of recent terrorist acts, early state intervention is essential, before rather than after the attack.[52]

47 J. Richards (2016) *Needles in Haystacks: Law, Capability, Ethics, and Proportionality in Big Data Intelligence-Gathering*. In A. Bunnik, A. Cawley, M. Mulqueen and A. Zwitter, *Big Data Challenges* (Palgrave Macmillan), p.74. See also L. Zedner (2007) Pre-Crime and Post-Criminology? *Theoretical Criminology*, 11(2), 730–741, 731.

48 Terrorism Act 2000, ss 57 and 58, and Terrorism Act 2006, ss 1 and 2.

49 *Supra* as per U. Beck (2002).

50 C. Walker (2008a) Terrorism: Terrorism Act 2000 s.57 – Direction to Jury on Defence of Possession of Items for Defensive Purposes, Case Comment, *Criminal Law Review*, 72–80, 74.

51 *Ibid.*

52 For attack on Turkey see http://edition.cnn.com/2016/03/13/world/ankara-park-blast. For Ivory Coast attack see http://www.nytimes.com/2016/03/14/world/africa/gunmen-carry-out-fatal-attacks-at-resorts-in-ivory-coast.html?_r=0. For Northern Ireland terror attack see http://www.telegraph.co.uk/news/uknews/terrorism-in-the-uk

Statutory preventative measures: possession of articles and collecting materials and information for use in terrorist activities

Statutory preventative measures form part of this anticipatory risk management approach, although enacted prior to Walker's point made above, and not in direct response to a terrorist attack. Under section 57 of the Terrorism Act 2000 if a person possesses an article in circumstances that give rise to a reasonable suspicion that such possession is for a purpose connected with the commission, preparation or instigation of an act of terrorism, they commit an offence. Similarly, under section 58 a person commits an offence if they collect or made a record of information of a kind likely to be useful to a person committing or preparing an act of terrorism, or they possess a document or record containing information of that kind. This includes photographic and electronic communications data, both of which will increasingly become available to law enforcement by way of IPA.

Although section 58 introduces measures requiring less proof of intent than section 57, both are designed to allow for the early prosecution of the would-be-terrorist, during the planning stage, rather than simply waiting for them to commit the physical act planned. Also known as anticipatory offences, these sections provide a correlative broad scope, meaning that more citizens are potentially brought under the scope of terrorist activity, therefore providing law enforcement agencies with an avenue to conduct surveillance, largely under IPA and RIPA. This has resulted in argumentation surrounding what exactly amounts to an article for the purposes of section 58.

In *R v K* the UK Court of Appeal made it clear that section 58 was not intended to criminalise possession of theological or propagandist material, and therefore must provide practical assistance.[53] The Court further made it clear that 'a document that simply encourages the commission of acts of terrorism' does not fall within the definition, thereby effectively curtailing the scope of section 58.[54] A year later in *R v G, R v J* the UK House of Lords appears to have built upon this judgment confirming that the defendant must be aware of the nature of the information contained in the article.[55] Ultimately, *J* argued infringement of his ECHR Article 7 and 10 rights in the European Court of Human Rights (ECtHR), which failed.[56] According to Ackerman this judicial interpretation adds weight to the argument that the UK's counterterror legislation is overbroad and merely moderated by the judiciary, police and CPS restraint, possibly providing an excuse for executive excess.[57] Ackerman continues to argue the real threat to the public comes not from terrorism, but from counterterrorism measures such as

and http://www.bbc.co.uk/news/northern_ireland. For Paris attack 2016 see http://www.bbc.co.uk/news/world-europe-34818994 accessed 30 March 2018.

53 [2008] EWCA Crim 185, [13].

54 *Ibid.*

55 [2009] UKHL 13, [47]–[50].

56 *Jobe v UK* [2011] 48278/09: ECHR Article 7 no punishment without law and Article 10 Freedom of Expression.

57 B. Ackerman (2007) Before the Next Attack – Preserving Civil Liberties in an Age of Terrorism, *Public Law*, 181–187.

these.[58] Gearty raises similar concerns, noting that the Convention rights are under 'severe attack from a variety of sources'.[59] According to Imran, what is now clear is that many 'of the questions raised in *K* may be rendered superfluous by the intervention of alternative provisions that reduce the necessity for reliance on section 58'.[60]

Inciting terrorism: encouragement and glorification

A person commits an offence of incitement under section 59 of the Terrorism Act 2000, if they incite another person to commit an act of terrorism, within or outside UK borders, if the act would constitute one of the following offences:

1 Murder (contrary to UK Common Law);
2 A section 18 offence of wounding with intent under the Offences Against the Person Act 1861;
3 Administering poison to a person under section 23 Offences Against the Person Act 1861;
4 Damage to property endangering life, as under section 1 Criminal Damage Act 1971.

The issue here is that the offence of incitement is restricted to these four constitutions and evidentially it renders a high threshold, hence it can be quite difficult to prove. To fill the vacuum between incitement and encouragement, thereby serving to lower the threshold allowing UK law enforcement to broaden the net of suspicion, sections 1 and 2 of the Terrorism Act 2006 may serve to provide Imran's reduction, and provide ever more 'expansive possibilities for the prosecution and conviction'.[61] Enacted as a result of the terrorist attack on London on 7 July 2005, and to reflect the provisions of Article 5 of the 2005 Council of Europe Convention on the Prevention of Terrorism, section 1 makes it an offence to encourage an act of terrorism, and section 2 makes it an offence to disseminate terrorist publications. Section 1 in particular may have perhaps been enacted as a result of the earlier ruling in *R v K*.

Encouragement and glorification of terrorism

The Terrorism Act 2006 was aimed at criminalising 'speeches at meetings, sermons at places of worship, chants and placards at demonstrations, broadcasts and

58 *Ibid.*
59 C. Gearty (2007) Rethinking Civil Liberties in a Counter-Terrorism World, *European Human Rights Law Review*, (2), 111–119.
60 A. Imran (2011) Slaying the Monster: Sentencing, *Criminal Law and Justice Weekly* 175(11), 151–152, 151.
61 *Ibid.*

material posted on the Internet', as discussed in Chapter 2.[62] A person will commit an offence of publishing a statement to directly encourage terrorism if:

a he publishes a statement or causes another to publish such a statement; and
b at the time he publishes it or causes it to be published,
c he intends members of the public to be directly or indirectly encouraged or otherwise induced by the statement to commit, prepare or instigate acts of terrorism or Convention offences; or
d is reckless as to such and
e the statement that is likely to be understood by some or all of the members of the public to whom it is published as a direct or indirect encouragement or other inducement to them to the commission, preparation or instigation of acts of terrorism or Convention offences.[63]

For Jones *et al.*, the 'notion of direct encouragement causes little difficulty'.[64] The criminal act of publishing the material with intent is little different from the offence of incitement under the Terrorism Act 2000. The section 1 of the Terrorism Act 2006 offences can be committed with intent, or recklessly as to whether members of the public will be directly or indirectly encouraged or otherwise induced.[65]

Indirect encouragement: glorification

The glorification element posed one of the most contentious issues during the passage of the Terrorism Act 2006 through UK Parliament.[66] The main concern centred on how broadly the offence had been drawn and the possible implications on civil liberties and human rights, namely Article 10 ECHR the freedom of expression. The Third Report of the Joint Committee on Human Rights raised such concern in 2005. The Committee accepted on balance that a new law was required but considered:

> that the offence of encouragement in clause 1 is not sufficiently legally certain to satisfy the requirement in Article 10 that interferences with freedom of expression be "prescribed by law" because of (i) the vagueness of the glorification requirement, (ii) the breadth of the definition of "terrorism" and (iii) the lack of any requirement of intent to incite terrorism or likelihood of such offences being caused as ingredients of the offence.[67]

62 A. Jones QC, R. Bowers and H. D. Lodge (2006) *Blackstone's Guide to The Terrorism Act 2006* (Oxford University Press) p.13.
63 Terrorism Act 2006, s 1(2)(b)(i)(ii).
64 *Supra* as per A. Jones QC, R. Bowers and H. D. Lodge (2006) p.16.
65 Terrorism Act 2006, s 1(2)(b)(i) and (ii).
66 *Supra* as per A. Jones QC, R. Bowers and H. D. Lodge (2006) p.13.
67 Counter-Terrorism Policy and Human Rights: Terrorism Bill and related matters, House of Lords, House of Commons Joint Committee on Human Rights, Third Report of Session 2005–06, HL Paper 75-I HC 561-I, summary p.3.

In order to render the new offence ECHR compatible, the Committee recommended that the references to glorification be removed, thereby creating 'a more tightly drawn definition of terrorism', ensuring intent or at the very least a subjective recklessness test.[68] It was also recommended that a reasonable excuse or public interest defence be inserted to further satisfy ECHR standards.[69] However, the Government refused to implement the amendments suggested by the House of Lords and the then Labour Home Secretary Charles Clarke stated in Parliament that section 1 of the Terrorism Act 2006 intended to provide an exemplary description of what would constitute glorification.[70] As a result, under section 1 the statement made must glorify the commission or preparation, including past, future or in general terms, terrorist attacks, and is a statement that members of the public could reasonably be expected to infer that they should emulate the glorified conduct. Clarke, however, made it clear that this description was not exhaustive.

Therefore a statement made that provides indirect encouragement is not limited to such glorification. Forming part of the UK's pre-emptive approach this section, coupled with section 5, creates a broader offence of preparation of terrorist acts, being closer to containing an offence of involvement, future intention or even just espousal of the cause, rather than the commission of an established crime.[71] It was argued this would appear to close off paths to enlightened discussion and debate utilising materials, as this could be perceived as supporting acts of terrorism, rather than condemning it.[72] Given the gravity of the radicalisation problem outlined above one can appreciate the political approach to the necessity of these powers. A similar approach is seen when looking at dissemination of terrorist materials.

Dissemination of terrorist publications

Following section 2 of the Terrorism Act 2006, a person engages in conduct falling within it if they distribute or circulate a terrorist publication, including the sale or lending of a publication, or the offering for sale or loan, or provide a service to others that enables the obtainment of the publication, including the transmission of the publication electronically. The offence of dissemination is completed if they intend their conduct to directly or indirectly encourage, or provide assistance in the commission, preparation or instigation of acts of terrorism, or is reckless as to such.[73] The Third Report of the Joint Committee on Human Rights raised the same concerns as those for the glorification of terrorism. They argued this provision 'suffers from some of the same compatibility problems as those identified in relation to the proposed encouragement offence'.[74] This included 'the lack of

68 *Ibid.*
69 *Ibid.*
70 *Ibid.*
71 *R v Rowe* [2008] Crim LR 72, see commentary.
72 *Ibid.*
73 Terrorism Act 2006 s 2(1).
74 *Supra* as per Counter-Terrorism Policy and Human Rights, HL Paper 75-I HC 561-I, summary p.3.

connection to incitement to violence and the absence of any requirement that such incitement be either intended, carried out with reckless indifference, or likely'.[75] Again the Committee suggested a reasonable excuse or public interest clause be inserted, primarily aimed at providing a defence and protection for legitimate activities of the media and academics.[76] On balance the requirement for this power appears to be necessary given the amount of data disseminated through the Internet, within which section 3 of the Terrorism Act 2006 makes specific provision for the application of sections 1 and 2 to Internet activity, thereby preventing terrorist material from making its way onto the Internet and attempting to halt terrorist communication. As highlighted, the enthused and encouraged would-be terrorist could potentially attempt to join terrorist groups currently fighting overseas.

These pre-emptive tools have proved not to be as effective as first hoped. In fact only three people have ever been successfully prosecuted under the Terrorist Act 2006. The tools could now be somewhat reinvigorated, however, given the bulk powers under IPA, and decryption methods. Taken as a whole, the legislation discussed to this point serves to provide severe human rights restrictions, specifically an individual's right to data privacy and to freedom of expression, protected by both the ECHR and EU law.

Conclusion

In addition to the unquantifiable threat highlighted in the previous chapter, this chapter has illustrated the frustrated scenario fashioned by sudden increases in independent operational abilities. This has resulted in the introduction of preemptive legislative measures and a risk management style of policing. To this end the chapter has highlighted the interconnection between the risk society theory and predictive policing.

Such pre-emptive measures include temporary travel restrictions and the criminalisation of neutral behaviour. Taking a doctrinal approach, terms used such as mass data surveillance and pre-crime measures have been discredited. Indeed, it would be physically impossible for law enforcement to conduct surveillance on the whole of the UK population's electronic communications data. It has further been shown that the term 'pre-crime' is simply a fabrication and misleadingly used, given that pre-emptive measures are in fact criminal offences.

The requirements for pre-emptive measures have been evidenced throughout both the previous and this chapter This chapter, in particular, highlights the fact that currently counterterrorism legislation fails to eliminate terrorist groups' propaganda and terrorist encrypted electronic communications data, both of which play an integral part in increasing the security risks posed to the UK. It further fails to provide clarity in practical terms, given that the Terrorism Act 2006 appears to have undercut sections 57 and 58 of the Terrorism Act 2000, where it could be

75 *Ibid.*
76 *Ibid.*

argued the latter merely provides 'a useful side-arm'.[77] Nonetheless, the balance between collective security and individual data privacy rights in the UK is fairly stable, and the same can be said for the pre-emptive legislative measures examined. Again this is because of the role and importance of judicial review, judicial independence and the overarching scrutiny provided by commissioners and parliamentary committees. Now that IPA has been passed, an increase in the usage of these dedicated pre-emptive measures is anticipated, thereby serving to provide the state with positive outcomes.

77 *Supra* as per A. Imran (2011).

5 Implications of the UK's legal response: striking the right balance between individual privacy and collective security in the digital age

Introduction

This chapter will assess if the bulk powers under IPA can stand to legal challenges over breaches of data protection and privacy rights. The chapter starts by examining the EU's constitutional and legal influence on the UK legislature, specifically with regard to data protection and the rule of law. This is simply because the EU has been instrumental in the UK's development in terms of data protection and data privacy, and data retention of electronic communications data.

As a result of the CJEU's ruling in *Digital Rights Ireland*, a new criterion will be developed with which to test new UK legislation, ensuring it remains within the limits set by EU law.[1] Applying this criterion specifically to IPA, the chapter will illustrate that having been tested by the CJEU, the initial bulk interception powers may be constrained. In addition, the new Judicial Commissioners' role will be examined focusing on the available powers, limited to judicial review rules. The overall aim of this chapter is to assess if IPA strikes the right balance between individual privacy and collective security in the digital age, and stands up to CJEU and ECtHR judicial scrutiny.

UK data protection

The Data Protection Act 1998 (DPA) provides statutory control over how a citizen's personal information is used by organisations, private businesses and the Government.[2] Those responsible for using the data must abide by the data protection principles ensuring data is:

1 used fairly and lawfully;
2 used for limited and/or specific expressed purposes;
3 accurate and used adequately;

1 *Digital Rights Ireland Ltd v Minister for Communications, Marine and Natural Resources and others and the conjoined case of Kärntner Landesregierung, Michael Seitlinger, Christof Tschohl and others* delivered on 8 April 2014 and reported at [2015] QB 127. Hereafter referred to as *Digital Rights Ireland*.
2 The Data Protection Act 1998, Introductory Text.

4 deleted when no longer required;
5 kept secure;
6 not transferred outside the European Economic Area without adequate protection.[3]

Should the data contain sensitive information, such as sexual health, criminal records or ethnicity and religious beliefs, then stronger protections must be in place.[4] When it was enacted, the impact of DPA was felt right across the public and private sectors. For the purposes of this chapter, the seventh data protection principle relates to security, and it states that 'appropriate technical and organisational measures shall be taken against unauthorised or unlawful processing of personal data and against accidental loss or destruction of, or damage to, personal data'.

This is particularly relevant to the issues raised in Chapters 2, 3 and 4 combined, where the use of Internet and email raises problems when private or public organisations wish to monitor its use. Briefly, an organisation has a right, even a duty, to monitor the use of the Internet and emails to prevent them being used for unlawful purposes or to distribute offensive material. However, running concurrent to this obligation is the fact an individual has a right to data privacy and protection. It is the duty of all organisation to provide access to email and the Internet to balance these two conflicting principles. In specific policing terms section 29 of DPA deals with crime and taxation exemptions that permit personal data to be processed and withheld from the individual concerned for the purposes of the prevention or detection of crime. Such exemption must be proportionate, and the 'data controller' must record the data being processed. This means of course that a person may not be able to ascertain what information law enforcement has collected.

Key human rights instruments: influencing the UK's approach

The right to data privacy is enshrined in the EU at the constitutional level through Article 8 of the Charter of Fundamental Rights (CFR or Charter) and at the legislative level by way of two directives, namely the Data Protection Directive in 1995 and the e-Privacy Directive in 2002.[5] In the interests of fullness, the 2002

3 The Data Protection Act 1998, Schedule 1.
4 The Data Protection Act 1998, s 2 and Schedule 3.
5 European Union Directive 95/46/EC of the European Parliament and of the European Council of 24 October 1995 on the protection of individuals with regard to the processing of personal data and on the free movement of such data. Also European Union Directive 2002/58/EC of the European Parliament and of the Council of 12 July 2002 concerning the processing of personal data and the protection of privacy in the electronic communications sector. See also *S and Marper v UK* [2008] 48 ECHR 1581, [66]–[67], the Court noted the concept of private life is a broad term not susceptible to exhaustive definition.

Directive repealed the earlier 1997 version aimed primarily at the telecommunications sector, so it is no longer relevant.[6]

EU constitutional protection: the Treaty of Lisbon

As a result of the ratification of the Treaty of Lisbon 2007, which came into effect in 2009, the Charter of Fundamental Rights 2000 was given legal status. Therefore, constitutionally speaking, data privacy and protection is afforded by Article 8 of the Charter which states individuals have a right to the protection of personal data:

> Such data must be processed fairly for specified purposes and on the basis of the consent of the person concerned or some other legitimate basis laid down by law. Everyone has the right of access to data, which has been collected concerning him or her, and the right to have it rectified.

The Charter also states compliance must be subject to control by an independent authority. However, the right afforded here requires implementation into EU surveillance legislative instruments to make them effective. The EU's instruments have so far failed in this regard as they do not provide sufficient oversight. Since the terrorist attack on the US on 11 September 2001, data protection appears to have been almost ignored as governments focus on data collection and mining.[7] Analysis illustrates that 'creating a stable and unequivocal system of data protection was not a priority'.[8]

EU legislative protection

The 1995 Directive was implemented in the UK by way of the Data Protection Act 1998, and the 2002 Directive was implemented through the Privacy and Electronic Communications (EC Directive) Regulations 2003. Following this in 2008, the EU adopted a framework decision aimed at providing similar legislative protection, but focused primarily on police and judicial cooperation when dealing in criminal matters.[9] The e-Privacy Directive in 2002 dealt with most aspects of protecting privacy in electronic communications, such as:

6 European Union Directive 97/66/EC of the European Parliament and of the European Council of 15 December 1997 concerning the processing of personal data and the protection of privacy in the telecommunications sector.
7 H. Hijmans and A. Scirocco (2009) Shortcomings in EU Data Protection in the Third and the Second Pillars, *Common Market Law Review*, 46, 1485–1525, 1496.
8 *Ibid.*
9 European Council Framework Decision on the protection of personal data processed in the framework of police and judicial co-operation in criminal matters 2008/977/JHA.

- *Security*: Article 4 requires the service provider to take appropriate technical security measures. Subscribers must be informed if there is a risk of a security breach;
- *Confidentiality*: Article 5 requires legislative assurance of confidentiality of communications made through public electronic communications services, or to such. Monitoring or storing communications is prohibited unless required for national security or crime prevention;
- *Location data*: Article 9 prohibits using location data unless it remains anonymous, or has the user's consent. It can only be used to provide a value added service, such as local weather details. Article 10, however, permits the use of location data in life threatening circumstances, such as mobile contact with emergency services;
- *Billing*: Article 6 stipulates that billing data must be erased or made anonymous once the service providers' reasons for retention have expired (i.e., the bill has been paid). Under Article 8, service users have a right to receive non-itemised billing;
- *Automatic call forwarding*: Article 11 provides service users the right to prevent automatic call forwarding by third parties;
- *Unsolicited marketing*: Article 13 prohibits unsolicited communication unless consented to by the service user.[10]

For Hijman and Scirocco, however, the protection afforded by way of these instruments lacked comprehensive cover for all data processing and thereby illustrated issues of practicality.[11] Balancing an individual's right to data privacy with the needs of national security has not been an easy task to fulfil, either within the UK or the EU. For example, the DPA introduced safeguards applied to access to communications data. The problem is that law enforcement agencies could only make use of electronic communications data for a limited period, and were thereby 'obliged to rely solely on data routinely retained by communications companies for their own purposes'.[12] This usually meant that the data was deleted following the payment of the last outstanding bill. In light of this, and the fact that no mandatory data retention regime existed, the EU introduced a number of Data Retention Directives. The first dealt with fixed networks and mobile telephony only, and was incorporated into UK law by way of the Data Retention (EC Directive) Regulations 2007 (S.I. 2007/2199). These were then superseded by the Data Retention (EC Directive) Regulations 2009 (S.I. 2009/859), 'which contained additional provisions relating to Internet access, Internet telephony and email'.[13]

10 *R (on the application of David Davis MP, Tom Watson MP, Peter Brice and Geoffrey Lewis) v The Secretary of State for the Home Department* [2015] EWHC 2092, summary.

11 *Supra* as per H. Hijmans and A. Scirocco (2009) 1496.

12 *R (on the application of David Davis MP, Tom Watson MP, Peter Brice and Geoffrey Lewis) v The Secretary of State for the Home Department* [2015] EWHC 2092, [37]–[38].

13 *Ibid*, [42].

The start of a new focus on data retention began when the EU's Council Action Plan on Combating Terrorism highlighted the emphasis to broaden security.[14] At this time, the EU focused on creating the next generation of Schengen, a visa information system and biometric passports with a focus on information gathering, analysis and exchange.[15] In meeting this agenda, the EU's Action Plan paved the way for framework decisions aimed at simplifying information exchange between the law enforcement agencies, Europol and Eurojust, and called for a Data Retention Directive.[16]

Bulk retention of electronic communications data: key human rights instruments

Mitsilegas followed this change in the use of EU level surveillance and noted five transformational trends: the linking of immigration with security and counter-terrorism; increasing biometric data; a sharp shift towards prevention; broadening the access to data by law enforcement agencies; and taking a risk assessment approach.[17] These links and growth in the use of surveillance highlight a utilitarian logic where 'information must be seen as a tool for collective benefits like fighting terrorism', ensuring 'that information is available when needed'.[18] This idea of the availability of data counters the EU's data protection principle, the aim of which is to limit the use of data to a specified purpose.

For Murphy, surveillance represents the broadest counterterrorism action taken by the EU.[19] In the 21st Century, national surveillance systems, such as the UK's IPA, subject to warrants and authorities can potentially affect a large section of the population and are not simply targeted towards immigrants, asylum seekers or suspected criminals. The EU's 2006 Data Retention Directive represents a classic example of targeting the whole population. For this reason, Murphy describes it as unpalatable.[20] The Directive:

> [a]ims to harmonise Member States' provisions concerning the obligations of the providers of publicly available electronic communications services or of public communications networks with respect to the retention of certain data which are generated or processed by them, in order to ensure that the data are

14 European Union Council (2007) *EU Action Plan on Combating Terrorism*, Brussels, 9 March.

15 *Ibid.*

16 *Ibid.*

17 V. Mitsilegas (2010) The Transformation of Border Controls in an Era of Security: UK and EU Systems Converging? *Journal of Immigration Asylum and Nationality Law*, 24(3), 233–245, 233.

18 *Supra* as per H. Hijmans and A. Scirocco (2009), 1490.

19 C. C. Murphy (2015) *EU Counter-Terrorism Law: Pre-Emption and the Rule of Law* (Hart Publishing).

20 *Ibid.*

available for the purpose of the investigation, detection and prosecution of serious crime, as defined by each Member State in its national law.[21]

Prior to the terrorist attack in London on 7 July 2005, the EU's attempts to create such a measure failed due to heavy opposition from the European Parliament.[22] However, in the aftermath of this attack the UK effectively suppressed any opposition, arguing that mobile telephones were used in the coordination of the attacks, as well as in the earlier Madrid attack on 3 March 2004, and unsubstantiated claims were made confirming telecommunications information was vital to the investigation.[23] This Directive amended the earlier e-Privacy Directive and as such, following adoption of the Data Retention Directive on the basis of Article 95 EC (now Article 114 Treaty on the Functioning of the European Union (TFEU)), Ireland supported by Slovakia brought forward an application to have it annulled by the CJEU. In *Ireland v European Parliament and European Commission* the CJEU reached the decision that the amendment was within the legal scope under the current Article 114 TFEU. In drawing a comparison to an earlier ruling concerning Passenger Name Record data, discussed in the next chapter, the Court confirmed the Directive merely aimed to harmonise the retention of data by private actors within the EU so that a distortion of competition within the internal market could be avoided.[24] Although the legality of the Directive is sufficient as it was adopted correctly, this further rationale represents a startlingly poor decision. The reason behind the adoption in the first place was to provide a lawful basis for the retention of data, both the traffic and location data of individuals, effectively permitting a total derogation from Articles 7 and 8 of the CFR, which would require the deletion of such information once the billing purpose was satisfied.

21 Article 1 of the Directive 2006/24/EC of the European Parliament and of the Council of 15 March 2006 on the retention of data generated or processed in connection with the provision of publicly available electronic communications services or of public communications networks and amending Directive 2002/58/EC.

22 Draft Framework Decision on the retention of data processed and stored in connection with the provision of publicly available electronic communications services or data on public communications networks for the purpose of prevention, investigation, detection and prosecution of crime and criminal offences including terrorism 2004/0813/CNS.

23 European Commission (2005) Proposal for a Directive of the European Parliament and of the Council on the retention of data processed in connection with the provision of public electronic communication services and amending Directive 2002/58/EC COM (2005) 438 final, Brussels, 21 September 2005. See also Euractiv.com, Data Retention: Parliament caves in to Council pressure, 14 December 2005, available at http://www.euractiv.com/section/digital/news/data-retention-parliament-caves-in-to-council-pressure accessed 30 March 2018.

24 *Ireland v European Parliament and European Commission* [2009] ECR-I-593, [60]–[69].

The breadth of the 2006 EU Directive

It is particularly concerning when one notes the sheer breadth of the 2006 Directive, which effectively includes a plethora of crimes for which the data may be utilised, with regard to both the number of people who can access the data and the retention period. The 'excess of crimes' argument stems from the fact Member States cannot agree upon a definition of serious crime, and therefore Member States have implemented the directive in their own very individual way, contrary to EU law.[25] The same can be said for the different law enforcement agencies' permitted access to the data stored, with some Member States allowing not only security and policing agencies to have access, but also military services, tax and customs officials and border authorities.[26] Retention periods also fluctuate given the Directive allows for such divergence, permitting between 6 and 24 months.[27]

These facts prove beyond doubt the 2006 Directive derogated from the very purpose of EU directives. Even though the situation may have been improved given the previous total lack of uniformity, some divergence remains, illustrative of the failure of the instruments' claim to harmonise the internal market.[28] A rather peculiar clause within the Directive, although subject to EU Commission approval, allows the Member State to extend the retention period beyond the two years should particular circumstances exist.[29] It is startling to note that the Commission only reviews the Member States' decision checking for compliance with the internal market, rather than data protection rights.[30] The lack of clarity surrounding the necessity of this provision and the fact it has not been used deem it somewhat superfluous and arguably unpalatable, given the lack of focus on fundamental data protection.[31]

It terms of human rights infringements, the Directive directly reversed the requirements under the e-Privacy Directive 2002, which as per above required immediate deletion of traffic and location data once the billing process has been completed.[32] This was challenged through the judicial process where the CJEU

25 Council of the European Union, Document 9439/11, Brussels, 27 April 2011.

26 European Commission (2011) Report from the Commission to the Council and the European Parliament: Evaluation report on the Data Retention Directive 2006/24/EC COM (2011) 225 final, Brussels, 18 April 2011 p.9.

27 Article 6 Data Retention Directive, Directive 2006/24/EC of the European Parliament and of the Council of 15 March 2006 on the retention of data generated or processed in connection with the provision of publicly available electronic communications services or of public communications networks and amending Directive 2002/58/EC.

28 The Commission noted a wide range of retention periods existed prior to the Data Retention Directive, from three months to four years. See *supra* European Commission (2005) p.1.

29 Article 12 and Article 12(2) Data Retention Directive 2006/24/EC.

30 M. Vilasau (2007) Traffic Data Retention v Data Protection: The New European Framework, *Computer and Telecommunications Law Review,* 13(2), 52–58, 58.

31 See *supra* European Commission (2005) p.13.

32 Article 6 Directive 2002/58/EC of the European Parliament and of the Council of 12 July 2002 concerning the processing of personal data and the protection of privacy in the electronic communications sector.

dismissed the first claim that was based on the legality under what is now Article 114 TFEU, as discussed above.[33] However, in 2010 the Irish High Court granted a motion brought by a campaign group known as Digital Rights Ireland, where they specifically requested the CJEU look at the compliancy of the Directive with Article 5(4) of the Treaty on the European Union (TEU) and with certain fundamental rights protected under the CFR.[34] Additionally, in 2012 a number of applicants brought an action in the Austrian Constitutional Court claiming the national law transposing the Directive infringed Article 8 of the CFR. The two claims were merged together by the CJEU where it was finally held that the Directive was invalid, overall, because the EU legislature had exceeded the limits imposed by Articles 7, 8 and 52(1) of the CFR.[35]

They decided the Directive failed to provide sufficient safeguards against unlawful access to and the use of retained data, particularly by public authorities.[36] Although noting the sheer breadth of the Directive and that, in effect, no limits on the power to retain data existed, the CJEU failed to expressly lay down particular restraints or conditional requirements should such retention be necessary.[37] The Court did, however, confirm:

1 The protection of the fundamental right to respect for private life requires that derogations and limitations in relation to the protection of personal data *must apply only* in so far as is strictly necessary. Consequently the legislation in question must lay down *clear and precise rules* governing the scope and application of the measure in question and imposing *minimum safeguards* sufficient to give effective protection against the risk of abuse and against any unlawful access to and use of that data;[38]
2 Any legislation establishing or permitting a general retention regime for personal data *must* expressly provide for access to and use of the data to be strictly *restricted* to the purpose of preventing and detecting *precisely defined* serious offences or of conducting criminal prosecutions relating to such offences;[39]
3 Above all, access by the competent national authority to the data retained *must* be made dependent on a *prior review by a court* or an independent administrative body whose decision seeks to *limit access* to the data and their use to what is *strictly necessary* for the purpose of attaining the objective pursued, and which intervenes following a reasoned request of those authorities.[40] [My emphasis]

33 C-301/06 *Ireland v European Parliament and European Commission* [2009] ECR-I-593.
34 *Ibid.*
35 *Digital Rights Ireland.*
36 *Ibid*, [57]–[59], [60]–[67].
37 *Ibid*, [58], [59].
38 *Ibid*, [52], [54].
39 *Ibid*, [61].
40 *Ibid*, [62], this was also highlighted by Bean LJ in *R (on the application of David Davis MP, Tom Watson MP, Peter Brice and Geoffrey Lewis) v The Secretary of State for the Home Department* [2015] EWHC 2092, [91].

Albeit the Court invalidated the Directive, a generalised rationale for the existence of such a data retaining measure was legitimised: 'the retention of data for the purpose of allowing the competent national authorities to have possible access to those data ... genuinely satisfies an objective of general interest'.[41]

The impact of the CJEU's *Digital Rights Ireland* decision on the UK cannot be overstated, given it effectively neutered any national law giving effect to the Directive, which was transposed into UK national law by way of the Data Retention (EC Directive) Regulations 2009.[42] Immediately following the CJEU's landmark decision, the then Home Secretary Theresa May put before the UK Parliament the Data Retention and Investigatory Powers Bill, specifying the UK must merely retain the powers under the invalid Directive, by fashioning such primary legislation.[43] This is made clear in the opening words of the statute, confirming that it was '[a]n Act to make provision, in consequence of a declaration made by the [CJEU] in relation to Directive 2006/24/EC, about the retention of certain communications data'.[44] To ensure *Digital Rights Ireland* had no bearing on the legislation, it did not purport to transpose any EU law.[45] It was introduced on 14 July 2014 and rushed through UK Parliament as emergency legislation, receiving Royal Assent some four days later on 17 July 2014.[46] A sunset clause was applied, to take effect on 31 December 2016, in order to alleviate MPs' fears with regard to rushed and inadequately debated legislation, which contains far-reaching powers.[47]

As a result and following the enactment Ministers David Davis and Tom Watson brought a judicial review action to the UK High Court, arguing the provisions were incompatible with the EU law, namely the CFR and CJEU's decision in *Digital Rights Ireland*, and additionally the ECHR.[48] Lord Justice Bean discussed the *Digital Rights Ireland* cases, specifically referring to the CJEU's interpretation of Articles 7 and 8 of the CFR. Bean LJ replied in part on an earlier decision reached by Lord Kerr in the UK Supreme Court, in *Rugby Football Union v Consolidated Information Services Ltd.*, confirming the CFR has direct

41 *Ibid*, [44].
42 The Data Retention (EC Directive) Regulations SI 2009/859, adopted pursuant to the European Communities Act 1972 s 2(2). Regulations under the ECA 1972 depend upon the existence of a valid EU instrument. See also A. Roberts (2015) Privacy, Data Retention and Domination: *Digital Rights Ireland Ltd v Minister for Communications, The Modern Law Review*, 78(3), 522–548, 536.
43 *Supra* as per D. Anderson QC (2015) p.16. See also V. Mitsilegas (2015) *The Criminalisation of Migration in Europe: Challenges for Human Rights and the Rule of Law* (Springer) p.39.
44 *R (on the application of David Davis MP, Tom Watson MP, Peter Brice and Geoffrey Lewis) v The Secretary of State for the Home Department* [2015] EWHC 2092, [44]–[46].
45 *Supra* as per A. Roberts (2015) p.537.
46 *Supra* as per D. Anderson QC (2015) p.15.
47 Data Retention and Investigatory Powers Act 2014, s 8(3).
48 *R (on the application of David Davis MP, Tom Watson MP, Peter Brice and Geoffrey Lewis) v The Secretary of State for the Home Department* [2015] EWHC 2092.

effect in UK national law, when implementing EU law.[49] Given UK data protection law has been within the scope of EU law since 1995, Bean LJ really had no option but to illustrate the fact he was dealing with the implementation of EU law.[50]

Referring to the ruling in *Digital Rights Ireland* rendering the Directive invalid, Bean LJ went on to say:

> The invalidation of the Data Retention Directive by the CJEU put in doubt the legal basis for requiring the continued retention of communications data under the [UK's Data Retention (EC Directive)] 2009 Regulations. Although the 2009 Regulations remained in force, they had been made under s. 2(2) of the European Communities Act 1972 to implement the Data Retention Directive and were already subject to a legal challenge that had been stayed pending the outcome of the Digital Rights Ireland case. We were told that following the Digital Rights Ireland judgment, some CSPs [Crown Prosecution Services] expressed the view that there was *no legal basis* for them to continue to retain communications data, and indicated that they would start to delete data that had been retained under the 2009 Regulations.[51] [My emphasis]

Therefore, in the absence of a clear legal power to retain electronic communications data, the UK's law enforcement agencies' ability to use the Data Retention (EC Directive) Regulations 2009 was endangered. In disseminating the CJEU's judgment in *Digital Rights Ireland*, Bean noted the Court's failure to stipulate possible conditions. However, following the ratio it is clear that 'legislation establishing a general retention regime for electronic communications data infringes rights under Articles 7 and 8 of the CFR unless it is accompanied by an access regime which provides adequate safeguards for those rights'.[52]

The claimants' application for judicial review succeeded and the High Court declared that section 1 of DRIPA was inconsistent with EU law in so far as:

a it does not lay down *clear and precise rules* providing for access to and use of communications data retained pursuant to a retention notice to be *strictly restricted* to the purpose of preventing and detecting precisely defined serious offences or of conducting criminal prosecutions relating to such offences; and
b access to the data is not made dependent on a *prior review* by a court or an independent administrative body whose decision limits access to and use of

49 See *Rugby Football Union v Consolidated Information Services Ltd., (formerly Viagogo Ltd)* [2012] 1 WLR 3333, [27]–[28].

50 *R (on the application of David Davis MP, Tom Watson MP, Peter Brice and Geoffrey Lewis) v The Secretary of State for the Home Department* [2015] EWHC 2092, [6]–[8], [11].

51 *Ibid*, [44]–[46].

52 *Ibid*, [89].

the data to what is strictly necessary for the purpose of attaining the objective pursued.[53] [My emphasis]

The High Court therefore made an order suspending section 1 of DRIPA postponed until 31 March 2016 to give Parliament time to consider their judgment and introduce measures consistent with EU law.[54] The High Court's decision is not surprising given that inherently bulk collection of evidence has not been particularly welcomed or upheld, quite separately from constitutional EU law principles, within the jurisprudence of the ECtHR.[55]

European Court of Human Rights jurisprudence

The ECHR and the ECtHR provide an additional layer of judicial accountability of UK statutes. Although the examples illustrated below do not cover electronic communications data, they do concern the state retaining data of persons who have not been either charged or convicted of a criminal offence. The jurisprudence of the ECtHR has illustrated that the state cannot simply retain the information for future use, or as a 'just in case measure'.[56] This has been evident for some time, and by way of example, under section 64(1A) of the Police and Criminal Evidence Act 1997 (PACE), the state was permitted to keep on file DNA and fingerprint evidence of those either not charged or convicted of the crime of which they were suspected. This also included DNA from those who volunteered to give samples for elimination. Challenged by way of *R (S) v Chief Constable of South Yorkshire Police* in the House of Lords, it was held the Association of Police Officers (ACPO) policy of allowing retention of DNA and fingerprints was lawful.[57] Later the case became known as *S and Marper v UK* where the ECtHR decided that a blanket and indiscriminate policy amounted to a breach of Article 8 ECHR.[58] This particular case highlights the clash between the UK judiciary and the jurisprudence of the ECtHR, where Lord Steyn in dismissing the appeal affirmed, whilst accepting the necessity that the Court interpret the ECHR in a harmonious way with the ECtHR's jurisprudence: 'The whole community, as well as the individuals whose sample was collected, benefits from there being as large a database as it is possible ... The benefit to the aims of accurate and efficient law enforcement is thereby enhanced.'[59]

The dichotomy is interesting here, given Lord Steyn favoured the interests of the wider community over the individual, and the ECtHR ultimately favoured the opposite, highlighting particular areas of concern: 'have due regard to the specific

53 *Ibid*, [114].
54 *Ibid*, [121].
55 *R (GC) v Commissioner of the Metropolis* [2011] 1 WLR 1230.
56 *Ibid.*
57 [2004] UKHL 39.
58 [2008] (Application Numbers 30562/04 and 30566/04), [67], and see also [2008] 48 EHRR 1169.
59 [2004] UKHL 39, [78].

context in which information at issue is recorded and retained, the nature of the records, the way in which these records are used and processed and the results that may be obtained'.[60]

In light of the final ECtHR ruling, ACPO decided to do nothing, believing it should follow the earlier ruling in the House of Lords. This inevitably led to the database being further challenged in *R (GC) v Commissioner of the Metropolis* in the UK Supreme Court.[61] It held that the ECtHR's decision should be followed and therefore retaining the database was unjustified interference with Article 8 of the ECHR. Although the decision was welcomed, the Supreme Court did not make a declaration of incompatibility under the Human Rights Act 1998 with regard to section 64(1A) of PACE, stating Parliament had intended discretion to be used as to what could be kept on the database. The Court did, however, clarify that should Parliament not remedy the situation within a reasonable time then citizens would have viable public law challenges. As a result Parliament introduced the Protection of Freedoms Act 2012, where section 1 brought about the removal of DNA and fingerprints being kept on the database for those citizens not convicted.

Considering the ECtHR's approach and particular emphasis in *S and Marper* that in order for the powers to be in accordance with the rule of law, and ECHR compatible, there must be adequate legal protection against arbitrariness and sufficient clarity about the discretionary scope given to authorities with a focus on the way the powers are exercised.[62] The Court findings are not that surprising given their earlier ruling in *Klass v Germany* where they emphasised proportionality and a focus on the individual's rights.[63] It is clear that blanket policies do not sit well within the ECHR framework, and where the ECtHR sees the dignity of the individual prevailing over the interests of the wider community. Although the ECtHR disapproves of blanket policies the CJEU appears to be somewhat in favour, providing that minimum safeguards are put in place. It was evident from the *Digital Rights Ireland* case that the collection of data was not the main issue, rather the safeguards surrounding the access to it.

More recently, however, in *Zakharov v Russia* the ECtHR held that any authorisation for the use of surveillance powers must be capable of:

> verifying the existence of a reasonable suspicion against the person concerned, in particular, whether there are factual indications for suspecting that person of planning, committing or having committed criminal acts or other acts that may give rise to secret surveillance measures, such as, for example, acts endangering national security.[64]

60 [2008] (Application Numbers 30562/04 and 30566/04), [67].
61 [2011] 1 WLR 1230.
62 [2008] (Application Numbers 30562/04 and 30566/04), [95].
63 [1978] (Application number 5029/71), [68].
64 47143/06, 4 December 2015, [260].

Accordingly, the ECtHR has made it quite clear here that privacy and the freedom of expression are important principles that must be protected.

Therefore, the ECtHR's findings would be, to my mind at least, entirely reliant upon whether or not it views the initial retention of electronic communications data as a form of surveillance. If it does take this view, then the court will undoubtedly find it unjustifiable for a government to conduct surveillance on the private communications data of potentially millions of people who it does not suspect of being involved in criminal or terrorist-related activity.[65] This would have a profound impact on law enforcement's capabilities as highlighted in the previous chapters, and unbalance the scales weighting the right to life and right to privacy.

It is argued, however, that the initial collection and retention of data is not surveillance, given that much of the data is never viewed by law enforcement, and disregarded following autonomous filtering. Likewise, the autonomous electronic screening of this retained data does not equate to surveillance, and it is deleted after 12 months. As discussed, the use of the bulk powers is heavily curtailed, requiring warranted and independent judicial approval, and is subject to four additional layers of independent scrutiny.[66] They are essential to finding the ever-elusive terrorist, a fact made clear when a terrorist suspect was found working at a UK airport, planning to use his security access to plant bombs for al-Qaeda.[67] It remains essential, of course, that ensuring restrictive laws provide for data protection and privacy remains a high priority when the UK leaves the EU, in terms of intelligence exchange, as explored in the next chapter.

Creating a new data retention law: the digital rights criterion

Returning to EU law, in order for UK legislation to fit with constitutional EU law and the jurisprudence of the CJEU, and the ECtHR, the following criteria are proposed to ensure compatibility:

1. Primary legislation must lay down clear and precise rules governing the scope and application of the measure;
2. Minimum safeguards must be imposed sufficiently reducing the risk of abuse or unlawful access to the data;
3. Access to the data must be expressly provided for, limiting the number of persons authorised to have such access and restricted to the purpose of preventing and detecting precisely defined serious criminal offences;

65 *Ibid.*

66 The four layers are: the UK's independent reviewer of anti-terrorist legislation, currently Max Hill QC; the Intelligence Services Committee; Investigatory Powers Commissioner; and the Investigatory Powers Tribunal.

67 See http://news.bbc.co.uk/1/hi/4778575.stm accessed 30 March 2018.

4 Access to the data will only be granted after a prior assessment has been made by an independent administrative body or court, with the primary focus on human rights and the proportionality of the measure;
5 Retained data will be deleted after 12 months unless an independent administrative body or court decides otherwise, having weighed the evidence and conducted a proportionality test.

Focusing on EU law, it could be argued IPA is purely domestic legislation and thereby not subject to the CFR, namely Article 8 right to data protection. DRIPA was arguably different, enacted to give effect to an EU instrument. One could generalise and state that the EU lacks competence in legislating within the field of fundamental rights and Member States must only respect the CFR when implementing EU law. However, legally it is much more complex as the CJEU expansively magnifies the term 'implementing EU law' particularly when Member States seek to rely on a derogation from EU law principles.[68] The IPA in fact specifies under Schedule 10 Part 1 that the Privacy and Electronic Communications (EC Directive) Regulations 2003 do not apply in relation to any personal data breach which is to be notified to the Investigatory Powers Commissioner in accordance with a code of practice.[69] Considering UK data protection laws have been founded on EU law, particularly the e-Privacy Directive, it is argued IPA is based upon EU derogation and it will undoubtedly be classed as implementing EU law by the CJEU. For this reason, the Act must respect the CFR and implement the digital rights criterion.

The Investigatory Powers Act 2016: striking the right balance

It has been recognised IPA needs to strike the right balance between individual privacy and collective security in the digital age. It has been said that holding privacy and security concerns to be irreconcilable is unhelpful and constraining given 'we all share an interest in maximising both our individual privacy on the one hand and collective security on the other'.[70] Particularly since *Digital Rights Ireland*, it is vital any new intrusive surveillance powers that are passed do so with due regard to the CFR.[71] Although the IPA was written to last, not just for the remaining time the UK is within the EU, it is important that UK counterterrorism legislation meets the CFR thereafter, in order to secure and maintain intelligence

68 Case C-390/12 *Pfleger* EU:C:2014:281, Case C-418/11 Texdata Software EU: C:2013:588 [71]–[75].
69 S.I. 2003/2426.
70 House of Commons Second Reading, 15 March 2016, Column 824, available at http://www.publications.parliament.uk/pa/cm201516/cmhansrd/cm160315/debtext/160315-0001.htm#16031546000001 accessed 20 March 2018.
71 A. Murray and B. Keenan (2015) Ensuring the Rule of Law, LSE Law Department Briefings on the Investigatory Powers Bill, *LSE Law Policy Briefing*, 12, Social Science Research Network, available at http://ssrn.com/abstract=2703806 accessed 30 March 2018.

exchange. Accordingly, the right to data protection includes data security and was described in *Digital Rights Ireland* as the essence of this right.[72]

Bulk powers: digital rights criterion

In the previous chapter it was shown that the bulk powers of interception, retention and equipment interference have been instrumental, and sometimes pivotal, in preventing acts of terrorism and other serious crimes. The idea is to gather large volumes of data, which is then subject to stringent controls, used to filter out irrelevant material, so the security services can simply focus on the small fraction that provides intelligence on known and potential threats.[73] The issue here is regardless of the filtering process many innocent citizens' electronic communications data would have been collected in the course of the action. King argues that whilst there 'needs to be formidable intrusive powers for law enforcement agencies' to operate', they must be targeted only and proportionate, rather than catchall bulk powers.[74] The bulk powers are extraordinarily broad in scope and the 'catchall' part to the bulk collection does not sound proportionate, however, the practical effect of the breadth is limited by what can follow after the device has been accessed, or the telephone line tapped. It has been put forward that this stage makes the former proportionate.[75]

The question is, of course, does IPA meet the digital rights criterion? IPA clearly satisfies the first test insofar as it forms primary legislation that lays down clear and precise rules that govern the scope and application of the measures. The many accompanying codes of conduct, although not law, may perhaps go some way in further satisfying this test. The access to the data is expressly provided for, with the bulk powers in particular stating that only intelligence and security agencies can apply for the necessary warrants. This therefore limits the number of persons authorised to have such access and it is restricted to the purpose of preventing and detecting precisely defined serious crime.

In order to pass the digital rights criterion measures must introduce minimum safeguards that sufficiently reduce the risk of abuse or unlawful access to the data, and guarantee that access to the data will only be granted after an independent administrative body or court has made a prior assessment, with the primary focus on human rights and the proportionality of the measure. It is clear the UK

72 O. Lynskey (2015) Beyond privacy: the data protection implications of the IP Bill, LSE Law Department Briefings on the Investigatory Powers Bill, *LSE Law Policy Briefings*, 15, Social Science Research Network, available at http://ssrn.com/abstract=2704299 accessed 30 March 2018.

73 House of Lords Second Reading 27 June 2016, Volume 773, Column 1362, available at https://hansard.parliament.uk/lords/2016-06-27/debates/1606278000466/InvestigatoryPowersBill accessed 20 March 2018.

74 First Sitting Committee Debate Session 2015–16, Investigatory Powers Bill, Publications on the Internet, Column 14, 24 March 2016, available at http://www.publications.parliament.uk/pa/cm201516/cmpublic/investigatorypowers/160324/am/160324s01.htm accessed 30 March 2018.

75 *Ibid*, Column 6, 24 March 2016.

Government has listened to the recommendations made, and perhaps learned from past mistakes, and has taken a human rights approach highlighted by the opening part of IPA, which imposes certain duties and introduces general privacy protections and safeguards.[76]

The intrusive powers can only be used when it is necessary and proportionate to do so, and requires an independent judicial commissioner to review the Secretary of State's decision before the warrant is valid.[77] IPA's new double lock system creates a number of new posts, including judicial commissioners and an independent Investigatory Powers Commissioner.[78] This new position brings together the responsibilities of the Interception of Communications Commissioner, the Intelligence Services Commissioner and the Chief Surveillance Commissioner.[79] Additionally, the commissioners will be provided with inspectors, technical experts and independent legal advisers, and should an individual suffer as a result of an error the IPC will have the power to inform them.[80] These provisions certainly increase the difference between IPA and all other surveillance legislation including RIPA.

In deciding whether the warrant is necessary on relevant grounds and whether the conduct authorised is proportionate, judicial commissioners must apply the same principles as would be applied by a court on an application for judicial review.[81] The meaning of judicial review was discussed during the first sitting committee stage of IPA and criticised by Sara Ogilvie from Liberty as being inherently limited in terms of jurisdiction.[82] In response Suella Fernandes confirmed that the double lock involves, 'an intensive analysis of necessity and proportionality'.[83]

Checks and balances: judicial commissioners and other mechanisms

In labouring the point Ogilvie argued that the level of judicial review would naturally be less intensive due to the 'national security' argument. Although Fernandes did offer some assurance in that the process is not meant to be a 'rubber-stamping' exercise, it certainly appears that way considering section 229(6) confirms that judicial commissioners must not act in a way that is contrary to the public interest, or prejudicial to national security, the prevention or detection of

76 Investigatory Powers Bill 2015.

77 Investigatory Powers Bill 2015, ss 19 and 23; see also House of Commons Second Reading, 15 March 2016, Column 815, available at http://www.publications.parliament.uk/pa/cm201516/cmhansrd/cm160315/debtext/160315-0001.htm#16031546000001 accessed 20 March 2018.

78 *Ibid* Column 813.

79 *Ibid* Column 822.

80 Investigatory Powers Bill 2015, ss 19 and 23; see also *ibid.*

81 Investigatory Powers Bill 2015, s 23 (1)(2).

82 First Sitting Committee Debate Session 2015–16, Investigatory Powers Bill, Publications on the Internet, Column 17, 24 March 2016, available at http://www.publications.parliament.uk/pa/cm201516/cmpublic/investigatorypowers/160324/am/160324s01.htm accessed 20 March 2018.

83 *Ibid.*

serious crime or the economic well-being of the UK.[84] Adding further contention is the fact a judicial commissioner must not jeopardise the success of an intelligence or security operation, compromise the safety of those involved or unduly impede the operational effectiveness of an intelligence service.[85] Although these particular sections are not to be applied when performing the 'double-lock' function, it does indicate a peculiar set of functions to be placed on the role, requiring the commissioner to either agree or disagree with the Secretary of State.[86]

David Davis MP and Shami Chakrabarti both voiced similar concerns, referring to where IPA specifies the judicial commissioners have to make their decisions based on judicial review principles, rather than based on the evidence.[87] Both Davis and Chakrabarti do have an agenda, however, with the latter having been the director of Liberty for some years.[88] For Murray and Keenan., it seems relatively clear from IPA that 'the judicial commissioner will be asked to review the Secretary of State's action in issuing a warrant on judicial review principles alone, this is whether the action was illegal, unfair (illegitimate), irrational or disproportionate'.[89] This is simply another layer of accountability on state action by the judiciary. Although the IPA does not appear to read it this way, it could be further argued that the judicial commissioner's position would be untenable, if access to the data and evidence put forward to the Secretary of State remains unavailable to them. Murray *et al.* remain concerned that this lack of evidential transparency 'does not offer judicial independence required by the rule of law', and is not representative of an independent judiciary supposedly at the 'heart of the warrant process'.[90]

Notably, in terms of English public law, this new judicial position may challenge the doctrine of separation of powers, as the commissioners will be asked to 'cross the waterline between secrecy and transparency', and effectively draws judges into 'the realm of executive decision-making, thereby threatening the impression of impartiality on which the legal system ultimately depends'.[91] Prior independent judicial authorisation, however, is a new measure, so it is perhaps not possible to know with absolute certainty how it will work in practice. Inescapably, and to balance this view, the result of judicial approval means that public bodies do not simply have unlimited power to 'intrude upon the privacy of citizens' without proper 'justification and authorisation'.[92]

84 *Ibid.*
85 Investigatory Powers Act 2016, s 229(7).
86 Investigatory Powers Act 2016, s 229(8).
87 See http://www.theguardian.com/politics/blog/live/2015/nov/04/surveillance-internet-snoopers-charter-may-plans-politics-live accessed 20 March 2018.
88 See https://www.liberty-human-rights.org.uk accessed 30 March 2018.
89 A. Murray and B. Keenan (2015) *Ensuring the Rule of Law*, LSE Law Department Briefings on the Investigatory Powers Bill, LSE Law Policy Briefing Series, 12, *Social Science Research Network*, available at http://ssrn.com/abstract=2703806 accessed 27 March 2018.
90 *Ibid.*
91 *Ibid.*
92 House of Lords Second Reading 27 June 2016, Volume 773, Column 1363, available at https://hansard.parliament.uk/lords/2016-06-27/debates/1606278000466/InvestigatoryPowersBill accessed 20 March 2018.

Governmental committees: holding law enforcement to account

The Intelligence and Security Committee (ISC) simply adds another additional layer to state and law enforcement agencies' accountability. It was first established by the ISA to 'examine the policy, administration and expenditure of the Security Service, Secret Intelligence Service, and the Government Communications Headquarters'.[93] Since then the Justice and Security Act 2013 has increased the ISC's remit, including the oversight of operations, and has been granted greater powers.[94] The ISC can now look at other intelligence-related work carried out by the Cabinet Office and Defence Intelligence for the Ministry of Defence and the Office of Security and Counter Terrorism. The members of this committee are appointed by Parliament, who then report back to Parliament and to the prime minister, often dealing with sensitive information.

The ISC members, drawn from both the House of Commons and the House of Lords, are able to hear classified material, meaning they can hold the intelligence agencies to account. On 7 November 2013 the ISC held its first ever open evidence session with the heads of the Security Service, GCHQ and Secret Intelligence Service (SIS). Although the sessions are closed when assessing information that is deemed highly classified, the Committee intends to hold further public sessions in future.[95] In the ISC's 2016–2017 Annual Report, headed by the Chair the Rt. Hon. Dominic Grieve, the members confirmed they are of the view that the agencies' powers provided by IPA are justified. In November 2015, a Joint Committee was appointed to commence pre-legislative scrutiny of IPA. Given the role of the ISC in overseeing the intelligence agencies and its ability to take evidence on classified matters, the Committee provided the pre-legislative scrutiny focusing on 'those aspects of the draft Bill which relate primarily to the agencies' investigatory powers'.[96] In addition to the ISC report, the Joint Committee on the draft IPA made a total of 86 recommendations.[97] Whilst the former report focused on the overseeing arrangements surrounding the policing security agencies, due to its ability to take evidence on classified matters, the latter report

93 See Intelligence and Security Committee of Parliament website, available at http://isc.independent.gov.uk accessed 30 March 2018.

94 *Ibid.*

95 *Ibid.*

96 Intelligence and Security Committee of Parliament, Annual Report 2016–2017, HC655, paragraph 5, available at https://b1cba9b3-a-5e6631fd-s-sites.googlegroups.com/a/independent.gov.uk/isc/files/2016-2017_ISC_AR.pdf?attachauth=ANoY7coJr3ybKy_li-2Mo-wKmKDInUqpeClCvEUyKVZsWsr Bri8ckF6HZiA2JqGUnbHM4sCChlHhKpdIr6ph9b6rPf4ch0gStHReiFT KuDGwMQ_Wg8mrb9CCaExzz29DaQDu14EhwYefRq2lG3CnQnF vEFgRsQHfJxW-VVw24o-7eGfWLHY–rBwQdyR2kcUHT9b5vI NyKVhXE2Egr4ROrNPDiiRKgi3EGSI3gTx0AzK1BopkAO0Fws%3D&attredirects=0 accessed 27 March 2018.

97 Joint Committee on the Draft Investigatory Powers Bill (2016) Report of Session 2015–2016, 11 February, HL Paper 93 and HC 651 available at http://www.publications.parliament.uk/pa/jt201516/jtselect/jtinvpowers/93/9302.htm accessed 27 March 2018.

focused on issues of clarity, judicial oversight and the justification for the various powers.

The Home Affairs Select mechanism used to hold Government and law enforcement agencies to account. This was seen on 6 December 2016, when David Armond the Deputy Director General of the NCA was questioned on EU policing and security issues.[98] This hearing led on from the earlier October 2016 hearing focusing on UK policing after the UK's exit from the EU.[99]

In response to the issues raised by the various committees, according to Prime Minster Theresa May, IPA starts with a presumption of privacy, where privacy protections form the 'backbone' of the Act, and the safeguards introduced further 'bolster' this in ensuring that high thresholds exist when sanctioning the most intrusive powers, and it limits the public authorities that can use the powers.[100] The question of trust between the citizens and the state is an important one.

Privacy and trust: balancing individual privacy and collective security

The previous chapter made it clear that powers of surveillance, particularly the proposed bulk powers, impinge upon individual privacy. Goold states, 'A public that is unable to understand why privacy is important – or which lacks the conceptual tools necessary to engage in meaningful debates about its value – is likely to be particularly susceptible to arguments that privacy should be curtailed'.[101]

Although different perspectives and theories exist with regard to the term 'privacy', this chapter has focused on the term's legal meaning. Privacy is important as it not only allows individualised expression and autonomy, but the concept can empower citizens to challenge state decisions. In *R v Spencer* the Supreme Court of Canada described the protection of privacy as a prerequisite to individualised security, autonomy and self-fulfilment, which is essential in maintaining a thriving democratic society.[102] Privacy is not an absolute right as per the ECHR or the EU's CFR, but rather qualified and limited. On the one hand the state must protect the qualified rights of its citizens insofar as possible, but on the other hand it has a duty to protect the lives of its citizens and keep them safe from criminality. In order to achieve this, the state must intrude on the privacy of

98 See http://www.parliament.uk/business/committees/committees-a-z/commons-select/home-affairs-committee/news-parliament-2015/161202-europol-ev accessed 27 March 2018.

99 See http://www.parliament.uk/business/committees/committees-a-z/lords-select/eu-home-affairs-subcommittee/news-parliament-2015/counterterrorism-lead-evidence-brexit accessed 30 March 2018.

100 House of Commons Second Reading, 15 March 2016, Column 814, available at http://www.publications.parliament.uk/pa/cm201516/cmhansrd/cm160315/debtext/160315-0001.htm#16031546000001 accessed 20 March 2018

101 B. J. Goold (2009) Surveillance and the Political Value of Privacy, *Amsterdam Law Forum,* available at https://commons.allard.ubc.ca/cgi/viewcontent.cgi?referer=https://www.google.co.uk/&httpsredir=1&article=1153&context=fac_pubs accessed 20 March 2018

102 *R v Spencer* [2014] 2 SCR 212, [15]

individual citizens, usually of course as part of targeted intelligence-led policing, where proportionate, necessary and lawful to do so.

In terms of balancing individual privacy rights and maintaining collective security, debates turn on the level of individual privacy verses the level of state powers of surveillance. This focal point is unhelpful and dismisses less tangible aspects to be taken into account such as the individual's horizontal and vertical relationships, which form their perspectives on the social norm of privacy.[103] Sir Thomas Erskine May rather poetically captured the issue when he stated in stated in 1863:

> Men may be without restraints upon their liberty: they may pass to and fro at pleasure but if their steps are tracked by spies and informers, their words noted down for crimination, their associates watched as conspirators – who shall say that they are free? Nothing is more revolting to Englishmen than the espionage that forms part of the administrative system of continental despotisms. It haunts men like an evil genius, chills their gaiety, restrains their wit, casts a shadow over their friendships, and blights their domestic hearth. The freedom of this country may be measured by its immunity from this baleful agency.[104]

Modern attitudes towards surveillance are perhaps not as robust as during May's time, however, an element of mistrust exists.[105] It is also relevant that attitudes towards privacy depend heavily on the citizen's own perspective, informed by history, experience, environment, education and development.[106] Research has illustrated such positions are exceedingly contextual.[107]

Fears of the surveillance society: the Snowdon revelations

Anderson insinuates societal vertical relationships depend heavily on trust.[108] He leads the reader to what he calls is the 'Snowden effect', referring to the leaking of classified and sensitive US National Security Agency (NSA) documents by Edward Snowdon in 2013.[109] The documents emphasised the relationship between the NSA and the UK's GCHQ, whereby intelligence exchange ensued initiating widespread trepidation over the potential violations of human rights, arguably

103 Britain is surveillance society (2006) The threat of sleepwalking into a surveillance society was thought to be a reality by the Information Commissioner, introducing his Report on the Surveillance Society, 2 November 2006, available at http://news.bbc.co.uk/1/hi/uk/6108496.stm accessed 30 March 2018.

104 T. E. May (1863) *Constitutional History of England since the Accession of King George III*, (W. J. Widdleton) vol. 2, p.275.

105 *Supra* as per D. Anderson QC (2015), pp.32–33.

106 *Ibid*, pp.32–33.

107 *Ibid*, p.33.

108 *Supra* as per D. Anderson QC (2015), p.34.

109 *Ibid*.

flouting legal protection for individual data privacy.[110] The documents highlighted the fact that a program called PRISM allowed US Federal agencies direct access to Internet servers, infiltrating Internet firms such as Microsoft, Apple, Facebook and Google.[111] Hopkins reports that between May 2012 and April 2013, 197 PRISM program intelligence reports were passed to the UK's counterterrorism law enforcement agencies.[112] The NSA, according to the leaked documents, was additionally recording millions of telephone conversations of US citizens despite the fact they were not under any suspicion of unlawful behaviour.[113] Snowden passed secret documents to Glen Greenwald, a *Guardian* employee, who in the first of a series of reports revealed that since April 2013 and under PRISM the NSA had collected and was retaining indiscriminately the telephone records of millions of US customers.[114] Although initially sanctioned to collect the communications records of foreign nationals, Greenwald confirmed that the NSA moved very quickly to concentrate on domestic communications.[115] As Greenwald continued with the series, he reported that the GCHQ had gained access to intelligence that included sensitive personal information, which it then shared with the NSA.[116] Additionally it was also reported that the US Government had paid GCHQ over £100 million to secure access to the UK's intelligence gathering programs.[117]

This is where the legal and cultural differences between the EU and the US become quite distinct, in that the Snowden revelations had the potential to damage diplomatic relationships, not only between the EU and the US but the EU and the UK. This could have also affected international intelligence exchange between all parties as discussed further below. In light of this danger, UK and US politicians were somewhat forced to provide honest information, and defend the actions of the NSA and GCHQ. The then UK Foreign Secretary William Hague MP confirmed that both the UK and the US had operated within the rule of law and used the intelligence obtained to protect their citizens' freedom.[118] Despite

110 D. Lowe (2014) Surveillance and International Terrorism Intelligence Exchange: Balancing the Interests of National Security and Individual Liberty, *Terrorism and Political Violence*, 13 August 2014, 1.
111 *Ibid* 4.
112 N. Hopkins (2013) UK Gathering Secret Intelligence via Covert NSA Operation, *Guardian*, 7 June 2013, http://www.theguardian.com/technology/2013/jun/07/uk-gatheringsecret-intelligence-nsa-prism accessed 30 March 2018.
113 G. Greenwald (2013) NSA Collecting Phone Records of Millions of Verizon Customers Daily, *Guardian*, 6 June 2013, http://www.theguardian.com/world/2013/jun/06/nsa-phone-records-verizon-court-order accessed 30 March 2018.
114 *Ibid.*
115 *Ibid.*
116 E. MacAskell, J. Borger, N. Davies and J. Ball (2013) GCHQ Taps Fibre-Optic Cables for Secret Access to World's Communications, *Guardian*, 21 June 2013, available at http://www.theguardian.com/uk/2013/jun/21/gchq-cablessecret-world-communications-nsa accessed 30 March 2018.
117 N. Hopkins and J. Borger (2013) Exclusive: NSA Pays £100m in Secret Funding for GCHQ, *Guardian*, 1 August 2013, available at http://www.theguardian.com/uk-news/2013/aug/01/nsa-paid-gchq-spying-edward-snowden accessed 30 March 2018.
118 See http://www.bbc.co.uk/news/uk-politics-23053691 accessed 30 March 2018.

UK and US officials' assurances, the actions taken by the NSA and GCHQ reverberated even further when reports indicated that EU politicians were also spied on, in particular Angela Merkel the German Chancellor.[119]

In terms of the public trust, despite assurances the UK public's reaction has evidenced a suspicious attitude.[120] In light of Snowden, an Austrian citizen and privacy advocate, Maximillian Schrems, took action against the Data Protection Commissioner.[121] His argument turned on the fact that Facebook Ireland has transferred his personal data to the US, and that the USs did not ensure sufficient protection of his personal data.[122] Referring to NSA's practices as reported by Greenwald and leaked by Snowden, he claimed the NSA and other US agencies could have retained his personal data.[123] The US Foreign Intelligence Services Act 1978 permits the NSA access to personal data held on US servers. Therefore, because Facebook Ireland is a subsidiary of Facebook US, *Schrems'* details had in fact been transferred. The CJEU noted that the US Foreign Intelligence Surveillance Court did not offer a judicial remedy to EU citizens and declared the 2000/520/EC Decision invalid, bringing an end to the Safe Harbour Agreement.

Article 25 of the 1995 Data Protection Directive (discussed in Chapter 4) was critical to the CJEU, particularly concerning the Commission's responsibility to ensure adequate personal protection of transferred data.[124] The CJEU confirmed that the level of protection provided by the US need not be identical to that of the EU, but must evidence adequacy at the very least, ensuring it has a high level of fundamental rights protection in place, equivalent to that which is afforded by Article 25.[125] The leaking of this information and GCHQ's actions regarding the allegation of conducting mass surveillance led to the German Justice Minister Sabine Leutheusser-Schnarrenberger asking UK ministers for reassurance that actions taken were legal and whether they affected German citizens. He stated further, 'In our modern world, the new media provide the framework for a free exchange of opinions and information. Transparent governance is one of the most important prerequisites that a democratic state and the rule of law requires.'[126]

The legal director of Liberty also accused GCHQ of violating citizens' Article 8 rights to privacy, commenting on the then proposed IPA:

119 G. Greenwald (2014) *No Place to Hide: Edward Snowden, the NSA, and the US Surveillance State* (Metropolitan Books) p.141.

120 A. Travis (2015) Snowden Leak: Governments' Hostile Reaction Fuelled Public Distrust of Spies, *Guardian*, 15 June 2015, available at https://www.theguardian.com/world/2015/jun/15/snowden-files-us-uk-government-hostile-reaction-distrust-spies accessed 20 March 2018.

121 *Maximillian Schrems v Data Protection Commissioner* [2015] C-362/14.

122 *Ibid.*

123 *Ibid.*

124 Data Protection Directive 1995, 95/46/EC, Article 25.

125 *Maximillian Schrems v Data Protection Commissioner* [2015] C-362/14, [73], [141], [142], [147].

126 Germany Seeks UK Surveillance Assurances, *BBC News*, 25 June 2013, available at http://www.bbc.co.uk/news/uk-23048259 accessed 30 March 2018.

> Those demanding the [Investigatory Powers Act, also termed as the] Snoopers' Charter seem to have been indulging in out-of-control snooping even without it – exploiting legal loopholes and help from Uncle Sam [US]. No one suggests a completely unpoliced Internet but those in power cannot swap targeted investigations for endless monitoring of the entire globe.[127]

In light of such reports and adversarial commentary, the EU's Justice and Home Affairs Council (JHAC) showed concern for the level of protection of EU citizens' constitutional right to privacy, which resulted in Viviane Reding the EU Justice Commissioner stating:

> The European Commission is concerned about the possible consequences on EU citizens' privacy. The Commission has raised this systematically in its dialogue with the U.S. authorities, especially in the context of the negotiations of the EU-U.S. data protection agreement in the field of police and judicial co-operation …[128]

It is interesting to note the dichotomy between the civilian and the state when discussing powers of surveillance and personal data privacy. Citizens' behaviour presents something of a paradox in that they seem unconcerned about sharing information freely in a horizontal fashion, by means of social media, for example, where people seem quite happy for others to know everything about them, but become quite aggrieved when information is viewed vertically, by the state.[129] In this regard the previous chapters have shown the importance of personal privacy being paramount in the minds of citizens, with a generalised fear of a Big Brother state given weight by the law enforcement agencies' use of OSINT and SOCMINT data. Many fear the UK is moving towards a surveillance society, given that what follows a terrorist act or perceived threat usually takes the form of new legislation introducing more restrictive measures. The fluid relationship between terror threats and new legislative prowess has been emphasised throughout this book, in addition to proposed new legislation dealing with extremism.

Conclusion

Part One of IPA could be equated to simply paying 'lip service' because for some, overall, the introduction of bulk powers under IPA fails to extend human rights protection, specifically related to the right to privacy, protection of personal data and freedom of expression. Although these bulk powers may pass the digital rights

127 *Ibid.*

128 N. Watt (2013) PRISM Scandal: European Commission to Seek Privacy Guarantees from U.S., *Guardian*, 10 June 2013, available at http://www.theguardian.com/world/2013/jun/10/prism-european-commissions-privacy-guarantees accessed 30 March 2018.

129 K. D. Ewing (2010) *Bonfire of the Liberties: New Labour, Human Rights, and the Rule of Law* (Oxford University Press) p.54.

criterion and could be described as necessary in finding would-be-terrorists, IPA may ultimately come to fail the CJEU and ECtHR jurisprudence when testing the proportionality of the measures.

In terms of checks and balances, IPA does introduce a double lock system whereby a judicial commissioner must agree with the Secretary of State, in line with judicial review influences, that the powers permitted under the warrant are necessary and proportionate. The ISC and the Home Affairs Committee, both independent governmental scrutiny mechanisms, with the former able to see classified information relating to intelligence operations, provide another form of checks and balances. The Right Honourable Sir Adrian Fulford has been appointed Investigatory Powers Commissioner, and provides additional safeguards overseeing the security agencies' arrangements for access to the data.[130] The new double lock system under IPA has additionally fashioned 13 new judicial commissioners.[131]

It has been stipulated in IPA that judicial commissioners must apply judicial review principles. Although this is not particularly concerning, given the commissioners will undoubtedly view the evidence used by the Home Secretary in approving the authority, it is a new element and until it is seen working in practice it will be difficult to make any judgement. It will also be interesting to see if the bulk powers under IPA will survive in their current form given legal challenges will undoubtedly come from human rights organisations such as Liberty. Even if the UK has left the EU prior to any future CJEU ruling on the subject, it must still keep within current criteria to ensure international intelligence exchange with EU continues.

The EU has led data protection and data privacy initiatives, legally and constitutionally up to now. However, looking forward it may be the case that the ECtHR takes the lead, given the EU's focus on data retention. Should the UK's bulk powers under IPA be challenged in the ECtHR, which historically does not approve of blanket policies, or the keeping of data of innocent civilians, it may not survive. This would be detrimental, however, and it is argued the CJEU and ECtHR should accept that terrorism in the digital age means the Internet must be monitored, allowing for bulk analysis of electronic communications data.

The chapter found, however, that the balance between collective security and individual data privacy rights in the UK are fairly stable because of the role of judicial review, judicial independence and the overarching scrutiny provided by commissioners and parliamentary committees. It is further argued that a blanket approach to retaining electronic communications data is necessary to find the terrorist in the ever growing haystacks because sometimes privacy rights and data protection must be curtailed to ensure the state can protect citizens' rights to life.

130 See https://www.ipco.org.uk accessed 20 March 2018.

131 See https://www.ipco.org.uk/docs/JC%20Announcement%2020171018.pdf accessed 20 March 2018.

6 The international nature of the 21st Century terrorism threat: preserving international intelligence exchange and the implications of the UK leaving the European Union

Introduction

This chapter will explore the relationship between the EU and the UK following the UK's exit from the EU. International intelligence exchange is an essential element of national security illustrating an international terror threat requires an international response. Particularly since al-Qaeda's terrorist attack on the US on 11 September 2001, the EU and the US have sought to cooperate through sharing internal security data. Being a part of the EU he UK has been party to this agreement.

The EU's legislative landscape has been shown in the previous chapter to be cluttered with many measures aimed at data surveillance and counterterrorism action. In addition to collecting, storing and exchanging a greater volume of intelligence data within the EU, by means of using both targeted and bulk powers, there has been an increased emphasis on transnational data exchange.[1] It will be highlighted that these international trends have also been contrary to the EU's rule of law. Focusing on current intelligence exchange arrangements between the EU and the UK, particularly with regard to Passenger Name Records (PNR) data exchange; this chapter will assess what the new relationship will look like post the UK's exit from the EU, using the US as a case study.

This will show that differing cultures of the EU and the US surrounding privacy rights have created their own set of problems.[2] The protection of privacy, particularly data privacy is protected under EU law, but less clear in the US.[3] Based on eight key principles, the EU focuses on the dignity of the individual citizen, whereas the US focuses on the liberty of the individual.[4] Not forgetting that the protection of privacy forms the safeguarding role of the rule of law within the EU, thereby requiring compliance with EU constitutional and legislative standards, the

1 C. C. Murphy (2015) *EU Counter-Terrorism Law: Pre-Emption and the Rule of Law* (Hart Publishing).

2 S. Sottiaux (2008) *Terrorism and the Limitation of Rights: The ECHR and the US Constitution* (Hart Publishing) pp.265–322.

3 *Ibid* pp.266–268.

4 J. Q. Whitman (2004) The Two Western Cultures of Privacy: Dignity Versus Liberty, *Yale Law Journal*, 13, 1151–1221, 1219.

position is exacerbated by the lack of any formally expressed data protection law in the US.[5]

The UK and the EU: the exit

Since December 2016 it is clear that the UK's current government appears to be playing with its cards close to its chest when it comes to releasing the details of the exit plan.[6] The position remains extremely unclear and it will therefore not be possible to make any firm statements about the situation. What is clear, however, is that the UK will certainly be leaving the EU and the single market, and Foreign Secretary Boris Johnson has affirmed his position that the UK will remain part of a 'dedicated European power'.[7] This does not however answer the questions, will international intelligence exchange with the EU be affected and will the UK remain a part of the European Police Force (Europol)?

EU counterterrorism: security and intelligence

For Argomaniz, Bures and Kaunert counterterrorism laws and measures have been a driver in the EU's Area of Freedom, Security and Justice (AFSJ) construction.[8] The EU has become increasingly active on the world stage, and has focused on creating and maintaining internal and external intelligence exchange structures.[9] The EU has also sought to harmonise Member States' national legislation, as well as to co-ordinate policies and offer support for operational work.[10] Through this network, Member States have been encouraged to adopt the same conceptual precautionary and organisational measures and structures.[11] According to Boer

5 H. Hijmans and A. Scirocco (2009) Shortcomings in EU Data Protection in the Third and the Second Pillars. 46 *Common Market Law Review,* 1487–1489, 1485.

6 J. Elgot (2016) Brexit Debate in Parliament Would Give Game Away to Brussels, Says Minister, *Guardian*, 16 October 2016, available at https://www.theguardian.com/politics/2016/oct/16/brexit-debate-iwould-give-game-away-to-brussels-priti-patel accessed 20 March 2018.

7 M. Dathan (2016) No Room for Bojo among EU's Foreign Ministers! Top Diplomats Tease Boris and Block Him from Joining Photo-Shoot as They Begin Process of Excluding Britain from Brussels Club, *The Mail Online*, 2 September 2016, available at http://www.dailymail.co.uk/news/article-3770744/Britain-continue-helping-EU-tackle-migrant-crisis-Brexit-Boris-Johnson-pledges-tours-European-capitals.html accessed 30 March 2018.

8 J. Argomaniz, O. Bures and C. Kaunert (2015) A Decade of EU Counter-Terrorism and Intelligence: A Critical Assessment, *Intelligence and National Security*, 30, 2–3, 191–206, 192.

9 See http://www.consilium.europa.eu/en/policies/fight-against-terrorism/counter-terrorism-coordinator accessed 30 March 2018.

10 *Supra* as per J. Argomaniz *et al.* (2015), 196. See also M. L. Wade (2014) The European Union as a Counter-Terrorism Actor: Right Path, Wrong Direction? *Crime Law and Social Change*, 62, 355–383.

11 M. D. Boer, and I. Wiegand (2015) From Convergence to Deep Integration: Evaluating the Impact of EU Counter-Terrorism Strategies on Domestic Arenas, *Intelligence and National Security*, 30, 2–3, 377–401, 377.

and Wiegand, this relationship has resulted in a move from convergence to a deeply integrated legal counterterrorism arrangement.[12] This has allowed the EU, in terms of supranational governance, to approach counterterrorism initiatives through a convergence of national counterterrorism systems, rather than a top down method.[13] Harmonisation ensuring constitutional, institutional and cultural similarities allows for greater ease of communications and information exchange.[14]

Although this idea and approach has perhaps been useful for law enforcement agencies in practical terms, particularly when accessing shared intelligence, research conducted by Wiegand suggests that significant differences remain between the national counterterrorism approaches of the Member States, despite the best intentions of the EU.[15] The EU has focused on four areas of convergence: political-strategic, organisational, procedural and legal. Within the legal spectrum the EU has pushed to integrate objectives by developing internationalised regulatory mechanisms and dividing the focal points into four subdivisions namely: preparation and response, prevention, protection and prosecution.[16] Following the 175 measures adopted by the EU in the immediate aftermath of the attack on the US in 2001, Boers and Wiegand's study shows Member States were sluggish in implementing them resulting in a 'slow, slack and uneven' scenario.[17]

The UK's exit position

Regardless this level of integration means that because the UK's counterterrorism structure has been formed, largely by its membership of the EU, the effects of leaving on international intelligence exchange should be minimal. Given the UK was still a member of the EU on 25 May 2018, it was required to implement the latest EU PNR Directive. However, when the UK leaves the EU, it may become necessary to renegotiate this agreement given the UK will essentially be classed as a third country. In Jenni's opinion, there is no current model or framework the UK could look towards to give an indication of what a post UK exit would look like.[18] The point being no Member State has ever left the EU before. The Swiss model, for example, is not a solution but may provide some suggestions.[19] It is important to note that post the UK's exit, the UK will still be exchanging intelligence with EU Member States. Below is a good example of the points raised below concerning *Schrems*.

12 *Ibid* 387.
13 *Ibid* 378.
14 *Ibid.*
15 *Ibid* 379.
16 *Ibid* 381 and 383.
17 *Ibid.*
18 S. Jenni (2016) Is the Swiss Model a Brexit Solution? The UK in a Changing Europe, 23 March 2016, available at http://ukandeu.ac.uk/is-the-swiss-model-a-brexit-solution, accessed 30 March 2018.
19 *Ibid.*

The Swiss lessons

Jenni argues there may be four lessons from the Swiss model applicable to the UK. The first is that it may take many years to negotiate agreements, which may be determined on an *ad hoc* basis.[20] The Swiss model has further shown that the UK will not be able to draw up an agreement dealing with one particular area of concern, rather that the EU deals in package type agreements including trade-offs.[21] The second lesson is that leaving the EU will not end the EU's influence on the UK's law-making powers. Particularly in terms of maintaining international security and mutual recognition, the EU would effectively curtail the UK's decision-making powers, albeit perhaps not directly. This process would also be important in terms of the UK remaining within the single market, which feeds into the third lesson whereby proposed legislation is assessed to ensure EU law compatibility. The final lesson proves that tailor-made agreements are more difficult to achieve.[22] The EU can be uncooperative as evidenced by the Swiss model, whereby it simply refuses to agree upon the terms of a negotiation. In response to the Swiss affirming their position, their access to the electricity market was suspended and they were excluded from the EU's Horizon 2020 research funding.[23] In light of the fact the current terrorism threat requires international cooperation, this awkward postulated position by the EU could become rather problematic in terms of the UK's current cross-border counterterrorism capabilities. It could also be argued that the EU has and will purposefully make it rather difficult for the UK to negotiate a positive deal given the fact Juncker will not want more EU Member States to leave.

International security: the European Arrest Warrant

The European Arrest Warrant (EAW) was introduced in 2004 to make extradition of those suspected of serious crime and terrorist activity swifter and simpler.[24] Although not specifically linked with surveillance of electronic communications data and intelligence exchange within the EU, the exit of the UK from the EU in 2019 may mean it no longer continues. The EAW forms part of the legal convergence mechanism aimed at the harmonisation of Member States laws within the EU. It effectively removed central authorities from the extradition process, which is now dealt with by law enforcement agencies and judicial authorities. It also meant that EU Member States could not refuse to surrender their own citizens to another Member State on nationality grounds if they were suspected of committing a serious crime.[25] It has been suggested the UK may lose some of its

20 *Ibid.*
21 *Ibid.*
22 *Ibid.*
23 *Supra* as per S. Jenni (2016).
24 See European Commission, available at http://ec.europa.eu/justice/criminal/recognition-decision/european-arrest-warrant/index_en.htm accessed 30 March 2018.
25 *Ibid.*

international counterterrorism capabilities upon leaving the EU: the EAW and the relationship with Europol and Eurojust are some prime examples. Under the EAW mechanism extradition takes on average 48 days whereas prior to the EAW extradition used to take an average of one year.[26] This mechanism was used by the UK in apprehending Hussain Osman, who went on to be prosecuted in the UK for his part in the planned, but failed, attempted terrorist attack on London on 21 July 2005.[27] However, there are some who would like to see the UK come out of the EAW arrangement.[28] Pollard cites a recent case involving Stuart Ramsay, an award winning Sky News correspondent who reported on an alleged firearms-running network in Romania.[29] In response the Romanian Government has asserted the reporting was faked and charged Ramsay for spreading false information.[30] As part of the first step towards issuing an EAW, it has requested the UK to assist in the criminal investigation.[31]

Despite Kearney's assertion that the UK's exit will not affect the relationship with the EU because the UK has a unique and successful counterterrorism framework, this has been built upon the relationship within the EU.[32] In Peers' opinion the EAW remains an important aspect for the UK, and as a quick form of extradition is something the UK should keep. Without this it is possible that the UK may fall back on an ECHR focused system, albeit similar to the EAW. According to Peers' oral evidence to the recent Home Affairs Committee,

> it would be something like the European arrest warrant, perhaps with exceptions, like Norway and Iceland have, but there might not be enough time to negotiate those exceptions, so we run the risk of falling back, rather than

26 European Commission (2011) Report from the Commission to the European Parliament and the Council on the Implementation Since 2007 of the Council Framework Decision of 13 June 2002 on the European Arrest Warrant and the Surrender Procedures Between Member States, Brussels, 11 April 2011, Com(2011), 175 final, p.11, available at http://ec.europa.eu/justice/criminal/files/eaw_implementation_report_2011_en.pdf accessed 20 March 2018.

27 See http://www.dailymail.co.uk/news/article-467244/21-7-bombers-failed-kill-dozens-mastermind-maths.html accessed 20 March 2018.

28 S. Alegre and M. Leaf (2004) Mutual Recognition in European Judicial Cooperation: A Step Too Far Too Soon? Case Study – the European Arrest Warrant, *European Law Journal*, 10(2), 200–217. See also C. Kaunert (2007) Without the Power of Purse or Sword: The European Arrest Warrant and the Role of the Commission, *Journal of European Integration*, 29(4), 387–404. See also S. Molders (2005) European Arrest Warrant Act is Void – the Decision of the German Federal Constitutional Court of 18 July 2005, *German Law Journal*, 7(1), 45–58.

29 S. Pollard (2016) The Case That Shows Why We Must Not Stay in the European Arrest Warrant, *The Spectator*, 3 September 2016, available at http://www.spectator.co.uk/2016/09/the-case-that-shows-why-we-must-not-stay-in-the-european-arrest-warrant accessed 30 March 2018.

30 *Ibid.*

31 *Ibid.*

32 J. Kearney (2016) The Security Implications of Brexit, Compas *Breakfast Briefing Summary*, available at http://www.compas.ox.ac.uk/media/160520-security-web-text.pdf accessed 30 March 2018.

> being able to negotiate something. The advantages of the European investigation order, which is not in force yet, might not be obvious for a few years, so we might end up falling out of that as well, rather than trying to stay part of it.[33]

The UK's relationship with Europol is equally important, especially in light of technological growth and the use of digital electronic communications by terrorists.

International cooperation: Europol

In essence Europol is a centralised computer hub that contains the shared intelligence of 28 EU Member States and 20 third countries including the US, Canada, Russia and Turkey.[34] Coming from the old third pillar of the TEU, it was envisaged Europol would be utilised as a system of information exchange. For Loader, however, once confidence grew in the agency it was inevitable it would be promoted as a kind of US style FBI for Europe.[35] Since its foundation in 1998 Europol has grown in external competences, and now has external agreements with other agencies including Interpol, the United Nations Office on Drugs and Crime (UNODC) and the World Customs Organisation (WCO).[36] Europol is also a support centre for law enforcement operations and provides expertise. Although at first glance there does not seem to be any difference between being an internal and external partner of Europol in terms of support or access to intelligence, in Guild's opinion the extent to which third countries are always at the demanding side of Europol is concerning.[37] Accordingly, 'they are always at the requesting side and they are never fully participating'.[38] Another concern is that:

> a lot of the measures relating to policing and criminal justice are subject to the data protection directive, which the UK has opted out of. As a Member State that has opted out of the directive, the UK's position would be somewhat different.[39]

33 Home Affairs Committee, House of Commons, EU Policing and Security Issues, 6 December 2016, HC806, Oral evidence by S. Peers, available at http://data.parliament.uk/writtenevidence/committeeevidence.svc/evidencedocument/home-affairs-committee/eu-policing-and-security-issues/oral/44210.html accessed 20 March 2018
34 See https://www.europol.europa.eu/partners-agreements/operational-agreements?page=1 and https://www.europol.europa.eu/partners-agreements/strategic-agreements accessed 30 March 2018.
35 I. Loader (2002) Policing, Securitization and Democratization in European Criminal Justice, *The International Journal of Policy and Practice*, 2(2), 125–153, 128.
36 See https://www.europol.europa.eu/partners-agreements/other-agreements accessed 30 March 2018.
37 Home Affairs Committee, House of Commons, EU Policing and Security Issues, 6 December 2016, HC806, Oral evidence by E. Guild, available at http://data.parliament.uk/writtenevidence/committeeevidence.svc/evidencedocument/home-affairs-committee/eu-policing-and-security-issues/oral/44210.html accessed 20 March 2018.
38 *Ibid.*
39 *Ibid.*

In procedural terms Europol has a designated Europol National Unit (ENU) that serves as the liaison between the authorities in that country and Europol, although only seven third counties have opted to have one.[40] It would appear from news reports that the UK Government intends to remain within Europol despite the UK's exit from the EU.[41] Brandon Lewis, the UK's Policing Minister, appears to have recognised the reality that transnational crime will remain when the UK leaves the EU.[42] UK policing and security agencies benefit from the level of expertise at Europol, which provides unique intelligence on cybercrime in addition to terrorism. Operation Golf is one such example, where the Metropolitan Police and the Romanian National Police set up a Joint Investigation Team, which led to the rescue of 28 children and the arrests of more than 125 individuals for offences including trafficking human beings, money laundering and child neglect.[43] More recently, in May 2016, a similar operation took place involving France, Paraguay and Spain.[44] Specifically in terms of terrorism, Kearney argues Europol is largely irrelevant.[45] However, policing and security officials who deal with the UK's terrorist threat daily are of a different opinion, confirming Europol to be an essential element in combatting the threat.[46]

Europol also produce an annual TE-SAT report, with the 2016 edition assessing the terrorist threat posed from Islamist, ethno-nationalist and separatist, left-wing and right-wing groups, including single-issue threats.[47] The report shows that:

> In 2015 the European Union (EU) experienced a massive number of casualties caused by terrorist attacks. By far the most affected Member State was France, which had to cope with losing 148 citizens and seeing more than 350 injured in attacks perpetrated in January and November. Murders and injuries in 2015 resulted from both unsophisticated lone actor terrorist attacks and well-coordinated, complex attacks by groups of militants. The carefully

40 See https://www.europol.europa.eu/partners-agreements accessed 30 March 2018.
41 K. McCann (2016) UK Opts Back into Europol Despite Brexit Vote, *Telegraph*, 14 November 2016, available at http://www.telegraph.co.uk/news/2016/11/14/uk-opts-back-into-europol-despite-brexit-vote accessed 20 March 2018.
42 *Ibid.*
43 J. Taylor (2010) Police Smash Romanian 'Child Trafficking Ring', *Independent*, 12 October 2010, available at http://www.independent.co.uk/news/uk/crime/police-smash-romanian-child-trafficking-ring-2104694.html accessed 30 March 2018.
44 Europol Supports Successful Operation against Human Trafficking Network, 3 June 2016, Press Release, see https://www.europol.europa.eu/newsroom/news/europol-supports-successful-operation-against-human-trafficking-network accessed 20 March 2018.
45 *Supra* as per J. Kearney (2016).
46 J. Rankin (2016) Europol Chief Says Brexit Would Harm UK Crime-Fighting, *Guardian*, 22 June 2016, available at https://www.theguardian.com/politics/2016/jun/22/europol-chief-says-brexit-would-harm-uk-crime-fighting accessed 30 March 2018.
47 Europol (2016) *EU Terrorism Situation and Trend Report TE-SAT 2016* (Europol), pp.8–9.

> planned attacks demonstrated the elevated threat to the EU from a fanatic minority, operationally based in the Middle East, combined with a network of people born and raised in the EU, often radicalised within a short space of time, who have proven to be willing and able to act as facilitators and active accomplices in terrorism.[48]

The difficulty the UK has in terms of negotiating a relationship to maintain access to Europol is threefold. First, in Guild's opinion it is a question of value, as in the value of the UK's contribution to intelligence. From the counterterrorism perspective, Guild confirms that from what he has seen in the 'documents of the perspective, concerns and worries, the contribution there is perhaps not so evidently enormous as it is in the cybercrime field'.[49] According to Peers, however, it may come down to a matter of money, and the UK's level of personal data protection, as raised by Guild above.[50] Another further obstacle is the fact that although the Council and the Commission may well confirm the UK's data protection is adequate in providing safeguards, the European Parliament may cause difficulties, particularly should it send a particular data protection compliance complaint to the CJEU, or 'individuals might challenge it, as they have done in the US, for instance, through information commissioners and national courts'.[51] Peers elaborates and states that:

> Europol is quite closely connected to other EU legislation on data sharing because Europol has access to the EU's databases and uses that as part of its analyses, so it might be difficult to think about a deal on Europol access in isolation, especially if we are talking about a bespoke deal with different rights than other non-EU countries.[52]

In terms of personal data, there will undoubtedly be an assessment of how effective and strong the UK's personal data laws are, particularly in light of IPA that was passed in 2016, which in Peers' opinion will face legal challenges to it in the UK and in the ECtHR. Based on an appeal on the earlier challenge to DRIPA on 21 December 2016, the CJEU held that general and indiscriminate retention of electronic communications data by governments is illegal. This represents a parallel Swedish case where the Court 'set out a series of problems with the older legislation'. This now means of course the decision could potentially be read across to see if those problems also exist within the IPA.[53]

48 *Ibid.*
49 Home Affairs Committee, House of Commons, EU Policing and Security Issues, 6 December 2016, HC806, Oral evidence by E. Guild, available at http://data.parliament.uk/writtenevidence/committeeevidence.svc/evidencedocument/home-affairs-committee/eu-policing-and-security-issues/oral/44210.html accessed 20 March 2018.
50 *Ibid*, Home Affairs Committee, Oral evidence by S. Peers.
51 *Ibid.*
52 *Ibid.*
53 *Ibid.*

In Armond's opinion the most important aspect of the UK's relationship with the EU is the maintenance of the UK's access to EAWs, which must continue because:

> Since [EAWs] have been linked to [the Schengen Information System] SIS II, over 2,000 offenders have been arrested in the UK, and 150 offenders wanted by the UK have been arrested in the EU. That is a 25% increase in a year. They are not individuals who are wanted for minor offences; those are serious offences. I would argue that we are not doing work for Europe; we are actually defending the citizens' [sic] of the UK by arresting criminals who present a threat to society and are present in our shores. Those are the things that I would put at the top of the list.[54]

The Schengen Information System

The Schengen Information System (SIS) follows a similar story to that of Europol in terms of the UK's relationship and negotiation, and the UK's exit from the EU may affect the UK's access. The SIS is a large-scale information system and database that supports external border control and law enforcement cooperation, thereby protecting internal security. Although the UK is not a member of the Schengen Area, it does have access to the SIS within the context of law enforcement cooperation.[55]

However, SIS still relies on a certain level of data protection, similar to the EU and Europol. SIS is an important tool, used for 'facilitating European arrest warrants, which includes stolen vehicles, missing people, people wanted for discussion with the police and people under surveillance, maybe for counter-terrorism activities'.[56] Given the current relationship is somewhat removed from EU membership it is possible the UK's access will continue as a part of Europe. On 13 April 2015, UK law enforcement joined the SIS II increasing the sharing of intelligence.[57] Armond, Deputy Director General of the UK's National Crime Agency, stated:

> SIS II has been a game-changer since it came online in April 2015, and access to it must remain … it is so important not only in terms of our border

54 Home Affairs Committee, House of Commons, *EU Policing and Security Issues*, 6 December 2016, HC806, Oral evidence by D. Armond, available at http://data.parliament.uk/writtenevidence/committeeevidence.svc/evidencedocument/home-affairs-committee/eu-policing-and-security-issues/oral/44210.html accessed 20 March 2018.

55 European Commission, Migration and Home Affairs, Schengen Information System, available at http://ec.europa.eu/dgs/home-affairs/what-we-do/policies/borders-and-visas/schengen-information-system/index_en.htm accessed 27 March 2018. See also Figure 16, Map of Schengen Countries, taken from https://www.google.co.uk/url?sa=i&rct=j&q=&esrc=s&source=images&cd=&cad=rja&uact=8&ved=0ahUKEwiOmZats-fQAhWLnBoKHfSZCF4QjhwIBQ&url=http%3A%2F%2Fec.europa.eu%2Fdgs%2Fhome-affairs%2Fwhat-we-do%2Fpolicies%2Fborders-and-visas%2Fschengen%2Findex_en.htm&psig=AFQjCNGqJrZlSbhJ02wVSBHPA9vAbw4BDQ&ust=1481382862154127 accessed 27 March 2018.

56 *Ibid.*

57 European Arrest Warrant Statistics, National Crime Agency, available at http://www.nationalcrimeagency.gov.uk/publications/european-arrest-warrant-statistics accessed 30 March 2018.

security, but in relation to work that police officers conduct every day on the street because 66 million records are available to them in the street via their radios and the police national computer. It is a very important function.[58]

The sharing of intelligence data not only takes place through SIS, but also through other mechanisms, such as those dealing with airline passenger travel, the rules around which changed substantially following the 2001 attack on the US.

Passenger Name Records data and Advanced Passenger Information: case study in relations between the EU and third countries

Conducting a case study on intelligence data exchange is essential at this point given the UK is on course to leave the EU in 2019. It has been shown in the previous chapter that the EU takes data privacy protection seriously. Strict legislative controls are in place and the importance of remaining within the EU's ambit in this regard in order to maintain intelligence data exchange will be illustrated below. Advanced Passenger Information (API) covers the basic details concerning the passenger which include name, date of birth, nationality and passport number.[59] PNR, however, includes data usually submitted by the passenger at the time of making the travel arrangements, including details such as credit card details, personal contact information, dietary information and sensitive data on ethnic origin, health, political views and sexual orientation.[60] Due to the fact API carries less personal data, the EU Directive ensuring data exchange within the EU, for example, was quickly adopted in 2004.[61] PNR agreements, on the other hand, have been controversial to say the least, impacting upon citizens' right to data protection, enshrined at the EU constitutional and EU law levels as discussed in the last chapter.

The relationship between the EU and the UK: PNR and intelligence exchange

An internal PNR agreement between the 28 Member States has been slow. The first attempt failed in 2011 due to the fact it did not have sufficient safeguards in place to protect individual data privacy.[62] The second attempt at a PNR Directive was passed in April 2016, giving Member States until 25 May 2018 to implement

58 *Supra* as per Home Affairs Committee, Oral evidence by D. Armond.

59 M. Tzanou (2015) The War Against Terror and Transatlantic Information Sharing: Spillovers of Privacy or Spillovers of Security?, *Utrecht Journal of International and European Law*, 31(80), 87–103, 96.

60 E. Brouwer (2009) The EU Passenger Name Record System and Human Rights: Transferring Passenger Data or Passenger Freedom, *CEPS Working Document* no.320/September 2009, p.3.

61 European Union Directive (2004) on the obligation of carriers to communicate passenger data, 2004/82/EC, 29 April 2004,.

62 European Commission (2011) Proposal for a Directive of the European Parliament and of the Council on the use of Passenger Name Record data for the prevention, detection, investigation and prosecution of terrorist offences and serious crime, COM

it into national law.[63] Similar to the external PNR agreement with the US, this Directive has put various safeguards into place, such as a 'controller' who will oversee the processing and exchange of data, ensuring requests made are proportionate.[64] Member States must also provide a data protection officer, who will offer advice to the controller and other employees from the policing and security agencies, thereby monitoring compliance with the Directive.[65] Article 54 of the Directive also ensures that those citizens affected by the provisions will have a judicial remedy. The rationale behind this heightened protection is the CJEU's decision in the *Schrems* and *Digital Rights* cases.[66] Member States have been encouraged to implement the new PNR directive urgently and not wait two years as the Directive allows, and thereby harmonize the exploitation of the PNR data.[67]

The PNR data sharing agreement between the UK and the EU is another issue whereby the UK's continued access to it is essential. In Armond's opinion:

> [Access to PNR] is absolutely essential in terms of the profiling that we do to protect the UK. Of course, prior to recent agreements, it was long the case that because of free movement agreements in Europe, many European nations were not prepared to share passenger name record data with us. It is much more interesting, much more detailed and much more relevant than advance passenger information, and of course it gives us names, bank account details, phone numbers, details of previous travel and who people have travelled with. All of that material is really useful in terms of developing profiles and preventing the most dangerous people from coming to our country.[68]

As with the UK's continued access to Europol, any type of bulk data collection and retention must satisfy the digital rights criterion developed in Chapter 5. Representing a further impact on EU law making, the EU's Directive must safeguard personal data and ensure it is protected to in turn safeguard the Directive being invalidated by the CJEU. If the UK is to maintain access to PNR within the EU, then the UK's legislation must still provide adequate protection. Ensuring

(2011) 32 final, available at http://ec.europa.eu/homeaffairs/news/intro/docs/com_2011_32_en.pdf accessed 30 March 2018.

63 European Union Directive 2016/681 of the European Parliament and of the Council, of 27 April 2016, on the use of passenger name record (PNR) data for the prevention, detection, investigation and prosecution of terrorist offences and serious crime, available at http://eur-lex.europa.eu/eli/dir/2016/681/oj accessed 30 March 2018.

64 *Ibid* Article 3(8), 19 and 20.

65 *Ibid* Articles 32 and 34.

66 *Digital Rights Ireland.*

67 Council of the European Union, State of Play on Implementation of the Statement of the Members of the European Council of 12 February 2015, the JHA Council Conclusions of 20 November 2015, and the Conclusions of the European Council of 18 December 2015, Brussels, 4 March 2016, available at http://data.consilium.europa.eu/doc/document/ST-6785-2016-INIT/en/pdf accessed 30 March 2018.

68 *Supra* as per Home Affairs Committee, Oral evidence by D. Armond.

that the digital rights criterion and the lessons learned from *Schrems* are employed fully should mean that the UK could maintain a relationship equal to the current standard. However, this is unknown territory for the UK and therefore one should look to how other third countries have agreed upon intelligence and data exchange.

The PNR agreements between the US and EU: the Snowden effect

In Kaunert and Zwolski's opinion the first international PNR agreement between the EU and the US merely represented the EU's attempt to play a significant role in the war on terror, which did not involve military action that had proved divisive since the Afghan conflict following 9/11.[69] A noteworthy increase in EU-US counterterrorism cooperation was seen following the terrorist attack on the US on 9 September 2001.[70] Kaunert and Zwolski break this cooperation down into two areas, the Justice Dialogue and the Policy Dialogue on Borders and Transport Security.[71] Although the Justice Dialogue started in 1998 to ensure information was transferred to the US, it has become increasingly important since the development of 'new EU competences in criminal judicial and police cooperation'.[72] Particularly since 2002, the Dialogue has been essential for negotiating agreements on mutual legal assistance and extradition, including liaison issues with the newly continued enhancement of Eurojust and Europol.[73] During this time the US introduced several measures aimed at strengthening border security, including the Container Security Initiative, the collection of PNR and the use of biometric passports.

These measures are unsurprising given the international nature of the current terrorist threat; the point has been made in previous chapters that international security and national security carry the same weight in terms of importance.[74] By this border security extension however, the US Homeland Security policies, specifically surrounding intelligence, policing and law enforcement and the financing of terrorism and justice, had vast implications for the EU that resulted in reinforcing cooperation.[75]

Under the US Aviation and Transport Security Act 2001, all airline companies operating passenger flights to the US must provide US authorities with electronic access to PNR.[76] This requirement caused a problem for EU airline companies, putting them under an obligation to disclose as per US law, and an obligation not

69 C. Kaunert and K. Zwolski (2013) *The EU as a Global Security Actor: A Comprehensive Analysis Beyond CFSP and JHA*(Palgrave Macmillan) p.96.
70 *Ibid.*
71 *Ibid* p.97.
72 *Ibid.*
73 *Ibid.*
74 The RT Hon Lord Lloyd of Berwick (1996) *Inquiry into Legislation against Terrorism*, Volume One, Cm3420, Chapter 2, paragraph 2.4.
75 *Supra* as per C. Kaunert and K. Zwolski (2013) p.97.
76 *Supra* as per C. C. Murphy (2015) p.158.

to disclose as per EU law, placing them at risk of compromising EU data protection laws, which inevitably could result in EU financial fines of up to $6,000 (USD) per passenger.[77] This rock and hard-place scenario led to the EU Commission deciding to take on the challenge of negotiating with the US and they managed to delay the implementation of the measures on the grounds that the EU were required to comply with the 1995 EU Directive on the protection of personal data.[78] The 1995 Data Protection Directive orates that no personal data should be transferred to any third country unless the EU Commission has determined that its data protection system provides an 'adequate level of protection of basic freedoms and rights of individuals'.[79] For Lowe, this represented the central obstacle for the EU in agreeing to a PNR data exchange agreement with the US.[80] The legal cultures of the EU and the US are remarkably different, as the EU focuses on the dignity of citizens in protecting fundamental human rights and the rule of law, in addition to the legislative data privacy protection, whereas the US focuses on liberty, and thereby has no explicit protection for data privacy under the Bill of Rights.[81] Rather legal scholars simply infer one from the specific rights in the First, fourth, Fifth and Ninth Amendments.[82] Because the US privacy framework did not meet EU standards the EU Commission developed a rather original solution, namely the 'Safe Harbour' scheme.[83] This scheme was aimed at commercial practices and although the adequacy was challenged in 2002 and 2004, nothing changed. For Van Wasshnova, this scheme lacked basic adequacy being insufficiently clear and precise, hence why the EU Commission finally determined it was not possible for them to agree upon PNR with a US state department alone.[84] On the basis of the Commission's adequacy decision they agreed on the transfer of PNR intelligence, but required the US to guarantee an adequate level of data protection for the transferred data.[85] This agreement received EU Council approval in 2004.[86]

77 P. Pawlak (2009) Made in the USA? The Influence of the US on the EU's Data Protection Regime CEPS – Liberty and Security in Europe, Centre for European Policy Studies, available at http://aei.pitt.edu/15102/1/madeusa-influence-us-eus-data-protection-regime.pdf accessed 30 March 2018.

78 *Supra* as per C. Kaunert and K. Zwolski (2013) p.97.

79 D. Lowe (2016) The European Union's Passenger Name Record Data Directive 2016/681: Is It Fit for Purpose? *International Criminal Law Review*, 16(5), 856–884, 860.

80 *Ibid.*

81 *Supra* as per S. Sottiaux (2008) pp.265–322.

82 *Supra* as per J. Q. Whitman (2004), pp.1115–1221.

83 EU Commission Decision 2000/520/EC.

84 M. R. Van Wasshnova (2008) Data Protection Conflicts Between the United States and the European Union in the War on Terror: Lessons Learned from the Existing System of Financial Information Exchange, *Case Western Reserve Journal of International Law* 39(3), 827–865, 832.

85 European Council (2012) Council Adopts New EU-US Agreement on Passenger Name Records (PNR) 9186/12, PRESSE 173.

86 *Ibid.*

Criticisms of this agreement came primarily from the European Parliament (EP), having been marginalised throughout the negotiation instigated proceedings through the CJEU, arguing the level of protection guaranteed by the US was below EU standards, and the agreement was based on the wrong law dealing with transport being Article 95 EU (now Article 114 TFEU). For Ilbiz, Kaunert and Anagnostakis the latter point is much more prevalent given that early PNR data agreements such as this focused far too heavily on expanding and prioritising counterterrorism cooperation to the detriment of data protection rules.[87] In 2006 the CJEU focused on the former point and annulled the PNR agreement based on the fact it pertained to criminal justice cooperation and thereby the public security framework, and not to the regulations of the internal market.[88] The CJEU made this clear in confirming that the now Article 114 TFEU was incompatible with Article 25 of the Data Protection Directive, which excluded the processing of personal data for 'public security, defence, state security and the activities of the state in areas of criminal law'.[89] As a result the PNR agreement was annulled on the basis that the Commission could not lawfully use the Data Protection Directive, and the Council was not competent to conclude the agreement on that foundation.[90]

Unfortunately, the adequacy of data protection under the Directive received very little discussion, which meant that any future PNR agreements must be based within the framework of the third pillar, in turn excluding the EP from the decision-making process, arguably despite the future Treaty of Lisbon abolishing the old system and providing the EP with more decision-making powers.[91] This meant that the second PNR agreement had to be based on the CJEU's findings, which Gilmore and Rijpma describe as a 'poisoned chalice' in terms of improving human rights and data protection compliance agreements.[92] For Murphy, this result could be termed perverse in that the 'constitutional role of the rule of law played a part in undermining the principle's safeguarding role'.[93] The EU Council therefore would lead the negotiations with the assistance of the Commission. In the meantime an interim PNR agreement was put in place to ensure continued intelligence sharing.[94] The second agreement was approved in 2007, by 19 rather than 34, creating two main matters where the adoption was based

87 E. Ilbiz, C. Kaunert and D. Anagnostakis (2015) The Counterterrorism Agreements of Europol with Third Countries: Data Protection and Power Asymmetry, *Terrorism and Political Violence*, 29(6), 1–18, 2.

88 Joined Cases C-317/04 and C-318/04 *European Parliament v Council of the European Union and Commission of the European Communities* [2006] ECR I-4721.

89 Data Protection Directive 1995, 95/46/EC, Articles 3(2) and 25.

90 Joined Cases C-317/04 and C-318/04 *European Parliament v Council of the European Union and Commission of the European Communities* [2006] ECR I-4721, [61], [70].

91 *Supra* as per C. Kaunert and K. Zwolski (2013) p.98.

92 G. Gilmore and J. Rijpma (2007) Joined Cases C-317/04 and C-318/04, *European Parliament v Council and Commission*, Judgment of the Grand Chamber of 30 May 2006, [2006] ECR I-4721, *Common Market Law Review* 44, 1081–1099, 1098.

93 *Supra* as per C. C. Murphy (2015) p.162.

94 *Ibid* p.161.

upon the Court's findings and properly under Police and Judicial Co-operation in Criminal Matters (PJCCM), and where it was agreed the US would receive less fields of data than under the first agreement that could be 'pulled' from the airline carriers database.[95]

However, with regard to the latter point, Papakonstantinou and de Hert argue the reduction was not a reduction at all.[96] Instead the original 34 fields of data were merged to merely give the appearance of a reduction.[97] As part of the negotiation and in exchange for reducing the fields of data, the EU agreed that the US authorities could share the data with an increased number of internal agencies, and store the data for 15 years.[98] It was further agreed that the Department of Homeland Security be permitted to access 'sensitive data' where 'the life of a data subject or of others could be imperilled of seriously impaired'.[99] For Murphy, this broad test renders sensitive personal data 'open to widespread use by US law enforcement authorities'.[100] With regard to the former issue, concluding the agreement under the authority of PJCCM resulted in significant consequences for the regulatory framework within the operation. The roles of the EP and national Parliaments and the CJEU in terms of oversight were therefore reduced.[101] Not surprisingly the EP criticised this second agreement, mainly based on the lack of democratic oversight within the PNR agreement, coupled with the fact that the US agreement took little to no account of the PNR agreement with other nation states, such as Canada and Australia. For Kaunert this provided a lack of surety regarding 'higher standards of protection of personal data'.[102] The Canadian agreement, for example, allows the PNR data to be held for six years, with the Australian model allowing for five years and six months.[103]

95 European Council Decision (2007) Agreement between the European Union and the United States of America on the processing and transfer of Passenger Name Records (PNR) data by air carriers to the United States Department of Homeland Security (DHS) 2007/551/CFSP/JHA (hereafter Second Agreement).

96 V. Papakonstantinou and P. de Hert (2009) The PNR Agreement and Transatlantic Anti-Terrorism Co-operation: No Firm Human Rights Framework of Either Side of the Atlantic, *Common Market Law Review,* 46, 885–919, 914.

97 *Ibid.*

98 *Supra* as per C. Kaunert and K. Zwolski (2013) p.99.

99 Department of Homeland Security, US letter to the EU, III Types of Information Collected, OJL204/21, 4 August 2007, available at https://www.dhs.gov/sites/default/files/publications/privacy/pnr-2007agreement-usversion.pdf accessed 20 March 2018.

100 *Supra* as per C. C. Murphy (2015) p.163.

101 *Supra* as per G. Gilmore and J. Rijpma (2007).

102 *Supra* as per C. Kaunert and K. Zwolski (2013).

103 European Council Council Decision (2008) Agreement between the European Union and Australia on the processing and transfer of European Union-sourced passenger name record (PNR) data by air carriers to the Australian Customs Service Agreement between the European Union and Australia on the processing and transfer of European Union-sourced passenger name record (PNR) data by air carriers to the Australian customs service 2008/651/CFSP/JHA. And European Council Decision (2006) Agreement between the European Community and the Government of Canada on the processing of API/PNR data 2006/230/EC.

Rather unmistakably this second PNR agreement was favourable towards the US, rather than towards the EU. This adds weight to Lehrke and Schomaker's hypobook that because the EU is more embedded in its networks with the US, the US found itself able to exert influence on the EU Council and Commission.[104] According to Lowe, this hypobook

> builds on Pawlak's earlier study who states as the EU's security consciousness has not developed as rapidly as the US, the US has the opportunity to exert a big influence on the transatlantic agenda with the US dictating and shaping the EU's security agenda.[105]

This second agreement was in turn replaced by a third PNR agreement in 2012, following the adoption of the Lisbon Treaty 2007, which provided the EP with increased decision-making powers.[106] Introducing this third agreement the EU Council confirmed the legal framework for PNR data exchange would not only assist with border crimes, it would also greatly increase the capabilities inherent in the prevention and detection, investigation and prosecution of terrorist offences.[107] The third agreement strongly resembles the second in terms of broadness, retention periods and access to the data.[108]

The broadness of the external PNR agreements: access, crime and human rights

With regard to the third agreement, the CJEU added that legislation allowing public authorities access to the stored electronic communications data on a 'generalised basis' must be 'regarded as compromising the essence of the fundamental right to privacy'.[109] In addition to the 15 year retention period and the so-called reduced fields of data covered, the list of agencies permitted to access PNR data have been extended, including law enforcement agencies not generally associated with counterterrorism. The first PNR agreement included the Inland Revenue Service and Animal Plant Health Inspection Service, for example.[110] The interim and second agreements included an infinite number of agencies including the

104 J. P. Lehrke and R. Schmaker (2014) 'Mechanisms of Convergence in Domestic Counterterrorism Regulations: American Influence, Domestic Networks and International Networks', *Studies in Conflict & Terrorism*, 37(8), 689–712, 693.
105 *Supra* as per Lowe (2016) p.860.
106 C. Kaunert, S. Leonard and A. McKenzie (2012) The Social Construction of an EU Interest in Counter-Terrorism: US Influence and Internal Struggles in the Cases of PNR and SWIFT, *European Security*, 21(4), 474–496, 485.
107 European Council (2012) Council Adopts New EU-US Agreement on Passenger Name Records (PNR) 9186/12, PRESSE 173.
108 See Article 8, available at http://eur-lex.europa.eu/legal-content/EN/TXT/?qid=1416915581157&uri=CELEX:22012A0811(01) accessed 20 March 2018.
109 *Supra* as per D. Lowe (2016) p.860.
110 D. R. Rasmussen (2008) Is International Travel *Per Se* Suspicion of Terrorism? The Dispute Between the United States and the European Union over Passenger Name Record Data Transfers, *Wisconsin International Law Journal* 26, 551–590, 551.

Office of the Department of Homeland Security and all entities that directly support it.[111] The types of crimes listed under these agreements were also wide-ranging and broadly phrased to include other types of crimes besides serious crimes and terrorism.[112] Article 4 of the third PNR agreement provides the same extremely broad provisions, including threats to commit crime, and 'other crimes' punishable by a sentence of three years or more.[113] During the PNR agreement negotiations, the EP, the Article 29 Working Group, the European Data Protection Supervisor and national parliamentary organisations such as the UK House of Lords EU Committee all expressedgreat concerns relating to individual privacy protections.[114] These centred on the fact that transferring such data to the US may violate the EU's high-principled standards of data protection.[115] PNR data has been referred to as broader than what could be considered 'adequate, relevant and not excessive'.[116] It has been further argued that access to the data should be limited to reasons of terrorism and serious crime only, and that sensitive data should be abandoned entirely thereby ensuring compatibility with the Directive.[117]

Policing cooperation: EU and US intelligence

EU and US policing cooperation has mainly been based on agreements reached by the EU and US. Following the terrorist attack on the US on 9 September 2001, the EU demonstrated eagerness to show solidarity with the US and asked the then Director of Europol to draft an intelligence exchange agreement.[118] Focusing on strategic and technical information concerning serious forms of international crime, the first agreement was adopted by the EU Council in December 2001.[119] This agreement provided for the identification of personnel named as points of contact, information exchange, mutual consultation, exchange of expertise and

111 *Ibid* p.585.
112 *Ibid.*
113 Agreement between the United States of America and the European Union on the Use and Transfer of Passenger Name Records to the United States Department of Homeland Security, Europa, available at http://eur-lex.europa.eu/legal-content/EN/TXT/?qid=1416915581157&uri=CELEX:22012A0811(01) accessed 20 March 2018.
114 The Article 29 Data Protection Working Party was set up under the Directive 95/46/EC of the European Parliament and of the Council of 24 October 1995 on the protection of individuals with regard to the processing of personal data and on the free movement of such data. See http://ec.europa.eu/justice/data-protection/article-29/index_en.htm. For information on the UK House of Lords EU committee see http://www.parliament.uk/hleu accessed 20 March 2018.
115 *Ibid.*
116 Article 29 Data Protection Working Party, Opinion 4/2003 on the Level of Protection ensured in the US for the Transfer of Passengers' Data, 13 June 2003, p.7.
117 *Ibid* pp.7–8.
118 *Supra* as per C. Kaunert and K. Zwolski (2013), p.102.
119 Euroean Council (2001) Conclusions Adopted by The Council (Justice and Home Affairs), Doc. SN 3926/6/01, 20 September 2001.

liaison officers, specifically for crimes committed or likely to be committed in the course of terrorist activity.[120] The second agreement took longer to negotiate as the EU's direction in terms of personal data protection had developed and changed in comparison to that of the US. According to Rees the EU had passed a significant amount of data protection legislation due to the fact Member States had tended to keep large amount of their citizens' data, and in comparison the US's approach to this was more *ad hoc* and somewhat relaxed, whereby relatively small amounts of data were held and kept.[121] Regardless the agreement was passed in December 2002 and although criticised by civil liberties campaigners the agreement contains many data protection safeguards including the principle of 'purpose limitation', whereby intelligence can only be used for the specific purpose for which it was obtained.[122] These agreements remain in place to date despite the Snowden revelations that had the potential to damage this relationship.

Conclusion

The UK is in a unique position when it comes to the relationship with the EU as a Member State. This position will undoubtedly remain so given the legislative influence the EU has had on the UK since the enactment of the European Communities Act 1972. As a new third country to the EU, the UK may have to negotiate many provisions surrounding security, intelligence and data exchange and future counterterrorism measures. In striking the balance between national security and human rights, it could be argued that the US leans more to the interests of national security over individual human rights, whereas the EU Member States lean more towards the interests of human rights.

In order to maintain a relationship with the EU and the many agencies, the UK Government must retain its affiliation with human rights and preserve the data protection laws. It is currrently unclear whether or not the UK will continue to have access to Europol, the EAW or SIS II and PNR data. This chapter has shown that according to those who work within policing, the UK's continued membership and access to these are essential to keep the UK safe. Four obstacles to the UK's successful negotiation to this end have been highlighted:

1 *Money*: The EU funds Europol and other measures that will inevitably cost the UK should it wish to have access to them. However, Europol may not be separated from other institutions such as Eurojust and Frontex.
2 *Value of contribution*: The UK must evidence the level of contribution it could make to Europol.

120 *Ibid* Article 3.
121 W. Rees (2006) *Transatlantic Counter-Terrorism Cooperation: The New Imperative* (Routledge) p.92.
122 V. Mitsilegas (2003) The New EU-USA Cooperation on Extradition, Mutual Legal Assistance and the Exchange of Police Data, *European Foreign Affairs Review*, 8, 515–536, 519.

3 *Data protection*: Following the enactment of IPA this may become a problem. For the time being at least the bulk powers provisions under IPA are untested.
4 *Uncooperative*: Analysing the Swiss model shows that the EU can be very uncooperative. With Juncker in charge negotiations may be even more difficult.

Conclusion

The book began with an examination of the UK's legal definition of terrorism under section 1 of the Terrorism Act 2000. This is important because UK law enforcement agencies and the courts use the definition when ascertaining that the activity they are dealing with is terrorism. It was found that several elements of the definition, namely the lack of defined phrasing and the resulting broadness, impact upon the rule of law and individual human rights. Two problems. The first concerns the proliferation of undefined causes, which has resulted in some difficulty in deciding which to apply to a particular case, thereby affecting at least to some degree judicial application. The second problem is intrinsically linked to the first, but with an increased focus on the political currency attached to the term 'terrorism'. Neither problem is soluble due to both the extremely varied 21st Century terrorist threat and the political nature of international agreements. However, the analysis did find that a general criminal offence of terrorism may assist in taking the subject out of the political realm and putting it firmly into the legal arena. To this end, inserting exclusion clauses into this definition, covering actions taken by way of protest and industrial action and dissent or during an international armed conflict in accordance with customary international law would further assist.

Chapter 2 concluded that the dynamics of private life have changed as a result of the advances made in 21st Century communications technology, with people living their lives increasingly online. To that end private conversations simply no longer take place in citizens' homes or through using a landline telephone, but rather online through the Internet, social media and the ever-growing list of chat applications available on a smartphone, allowing encryption. What follows the legitimate use of technological advancements is criminal, or in this case terrorist exploitation. With terrorists using the Internet to communicate propaganda and with each other, the resulting law enforcement investigatory capabilities gap must be filled. The chapter highlights the growth in technology, which is estimated to double every two years. The chapter went on to show that IS have used this growth to fashion an extraordinary threat level whereby law enforcement have difficulty in recognising friend from foe. It simply cannot continue to be the case that law enforcement is denied investigatory powers within the realms of the Internet, when clearly there is a criminal exploitation and terrorist problem.

Chapter 3 explored the vast powers of surveillance provided to law enforcement to fulfil its task of protecting national security and the citizens' right to life. In conjunction with the EU, the UK has enacted new laws and regulations over time to close the capabilities gaps as and when they appear, due to technological advances. Allowing law enforcement to monitor Internet traffic has simply become an essential in the fight against terrorism, and in the state's duty to protect its citizens' lives. To this end, the UK Government has recently enacted IPA which introduces the ability to bulk collect and retain electronic data communications and to seek the operators' assistance in decryption. The examination highlighted the fact that although IPA attempts to take a human rights approach, the main contentious elements in the Act are those in relation to the authorities' capabilities to intercept and retain electronic communications data en masse, and to legally hack into the populations equipment, again en masse, often using backdoors into encrypted online services.

The analysis went on to evidence that terrorist groups and self-starters have embraced modern communication technology, using it to market the group and radicalise others and to coordinate a terrorism attack. It also concluded that some legislative measures have failed to combat terrorism communication, for example sections 1 and 2 of the Terrorism Act 2006, and sections 57 and 58 of the Terrorism Act 2000. Chapter 3 continued to critically analyse the legalised pre-emptive measures, including temporary travel restrictions and the criminalisation of neutral behaviour. Utilising the doctrinal methodology, terms used such as mass data surveillance and pre-crime measures have been discredited. It was shown it would be physically impossible for law enforcement to conduct surveillance on the whole of the UK population's electronic communications data. It was further shown that the term 'pre-crime' is simply a fabrication and used misleadingly, given that pre-emptive measures are in fact criminal offences.

It was argued that a unique threat has been created, allowing people to operate under an anonymity cloak. The advanced independent operational abilities of terrorists is concerning, giving them potential access to explosives and firearms purchased on the darknet. It was made clear that legislation is required aimed at policing Internet traffic. A cooperative approach with ISPs is essential to achieve this objective, ensuring the dark sides of the web are monitored and then removed should they be deemed to be providing illegal materials.

This in turn has resulted in new measures that provide bulk interception of communications data and bulk equipment interference, which have been deemed to be extraordinarily powerful tools to be wielded, having a much bigger impact upon individual privacy than traditional communications interception and surveillance might have had. Intercepting electronic communications data and content is not the same as intercepting a landline call as evidenced in Chapter 4. Additionally it is unhelpful and disappointing to note IPA does not expressly cover OSINT and SOCMINT collection, although the Government had plenty of time to implement such measures. Chapter 4 also showed that communications data, by the very nature of its digital form, is ideal for analysis and profiling individuals. Data mining will increasingly become autonomous as automatic computer algorithms carry out the first bulk interception step. Aimed at the population as a whole, who are not suspected of being involved in any criminal or terrorist activity, subject to authority these bulk powers have the potential to effectively destroy the privacy rights of millions of people in order to find the elusive terrorist in the haystack. Although IPA may pass the digital rights criterion as highlighted in Chapter 5, and could be described as necessary in finding would-be-terrorists, it may ultimately come to fail the ECtHR jurisprudence when testing the proportionality of the retention of data and the bulk power measures.

Chapter 5 further emphasised the fact that the EU has been influential on the UK's law-making processes. The CJEU in particular has proved the most instrumental judicial body in terms of individual data protection, through its key judgments in *Digital Rights Ireland.*[1] The CJEU has achieved this by applying the EU's constitutional and legal prowess in protecting data protection, such as Article 8 of the Charter of Fundamental Rights and by way of two directives, namely the Data Protection Directive in 1995 and the e-Privacy Directive in 2002.[2] It was concluded that in order to keep the capabilities gap closed, the UK Government must ensure the law endures by safeguarding the cohesiveness with the jurisprudence of the CJEU and the (ECtHR. These human rights courts focus on different elements, built around the Conventional rights, with the CJEU centred on data protection and the ECtHR on Article 8 right to privacy.

The level of data protection becomes even more important in Chapter 6 as in order to maintain or indeed build new agreements with regard to data intelligence exchange individual data must be protected to a level agreed by the EU. However, it is currently unclear whether or not the UK will continue to have access to Europol, the EAW or SIS II and PNR data after it leaves the EU. Chapter 6 explored these issues and illustrated that according to those who work within policing the UK's continued membership and access to these are essential to keep the UK safe. EU level data privacy protection has been highlighted to be one of the three pre-existing conditions that must be met in order to facilitate the UK's negotiation. Using the US and EU's PNR agreement as a case study for the UK demonstrates the importance the EU places on data privacy protection. Overall, provided the UK law is considered to afford adequate protection, looking forward and perhaps focusing on some of the potential stumbling blocks to successful negotiation, the situation may not be as bad as first thought.

1 *Digital Rights Ireland Ltd v Minister for Communications, Marine and Natural Resources and others and the conjoined case of Kärntner Landesregierung, Michael Seitlinger, Christof Tschohl and others.*

2 European Union Directive 95/46/EC of the European Parliament and of the European Council of 24 October 1995 on the protection of individuals with regard to the processing of personal data and on the free movement of such data and Directive 2002/58/EC of the European Parliament and of the Council of 12 July 2002 concerning the processing of personal data and the protection of privacy in the electronic communications sector. See also *S and Marper v UK* [2008] 48 ECHR 1581, [66]–[67], the Court noted the concept of private life is a broad term not susceptible to exhaustive definition.

It has been found that there are, and will perhaps always be, conflicting issues between collective security and upholding individual human rights protection, specifically regarding the gathering and retention of electronic communications data, the sanctioned use of bulk powers under IPA and the sharing of intelligence, both domestic and international. Following the analysis, it was found that this balance in the UK is fairly steady because of the role and importance of judicial review, judicial independence and the overarching scrutiny provided by commissioners and parliamentary committees. It must also be accepted that, at times, individual privacy rights must be secondary to the absolute human right to life.

The value of these powers has been evidenced through the book, and particularly emphasised by the professionals working within the policing and security agencies. This point has also been given credibility by the many Governmental Committee hearings into law enforcement's action. Reports continually suggest that there is no shortage of individuals mounting or attempting to mount terrorist attacks. This is further evidenced in the 2017 Europol TE-SAT report, which highlights that during 2016, there were 13 terrorist attacks in the EU resulting in 718 terrorist-related arrests, with an additional 123 in the Republic of Ireland.[3] The consequences of not preventing terrorist acts can be severe resulting in serious injury and death. In 2017 five terrorist attacks were recorded in the UK, including a far right inspired attack on a group of Muslim men, and the Manchester attack perpetrated by Salman Abedi. Evidence has shown that the perpetrators were on security intelligence databases, but were not identified as major threats. Regardless of this, these incidents can still occur because terrorist methods have changed and continue to do so. The success in preventing complex plots is largely due to increased international cooperation between states, however, it has been shown, a major concern for intelligence and policing agencies is the threat lone actors pose over and above the overall terrorist threat as they can go about undetected due to their low-level planning. This was demonstrated on 14 July 2016 in Nice, when a lone actor influenced by the Islamist narrative drove a heavy goods vehicle into the crowds watching the firework display on the promenade.

It is low-level attacks that largely justify state agencies having powers to conduct bulk surveillance into aspects of citizens' lives where the need necessitates it. The above examples show, however, that even when citizens are placed under a targeted surveillance authority, the lack of resources and financial pressures on law enforcement agencies means that individual suspects must be prioritised and often intelligence is missed and targets lost. It therefore follows that it would simply be impossible to monitor the entirety of Internet traffic and all UK citizens all of the time, despite the media's portrayal of law enforcement's arbitrary use of surveillance and detention powers. In the EU, UK and US the powers are not arbitrary. Powers to conduct surveillance of electronic communications must be applied proportionately and within the rule of law. These assertions and increased powers of surveillance have resulted in an emphasis on privacy that has in turn resulted in the growth of commercial encryption; particularly in light of the fact lives are

3 Europol (2016) EU Terrorism Situation and Trend Report TE-SAT 2016, 2.1.

being increasingly lived online.[4] Privacy advocates have therefore campaigned for reduced state powers or enhanced safeguards to protect the individual from what they judge to be a surveillance state.[5] In turn governments seem to fear the possibility of the emergence of electronic communication channels they cannot monitor, and the possibility of losing intelligence powers. Both sides of the divide see a future in which they lose control, where 'privacy advocates look at a world in which ever more data is produced, aggregated and mined and the authorities fear developments such as universal default encryption, peer-to-peer networks and the dark net'.[6]

The UK Government has the duty to protect and ensure citizens' absolute Article 2 ECHR right to life. In doing so it intimately interferes with citizens' qualified Article 8 right to privacy under ECHR, and Articles 7 and 8 under the CFR. It is impossible for a citizen to use and access qualified rights if their Article 2 right is not protected. Overall, it has been evidenced that the balance in the UK between collective security and individual data privacy rights is stable because of the role of judicial review, judicial independence and scrutiny by commissioners and parliamentary committees.

4 See https://globenewswire.com/news-release/2016/10/31/884765/0/en/Encryption-Software-Market-Expected-To-Reach-2-16-Billion-By-2020.html accessed 30 March 2018.

5 See https://www.privacyinternational.org/node/917 accessed 30 March 2018.

6 *Supra* as per D. Anderson QC (2015) p.34.

Bibliography

Aas, K. F. (2007) *Globalisation and Crime* (Sage)

Ackerman, B. (2007) Before the Next Attack – Preserving Civil Liberties in an Age of Terrorism, *Public Law*, 181–187

Alegre, S. and Leaf, M. (2004) Mutual Recognition in European Judicial Cooperation: A Step Too Far Too Soon? Case Study – the European Arrest Warrant, *European Law Journal*, 10(2), 200–217

Alonso, R. et al. (2008) *Radicalisation Process Leading to Acts of Terrorism*. A concise report prepared by the European Commission's Expert Group on Violent Radicalisation, *Official Journal of the European Union*, L 111/9, 25 April 2008

Alston, P. and Weiler, J. H. H. (1999) An 'Ever Closer Union' in Need of a Human Rights Policy: The European Union and Human Rights, in Alston, P. (ed.) *The EU and Human Rights* (Oxford University Press)

Anderson, D., QC (2014) *The Terrorism Acts in 2013* (The Stationary Office)

Anderson, D., QC (2017) *The Terrorism Acts in 2016* (The Stationary Office)

Anderson, D., QC Independent Reviewer of Terrorism Legislation (2015) *A Question of Trust: Report of the Investigatory Powers Review*, June 2015 (The Stationary Office)

Anderson, M. (1998) European Frontiers at the End of the Twentieth Century, in Anderson, M. and Eberhard, B. (eds) *The Frontiers of Europe* (Pinter)

Andrew, C. (no date) The Rise of the Islamist Terrorist Threat, MI5, available at https://www.mi5.gov.uk/the-rise-of-the-islamist-terrorist-threat accessed 12 March 2018

Andrews and Arnold Ltd. (2015) Written evidence (DIP0001) submitted to the Joint Committee on the Draft Investigatory Powers Bill, available at https://www.parliament.uk/documents/joint-committees/draft-investigatory-powers-bill/written-evidence-draft-investigatory-powers-committee.pdf accessed 30 March 2018

Argomaniz, J. (2012) *The EU and Counter-Terrorism* (Routledge)

Argomaniz, J., Bures, O. and Kaunert, C. (2015) A Decade of EU Counter-Terrorism and Intelligence: A Critical Assessment, *Intelligence and National Security*, 30, (2–3), 191–206

Arreguin-Toft, I. (2002) Tunnel at the End of the Light: A Critique of US Counter-Terrorist Grand Strategy, *Cambridge Review of International Affairs*, 15(3), 549–563

Ashour, O. (2009) *The De-Radicalisation of the Jihadists: Transforming Armed Islamist Movements* (Routledge)

Baker, C. (1998) Membership Categorization and Interview Accounts, in Silverman, D. (ed.) *Qualitative Research: Theory, Method and Practice* (Sage)

Baldwin, F. N. and DiPerna, T. A. (2007) The Rule of Law: An Essential Component of the Financial War Against Organized Crime and Terrorism in the Americas, *Journal of Financial Crime,* 16(2), 160–165

Ball, J. and Lewis, P. (2011) Twitter and the Riots: How the News Spread, *Guardian*, 7 December 2011, available at http://www.theguardian.com/uk/2011/dec/07/twitter-riots-how-news-spread accessed 30 March 2018

Balzacq, B., Bigo, D., Guild, E. and Carrera, S. (2006) *Security and the Two-Level Game*, CEPS Working Document No234/January 2006, Centre for European Policy Studies, available at https://www.ceps.eu/publications/security-and-two-level-game-treaty-prüm-eu-and-management-threats accessed 28 March 2018

Bamford, B. W. C. (2004) The United Kingdom's "War Against Terrorism", *Terrorism & Political Violence*, 16(4), 737–756

Bamford, B. W. C. (2005) The Role and Effectiveness of Intelligence in Northern Ireland, *Intelligence and National Security*, 20(4), 581–607

Barker, J. and Foster, S. (2010) The Use of Fatal Force, Article 2 of the European Convention and the Jean Charles de Menezes Case, *Coventry Law Journal*, 15(2), 39–49

Barnidge, R. P. (2008) *Non-State Actors and Terrorism: Applying the Law of State Responsibility and the Due Diligence Principle* (Cambridge University Press)

Bartlett, J., Miller, C., Crump, J. and Middleton, L. (2013) Policing in an Information Age, Centre for Analysis of Social Media, Demos, March, available at http://www.demos.co.uk/files/DEMOS_Policing_in_an_Information_Age_v1.pdf?1364295365 accessed 30 March 2018

Bartow, A. (2011) Facebook and the Fourth Amendment: Expecting Any Privacy may be Unreasonable, *Jotwell*, 18 April 2011, available at http://cyber.jotwell.com/2011/04 accessed 30 March 2018

Bassiouni, M. Cherif (1988) A Policy-oriented Inquiry of 'International Terrorism, in Bassiouni, M. Cherif (ed.) (1988) *Legal Responses to International Terrorism: U.S. Procedural Aspects* (Martinus Nijhoff Publishers)

Batty, D. (2016) Prevent Strategy 'Sowing Mistrust and Fear in Muslim Communities', *Guardian*, 3 February 2016, available at https://www.theguardian.com/uk-news/2016/feb/03/prevent-strategy-sowing-mistrust-fear-muslim-communities accessed 30 March 2018

Beck, U. (2002) The Terrorist Threat: World Risk Society Revisited, *Theory, Culture and Society*, 19(4), 39–55

Beinart, P. (2015) What Does Obama Really Mean by 'Violent Extremism'?, *The Atlantic*, February 2015, available at http://www.theatlantic.com/international/archive/2015/02/obama-violent-extremism-radical-islam/385700 accessed 30 March 2018

Bell, L. (2016) Millions of Apple Devices at Risk of Attack Due to a Security Bug, Wired Cyber Security, 22 July 2016, available at http://www.wired.co.uk/article/apple-security-bug-hackers-steal-your-password accessed 30 March 2018

Bentham, M. (2016) Lone Right Wing Extremists 'Kill and Harm More People than Lone Islamist Terrorists, *Evening Standard*, 21 June 2016, available at http://www.standard.co.uk/news/uk/lone-right-wing-extremists-kill-and-harm-more-people-than-islamist-terrorists-a3276876.html accessed 30 March 2018

Berenskoetter, F. (2012) Mapping the Field of UK EU Policing, *Journal of Common Market Studies*, 50(1), 37–53

Berger, J. M. and Morgan, J. (2015) The ISIS Twitter Census: Defining and Describing the Population of ISIS Supporters on Twitter, 20 March 2015, Center for Middle East Policy at Brooking, available at http://webcache.googleusercontent.com/search?q=ca

che:nUpiATbv50wJ:www.brookings.edu/~/media/research/files/papers/2015/03/isis-twitter-census-berger-morgan/isis_twitter_census_berger_morgan.pdf+&cd=1&hl=en&ct=clnk&gl=uk accessed 30 March 2018

Bergeron, J. (2013) Transnational Organised Crime and International Security, *The Rusi Journal*, 158(2), 6–9

Bernal, P. (2015) Supplementary Written Evidence (IPB0018) Submitted to the Joint Committee on the Draft Investigatory Powers Bill, available at https://www.parliament.uk/documents/joint-committees/draft-investigatory-powers-bill/written-evidence-draft-investigatory-powers-committee.pdf accessed 30 March 2018

Bertrand, N. (2015) ISIS is Taking Full Advantage of the Darkest Corners of the Internet, *Business Insider UK*, available at http://uk.businessinsider.com/isis-is-using-the-dark-web-2015-7?r=US&IR=T accessed 30 March 2018

Bigo, D. et al. (2013) Open Season for Data Dishing on the Web, CEPS Policy Brief No.293, 18 June 2013, European Parliament, available at https://www.ceps.eu/system/files/PB293%20Bigo%20et%20al%20Prism%20Programme.pdf accessed 28 March 2018

Bigo, D. et al. (2015) The EU Counter-Terrorism Policy Responses to the Attacks in Paris: Towards an EU Security and Liberty Agenda, CEPS Policy Brief No.81, February 2015, available at https://www.ceps.eu/system/files/LSE81Counterterrorism.pdf accessed 28 March 2018

Blake, M. (2017) Blackburn Activisty Becomes First British Woman to Join Fight against ISIS in Syria, *Guardian*, available at https://www.theguardian.com/uk-news/2017/feb/09/blackburn-activist-kimberly-taylor-becomes-first-british-woman-join-fight-isis-syria accessed 30 March 2018

Bockstette, C. (2010) Terrorists Exploit Information Technologies: Use of Strategic Communication Calls for United Response, *Pre Concordiam, Journal of European Security and Defense Issues, Terrorism*, 1 (3), 1–70

Boer, M. D. (2002) Towards an Accountable Regime for an Emerging European Policing Governance, *Policing and Society: An International Journal of Research and Policy*, 12 (4), 275–289

Boer, M. D. (2015) Counter-Terrorism, Security and Intelligence in the EU: Governance Challenges for Collection, Exchange and Analysis, *Intelligence and National Security*, 30 (2–3), 402–419

Boer, M. D. and Wiegand, I. (2015) From Convergence to Deep Integration: Evaluating the Impact of EU Counter-Terrorism Strategies on Domestic Arenas, *Intelligence and National Security*, 30(2–3), 377–401

Bogard, W. (2006) Welcome to the Society of Control, in Haggerty, K. D. and Ericson, R. V. (eds), *The New Politics of Surveillance Visibility* (University of Toronto Press)

Bonino, S. (2012) Policing Strategies against Islamic Terrorism in the UK after 9/11: The Socio-Political Realities for British Muslims, *Journal of Muslim Minority Affairs*, 32(1), 5–31

Bonner, D. (2006) Responding to Crisis: Legislating Against Terrorism, *Law Quarterly Review*, 122, 602–631

Booth, R., Dodd, V. and Parveen, N. (2016) Labour MP Jo Cox Dies After Being Shot and Stabbed, *Guardian*, 16 June 2016, available at https://www.theguardian.com/uk-news/2016/jun/16/labour-mp-jo-cox-shot-in-west-yorkshire accessed 30 March 2018

Borum, R. (2011) Radicalisation into Violent Extremism I: A Review of Social Science Theories, *Journal of Strategic Security*, 4(4), 7–36

Boyne, R. (2000) Post Panopticism, *Economy and Society*, 29, 285–307

Bradley, A. W. (2008) Relations between Executive, Judiciary and Parliament: An Evolving Saga? *Public Law*, 470–489

Bradley, A. W. and Ewing, K. D. (2011) *Constitutional and Administrative Law* (15th Edition, Pearson Education Ltd)

Brodeur, J. P. (2007) High and Low Policing in Post-9/11, *Times Policing*, 1(1), 70–79

Brown, C. S. D. (2015) Investigating and Prosecuting Cyber Crime: Forensic Dependencies and Barriers to Justice, *International Journal of Cyber Criminology*, 9(1), January–June, available at http://www.cybercrimejournal.com/Brown2015vol9issue1.pdf accessed 30 March 2018.

Brown, I. and Korff, D. (2014) Foreign Surveillance: Law and Practice in a Global Digital Environment, *European Human Rights Law Review*, 3, 243–251

Bulk Acquisition Draft Code of Practice, published for consultation alongside the Investigatory Powers Bill, Home Office, Spring 2016, available at https://www.gov.uk/government/uploads/system/uploads/attachment_data/file/505412/Bulk_Acquisition_draft_code_of_practice.PDF accessed 30 March 2018

Bures, O. (2008) Europol's Fledgling Counterterrorism Role, *Terrorism and Political Violence*, 20(4), 498–517

Burke, J. (2007) *Al-Qaeda* (Penguin Books)

Busuioc, M., Curtin, D. and Groenleer, M. (2011) Agency Growth between Autonomy and Accountability: The European Police Office as a 'Living Institution', *Journal of European Public Policy*, 18(6), 848–867

Buttarelli, G. (2015) Counter-Terrorism, De-Radicalisation and Foreign Fighters, Joint debate during the extraordinary meeting of the LIBE Committee. European Parliament, Brussels, 27 January 2015

Buxton, R. (2010) Terrorism and the European Convention, Case Comment, *Criminal Law Review*, (7), 533–542

Byman, D. (2015) *Al Qaeda, The Islamic State and the Global Jihadist Movement* (Oxford University Press)

Byrnes, A. (2002) Apocalyptic Visions and the Law: The Legacy of September 11, a professorial address by Byrnes at the Australian National University Law School for the Faculty's Inaugural and Valedictory Lecture Series, 30 May 2002, available at https://law.anu.edu.au/CIPL/StaffPapersTalks&Submissions/Byrnes30May02.pdf accessed 30 March 2018

Campbell, D. (2010) The Threat of Terrorism: David Campbell Responds to Clive Walker, *Public Law*, 459–463

Carpenter, J. S., Levitt, M. and Jacobson, M. (2009) Confronting the Ideology of Radical Extremism, *Journal of National Security Law & Policy*, 3, 301–327

Carter, D. L. and Carter, J. G. (2009) Intelligence Led Policing: Conceptual Considerations for Policy, *Criminal Justice Policy Review*, 20, 310–325

Carter, G. and Carter, D. L. (2012) Law Enforcement Intelligence: Implications for Self-Radicalized Terrorism, *Police Practice and Research*, 13(2), 138–154

Cassese, A. (2008) *International Criminal Law* (2nd Edition, Oxford University Press)

Chacos, B. (2013) Meet Darknet, the Hidden, Anonymous Underbelly of the Searchable Web, PC World, available at http://www.pcworld.com/article/2046227/meet-darknet-the-hidden-anonymous-underbelly-of-the-searchable-web.html accessed 30 March 2018

Chadderton, C. (2012) UK Secondary Schools under Surveillance: What are the Implications for Race? A Critical Race and Butlerian Analysis, *Journal for Critical Education Policy Studies*, 76–92

Chaliand, G. (1987) *Terrorism: From Popular Struggle to Media Spectacle* (Saqi Books)
Choi, S. W. and Luo, S. (2013) Economic Sanctions, Poverty, and International Terrorism: An Empirical Analysis, *International Interactions: Empirical and Theoretical Research in International Relations*, 39(2), 217–245
Choudhury, T. and Fenwick, H. (2011) The Impact of Counter-Terrorism Measures on Muslim Communities, *Equality and Human Rights Commission Research Report72*, (Durham University)
Cini, M. (2003) *European Union Politics* (Oxford University Press)
Clarke, R. (1991) Information Technology and Dataveillance, in Dunlop, C. and Kling, R. (eds), *Computerization and Controversy: Value Conflicts and Social Choices* (Academic Press, Inc.)
Coates, S. (2015) PM: Seven Terror Attacks in UK Stopped in Last Year, *The Times*, 16 November 2015, available at http://www.thetimes.co.uk/tto/news/uk/article4615198.ece accessed 30 March 2018
Cockayne, J., Millar, A., Cortright, D. and Romaniuk, P. (2012) *Reshaping United Nations Counterterrorism Efforts: Blue-Sky Thinking for Global Counterterroism Cooperation 10 Years After 9/11*, Centre on Global Counterterrorism Cooperation, available at http://globalcenter.org/wp-content/uploads/2012/07/Reshaping_UNCTEfforts_Blue-Sky-Thinking.pdf accessed 28 March 2018
Coco, A. (2013) The Mark of Cain, *Journal of International Criminal Justice*, 11(2), 425–440
Coleman, R. and McCahill, M. (2011) *Surveillance & Crime* (Sage Publications)
College of Policing (2015) Intelligence Collection, Development and Dissemination, available at https://www.app.college.police.uk/app-content/intelligence-management/intelligence-cycle accessed 30 March 2018
Colvin, M. (1998) *Under Surveillance: Covert Policing and Human Rights Standards* (Justice)
Comay, M. (1976) Political Terrorism, *Mental Health and Society*, 3, 249–261
Cook, A. H. and Lounsbery, M. O. (2011) Assessing the Risk Posed by Terrorist Groups: Identifying Motivating Factors and Threats, *Terrorism and Political Violence*, 23(5), 711–729
Council of Europe (2005) Special investigation techniques in relation to serious crimes including acts of terrorism: Recommendation Rec (2005) 10 and explanatory memorandum, (Council of Europe Publishing)
Council of the European Communities (2005) *Communication from the Commission to the Council and the European Parliament*, Brussels COM (2005) 124 6 April 2005
Council of the European Union (2005) *The European Union Counter-terrorism Strategy* 14469/4/05 30 November
Council of the European Union (2012)*Council Adopts New EU-US Agreement on Passenger Name Records* (PNR) (2012) 9186/12, PRESSE 173
Counter-Extremism Strategy, HM Government, October 2015, Cm9145
Countering International Terrorism: The United Kingdom's Strategy (2006) HM Government, July, Cm6888
Counter-Terrorism Policy and Human Rights: Terrorism Bill and Related Matters, Third Report of Session 2005–06, House of Lords, House of Commons, Joint Committee on Human Rights, HL Paper 75-I, HC 561-I
Crawford, A. (2002) *Crime and Insecurity: The Governance of Safety in Europe* (Willan Publishing)
Crish, P. (2016) Junior Doctors' Strikes will Continue as Minister Plans to Impose New Contracts, Chartered Institute of Personnal and Development, available at http://www.

cipd.co.uk/pm/peoplemanagement/b/weblog/archive/2016/02/12/junior-doctors-39-strikes-will-continue-as-minister-plans-to-impose-new-contracts.aspx accessed 30 March 2018

Crone, M. and Harrow, M. (2011) Homegrown Terrorism in the West, *Terrorism and Political Violence*, 23(4), 521–536

Crowcroft, O. (2015) What's the Correct Name for the World's Most Dangerous Terrorists? *International Business Times*, available at http://www.ibtimes.co.uk/why-isis-hate-being-called-daesh-whats-correct-name-worlds-most-dangerous-terrorists-1531506 accessed 30 March 2018

Curtis, M. (2010) *Secret Affairs: Britain's Collusion with Radical Islam* (Serpent's Tail)

Dathan, M. (2016) No Room for Bojo among EU's Foreign Ministers! Top Diplomats Tease Boris and Block Him from Joining Photo-Shoot as They Begin Process of Excluding Britain from Brussels Club, *Mail Online*, 2 September 2016, available at http://www.dailymail.co.uk/news/article-3770744/Britain-continue-helping-EU-tackle-migrant-crisis-Brexit-Boris-Johnson-pledges-tours-European-capitals.html accessed 30 March 2018

Davies, C. (2015) Girl Becomes First Briton Convicted of Trying to Join Fight against Islamic State in Syria, *Guardian*, 20 November 2015, available at https://www.theguardian.com/uk-news/2015/nov/20/girl-becomes-first-briton-convicted-of-trying-to-join-fight-against-islamic-state-in-syria and http://thekurdishproject.org/history-and-culture/kurdish-nationalism/pkk-kurdistan-workers-party accessed 30 March 2018

Deen, T. (2005) U.N. Member States Struggle to Define Terrorism, Inter Press Service, available at http://www.ipsnews.net/2005/07/politics-un-member-states-struggle-to-define-terrorism accessed 30 March 2018

Deflam, M. (2006) Europol and the Policing of International Terrorism: Counter-Terrorism in a Global Perspective, *Justice Quarterly*, 23(3), 336–359

Deflam, M. (2009) *The Policing of Terrorism: Organizational and Global Perspectives* (Routledge)

Deleuze, G. (1992) Postscripts on the Societies of Control, *The MIT Press*, October, Winter Ed, 59(3), available at https://cidadeinseguranca.files.wordpress.com/2012/02/deleuze_control.pdf accessed 30 March 2018

Delmas-Marty, M. (2007) The Paradigm of the War on Crime: Legitimating Inhuman Treatment?, *Journal of International Criminal Justice*, 5(3), 584–598

Den Boar, M., Hillebrand, C. and Nolke, A. (2008) Legitimacy under Pressure: The European Web of Counterterrorism Networks, *Journal of Common Market Studies*, 46(1), 101–124

Diaz-Paniagua, C. F. (2008) *Negotiating Terrorism: The Negotiation Dynamics of Four UN Counter-Terrorism Treaties, 1997–2005* (City University of New York)

Dixon, D. (1997) *Law in Policing, Legal Rules and Police Practices: Legal Regulation and Police Practices* (Oxford University Press)

Dobinson, I. and Johns, F. (2007) Qualitative Legal Research in McConville, M. and Chong Hui, W. (eds) *Research Methods for Law* (Edinburgh University Press)

Dodd, V. (2011a) British Airways Worker Rajib Karim Convicted of Terrorist Plot, *Guardian*, 28 February 2011, available at https://www.theguardian.com/uk/2011/feb/28/british-airways-bomb-guilty-karim accessed 30 March 2018

Dodd, V. (2011b) Police Accessed Blackberry Messages to Thwart Planned Riots, *Guardian*, 16 August 2011, available at https://www.theguardian.com/uk/2011/aug/16/police-accessed-blackberry-messages-thwart-riots 30 March 2018

Dodd, V. (2015) Europe Faces Highest Terror Threat Since 9/11, MPs Told, *Guardian*, 13 January 2015, available at http://www.theguardian.com/uk-news/2015/jan/13/europe-highest-terror-threat-911-europol-fighting-overseas accessed 30 March 2018

Dodd, V. (2016) Anjem Choudary Jailed for Five-and-a-Half Years for Urging Support for ISIS, *Guardian*, 6 September 2016, available at https://www.theguardian.com/uk-news/2016/sep/06/anjem-choudary-jailed-for-five-years-and-six-months-for-urging-support-of-isis accessed 30 March 2018

Dodd, V. and Topping, A. (2010) Roshonara Choudhry Jailed for Life over MP Attack, *Guardian*, 3 November 2010, available at https://www.theguardian.com/uk/2010/nov/03/roshonara-choudhry-jailed-life-attack accessed 30 March 2018

Dominiczak, P.et al. (2016) Theresa May Secures Article 50 Victory in the Commons as Parliament Passes Amended Brexit Motion by 448 to 75 – Latest Reaction and Analysis, *Telegraph*, 7 December 2016, available at http://www.telegraph.co.uk/news/2016/12/07/brexit-article-50-mps-vote-supreme-court-pmqs-live accessed 30 March 2018

Donohue, L. K. (2005) Terrorism and the Counter-Terrorist Discourse, in Ramraj, V. V., Hor, M. and Roach, K. (eds) *Global Anti-terrorism Law and Policy* (Cambridge University Press)

Donohue, L. K. (2008) *The Cost of Counterterrorism: Power, Politics and Liberty* (Cambridge University Press)

Douglas, R. (2010) Must Terrorists Act for a Cause? The Motivational Requirement in Definitions of Terrorism in the United Kingdom, Canada, New Zealand and Australia, *Commonwealth Law Bulletin*, 36(2), 295–312

Draft Framework Decision on the retention of data processed and stored in connection with the provision of publicly available electronic communications services or data on public communications networks for the purpose of prevention, investigation, detection and prosecution of crime and criminal offences including terrorism 2004/0813/CNS

Drury, I. (2015) Public Schoolboy Who Quit City to Fight ISIS Returns Home: Briton Who Spent Five Months Alongside Kurdish Forces Says He Can Justify Actions if Questioned by Police, *Mail Online*, 10 June 2015, available at http://www.dailymail.co.uk/news/article-3119071/ISIS-fighting-city-trader-returns-home-UK.html accessed 30 March 2018

Edwards, L. and Urquhart, L. (2015) Privacy in Public Spaces: What Expectations of Privacy Do We Have in Social Media Intelligence?, *International Journal of Law and Information Technology*, 24(3), 279–310

Eijkman, Q. A. M. and Waggemans, D. (2011) Visual Surveillance and the Prevention of Terrorism: What about the Checks and Balances?, *International Review of Law, Computers & Technology*, 25(3), 143–150

Elgot, J. (2016) Brexit Debate in Parliament Would Give Game Away to Brussels, Says Minister, *Guardian*, 16 October 2016, available at https://www.theguardian.com/politics/2016/oct/16/brexit-debate-iwould-give-game-away-to-brussels-priti-patel accessed 30 March 2018

Elliott, M. (2004) Parliamentary Sovereignty and the New Constitutional Order: Legislative Freedom, Political Reality and Convention, *Legal Studies*, 22, 340–376

Elliott, M. (2007) The 'War on Terror' and the United Kingdom's Constitution, *European Journal of Legal Studies*, (1)

English, R. (2009) *Terrorism: How to Respond* (Oxford University Press)

Epstein, L. and King, K. (2002) The Rules of Inference, *University of Chicago Law Review*, 69(1), 1–133

Equipment Interference Code of Practice, Pursuant to Section 71 of the Regulation of Investigatory Powers Act 2000, January 2016, Home Office (The Stationary Office), available at https://www.gov.uk/government/uploads/system/uploads/attachment_data/file/496069/53693_CoP_Equipment_Interference_Accessible.pdf accessed 30 March 2018

Erlenbusch, V. (2013) How (not) to Study Terrorism, *Critical Review of International Social and Political Philosophy*, 17(4), 470–491

European Commission (2005a) *Communication to the European Parliament, The Hague Programme – Ten Priorities for the Next Five Years – a Partnership for European Renewal*, Brussels COM (2005)

European Commission (2005b) Proposal for a Directive of the European Parliament and of the Council on the retention of data processed in connection with the provision of public electronic communication services and amending Directive 2002/58/EC COM (2005) 438 final, Brussels, 21 September 2005

European Commission (2005c) *Communication from the Commission to the Council and the European Parliament – The Hague Programme: Ten priorities for the next five years, a partnership for renewal*, Brussels; EU Commission

European Commission (2005d) *Communication of the Commission to the Council and the European Parliament: Establishing a Framework Programme on "Security and Safeguarding Liberties" for the Period 2007–2013*

European Commission (2005e) *Proposal for a Council Framework Decision on the exchange of information under the principle of availability*, Brussels COM (2005) 490 Final 12 December 2005

European Commission (2005f) *Proposal for a Framework Decision on exchange of information under the principle of availability, Memorandum MEMO/05/367* Brussels; EU Commission

European Commission (2005g) *Communication from the Commission to the Council and the European Parliament*, Brussels COM (2005) 124 Final 06 April 2005

European Commission (2005h) *Communication for the Commission to the Council and the European Parliament: Developing a strategic concept on tackling organised crime*, Brussels COM (2005) 232 Final 2 April 2005

European Commission (2007) *Report from the Commission based on Art 11 of the Council Framework decision of 13 June 2002 on combatting terrorism*, Brussels, COM (2007) 681 6 November 2007

European Commission (2011a) *Proposal for a Directive of the European Parliament and of the Council on the use of Passenger Name Record data for the prevention, detection, investigation and prosecution of terrorist offences and serious crime*, COM (2011) 32 final

European Commission (2011b) *Report from the Commission to the Council and the European Parliament: Evaluation Report on the Data Retention Directive 2006/24/EC*, COM (2011) 225 final, Brussels, 18 April 2011

European Commission (2011c) *Report from the Commission to the European Parliament and the Council on the Implementation since 2007 of the Council Framework Decision of 13 June 2002 on the European Arrest Warrant and the Surrender Procedures between Member States*, Brussels, 11 April 2011, COM (2011), 175 final

European Council (2001) *Conclusions Adopted by the Council (Justice and Home Affairs)*, Doc. SN 3926/6/01, 20 September

European Council (2002) Council Decision of 28 February 2002: Setting Up Eurojust with a View to Reinforcing the Fight against Serious Crime, *Official Journal of the European Communities*, 6 March 2002, L63/1

European Council (2003) 2889th Council Meeting – Justice and Home Affairs, Brussels 27–28 February 2003, Document 6162/03 (Presse 42)

European Council (2004) 2579th Council Meeting – Justice and Home Affairs, Luxembourg 20 April 2004, Document 8694/04 (Presse 123)

European Council (2005a) 2642nd Council Meeting – Justice and Home Affairs, Brussels 24 February 2005, Document 6228/05 (Presse 28)

European Council (2005b) *Communication from the Commission to the Council and the European Parliament,* Brussels COM (2005) 124 6 April 2005

European Council (2005c) Council Meeting – Justice and Home Affairs, Brussels 12 December 2005, 12645/05 (Presse 247)

European Council (2007) EU Action Plan on Combating Terrorism, Brussels 9 March 2007, 7233/07

European Council (2012), Council Adopts New EU-US Agreement on Passenger Name Records (PNR) 9186/12, PRESSE 173

European Council Framework Decision on the protection of personal data processed in the framework of police and judicial co-operation in criminal matters 2008/977/JHA

European Council Framework Decision on combating terrorism 2002/475/JHA

European Parliament (2005) *The Hague Programme – Ten Priorities for the Next Five Years – a Partnership for European Renewal,* Brussels COM (2005)

European Union Council (2007) *EU Action Plan on Combating Terrorism,* Brussels 9 March 2007, 7233/07.

European Union Presidency (2004) Presidency Conclusions, Brusssels 4–5 November 2004, Document 14292/04

Europol (2012) *EU Terrorism Situation and Trend Report TE-SAT 2012,* (Europol)

Europol (2016) *EU Terrorism Situation and Trend Report TE-SAT 2016,* (Europol)

Evans, J. (2012) The Olympics and Beyond, MI5, available at https://www.mi5.gov.uk/home/about-us/who-we-are/staff-and-management/director-general/speeches-by-the-director-general/the-olympics-and-beyond.html accessed 30 March 2018

Ewing, K. D. (1999) The Human Rights Act and Parliamentary Democracy, *The Modern Law Review,* 62, 79–99

Ewing, K. D. (2004) The Futility of the Human Rights Act, *Public Law,* Winter, 829–852

Ewing, K. D. (2005) The Futility of the Human Rights Act – A Long Footnote, *Bracton Law Journal,* 37, 41–47

Ewing, K. D. (2010) *Bonfire of the Liberties: New Labour, Human Rights, and the Rule of Law* (Oxford University Press)

Feldman, D. (2005a) Proportionality and Discrimination in Anti-Terrorism Legislation, *Cambridge Law Journal,* 64(2), 271–273

Feldman, D. (2005b) None, One or Several? Perspectives on the UK's Constitution(s), *Cambridge Law Journal,* 64(2), 329–351

Feldman, D. (2006) Human Rights, Terrorism and Risk: The Role of Politicians and Judges, *Public Law,* 364–384

Feldman, D. (2010) Disclosure of Information, Torture and the 'Special Relationship', *Cambridge Law Journal,* 69(3), 430–433

Felsen, D. and Kalaitzidis, A. (2005) A Historical Overview of Transnational Crime, in Reichel, P. (ed.) *Handbook of Transnational Crime and Justice* (Sage)

Fenwick, H. (2008) Proactive Counter-Terrorist Strategies in Conflict with Human Rights, *International Review of Law, Computers & Technology,* 22(3), 259–270

Fenwick, H. (2011) Preventative Anti-Terrorism Strategies in the UK and ECHR: Control Orders, TPIMs and the Role of Technology, *International Review of Law, Computers and Technology,* 25(3), 129–141

First Sitting Committee Debate Session 2015–16, Investigatory Powers Bill, Publications on the Internet, 24 March 2016, available at http://www.publications.parliament.uk/pa/cm201516/cmpublic/investigatorypowers/160324/am/160324s01.htm accessed 30 March 2018

Fischer, A., Oswald, M. E. and Seiler, S. (2013) Terrorists Among Us: Effects of a Suspect's Group Membership, Terrorist Past, and Knowledge on Lay Persons' Interrogation Severity Recommendations, *Swiss Journal of Psychology*, 72(1), 13–23

Foreign Policy Aspects of the War against Terrorism, Sixth Report of the Foreign Affairs Committee, Session 2004–05, June 2005, Cm6590

Foster, S. (2009) The Fight against Terrorism, Detention without Trial and Human Rights, *Coventry Law Journal*, 14(1), 4–20

Freedman, D. and Thussu, D. K. (2012) *Media & Terrorism Global Perspectives* (Sage Publications)

Freeman, M. (2005) Order, Rights and Threats: Terrorism and Global Justice, in Wilson, R. A. (ed.) *Human Rights in the War on Terror* (Cambridge University Press)

Freeman, M. (2011) The Sources of Terrorist Financing: Theory and Typology, *Studies in Conflict & Terrorism*, 34, 461–475

Friedlander, R. A. (1983) *Terror Violence: Aspects of Social Control* (Oceana Publications)

Fuch-Drapier, M. (2011) The European Union's Solidarity Clause in the Event of a Terrorist Attack: Towards Solidarity or Maintaining Sovereignty, *Journal of Contingencies and Crisis Management*, 19(4), 184–197

Fulford, A. (2008) How Have Things Changed Since the IRA Trials?, *Medicine, Science & the Law*, 48(3), 185–188

Furedi, F. (2007) The Only Thing We Have to Fear is the 'Culture of Fear' Itself: How Human Thought and Action are being Stifled by a Regime of Uncertainty, *Spiked*, available at http://frankfuredi.com/pdf/fearessay-20070404.pdf accessed 28 March 2018

Fussey, P. (2007) Observing Potentiality in the Global City: Surveillance and Counter-terrorism in London, *International Criminal Justice Review*, 17, 171–192

Gale, C. J. S. (2006) The UK Response to Terrorism: Human Rights and a Wider Perspective, *Working Paper Series, No 06/01* , 185–219

Gallagher, R. (2013) Software that Tracks People on Social Media Created by Defence Firm, *Guardian*, 10 February 2013, available at http://www.theguardian.com/world/2013/feb/10/software-trackssocial-media-defence accessed 30 March 2018

Ganor, B. (2002) Defining Terrorism: Is One Man's Terrorist Another Man's Freedom Fighter?, *Police Practice and Research: An International Journal*, 3(4), 287–304

Ganor, B. (2014) Defining Terrorism: Is One Man's Terrorist Another Man's Freedom Fighter?, in Lowe, D., Turk, A. and Das, D. K. (eds) *Examining Political Violence: Studies of Terrorism, Counterterrorism and Internal War* (CRC Press)

Garland, D. (2001) *The Culture of Control: Crime and Social Order in Contemporary Society* (Oxford University Press)

Gartenstein-Ross, D. and Grossman, L. (2009) *Homegrown Terrorists in the U.S. and U.K.: An Empirical Examination of the Radicalization Process* (Foundation for Defense of Democracies Press)

Gearty, C. (2005) Terrorism and Human Rights, *European Human Rights Law Review*, 1, 1–6

Gearty, C. (2007) Rethinking Civil Liberties in a Counter-Terrorism World, *European Human Rights Law Review*, 2, 111–119

Gearty, C. (2012) Is Attacking Multiculturalism a Way of Tackling Racism – or Feeding It? Reflections on the Government's Prevent Strategy, *European Human Rights Law Review* (2), 121–129

Geltzer, J. A. (2011) Taking Hand-Outs or Going It Alone: Nationalization versus Privatization in the Funding of Islamist Terrorist Groups, *Studies in Conflict & Terrorism*, 34, 144–170

Gillespie, A. (2009) Regulation of Internet Surveillance, *European Human Rights Law Review*, 4, 552–565

Gilmore, G. and Rijpma, J. (2007) Joined Cases C-317/04 and C-318/04, *European Parliament v Council and Commission*, Judgment of the Grand Chamber of 30 May 2006, [2006] ECR I-4721, *Common Market Law Review*, 44, 1081–1099

Gioia, A. (2006) The UN Conventions on the Prevention and Suppression of International Terrorism, in Nesi, G. (ed.) *International Cooperation in Counter-terrorism: The United Nations and Regional Organizations in the Fight Against Terrorism* (Ashgate)

Githens-Mazer, J. (2008) Causes of Jihadi Terrorism: Beyond Paintballing and Social Exclusion, *Criminal Justice Matters*, 73(1), 26–28

Goold, B. J. (2009) Surveillance and the Political Value of Privacy, *Amsterdam Law Forum*, available at https://commons.allard.ubc.ca/cgi/viewcontent.cgi?referer=https://www.google.co.uk/&httpsredir=1&article=1153&context=fac_pubs accessed 20 March 2018Gottlieb, S. (2010) *Debating Terrorism and Counterterrorism: Conflicting Perspectives on Causes, Contexts and Responses* (CQ Press)

Graham, R. (2016) How Terrorists Use Encryption, Combating Terrorism Center, available at https://www.ctc.usma.edu/posts/how-terrorists-use-encryption accessed 30 March 2018

Greenwald, G. (2014) *No Place to Hide: Edward Snowden, the NSA, and the US Surveillance State* (Metropolitan Books)

Greenwald, G. (2016) Why is the Killer of British MP Jo Cox not Being Called a 'Terrorist'?, *The Intercept*, 17 June 2016, available at https://theintercept.com/2016/06/17/why-is-the-killer-of-british-mp-jo-cox-not-being-called-a-terrorist accessed 30 March 2018

Greer, S. (2010) Anti-Terrorist Laws and the United Kingdom's "Suspect Muslim Community": A Reply to Pantazis and Pemberton, *British Journal of Criminology*, 50(6), 1171–1190

Grierson, J., Dodd, V. and Rodrigues, J. (2016) Anjem Choudary Convicted of Supporting Islamic State, *Guardian*, 16 August 2016, available at https://www.theguardian.com/uk-news/2016/aug/16/anjem-choudary-convicted-of-supporting-islamic-state accessed 30 March 2018

Guille, L. (2010) Policing in Europe: An Ethnographic Approach to Understanding the Nature of Cooperation and the Gap between Policy and Practice, *Journal of Contemporary European Research*, 6(2), 257–271, available at http://www.jcer.net/ojs/index accessed 30 March 2018

Hacker, F. J. (1980) Terror and Terrorism: Modern Growth Industry and Mass Entertainment, *Studies in Conflict and Terrorism*, 4, 143–159

Haggerty, K. (2006) Tearing Down the Walls: On Demolishing the Panopticon, in D. Lyon (ed.) *Theorizing Surveillance: The Panopticon and Beyond* (Willan)

Haider, M. (2013) European Parliament Identifies Wahabi and Salafi Roots of Global Terrorism, *Dawn News*, available at http://www.dawn.com/news/1029713 accessed 30 March 2018

Hayes, B. (2002) The Activities and Development of Europol: Towards an Unaccountable FBI in Europe, *Statewatch*, available at http://www.statewatch.org/news/2002/feb/eufbi.pdf accessed 30 March 2018

Head, M. (2010) Calling Out the Troops and the Civil Contingencies Act: Some Questions of Concern, *Public Law*, 340–361

Henderson, B. and Sabur, R. (2016) Nice Terrorist Attack on Bastille Day: Everything We Know So Far on Monday, *Telegraph*, 18 July 2016, available at http://www.telegraph.

co.uk/news/2016/07/15/nice-terror-attack-on-bastille-day-everything-we-know-so-far-on accessed 30 March 2018

Henne, P. S. (2012) The Ancient Fire: Religion and Suicide Terrorism, *Terrorism and Political Violence*, 24(1), 38–60

Hewitt, S. (2008) *The British War on Terror* (Continuum Books)

Hijmans, H. and Scirocco, A. (2009) Shortcomings in EU Data Protection in the Third and the Second Pillars, *Common Market Law Review*, 46, 1485–1525

Hillyard, P. (1993) *Suspect Community: People's Experience of the Prevention of Terrorism Act in Britain* (Pluto Press)

HM Government (2010a) *A Strong Britain in an Age of Uncertainty: The National Security Strategy*, October 2010 (HM Government, Cm7953)

HM Government (2010b) *Securing Britain in an Age of Uncertainty: The Strategic Defence and Security Review*, October 2010 (HM Government, Cm7948)

HM Government (2011) *Review of Counter-Terrorism and Security Powers, Review Findings and Recommendations*, January 2011 (HM Government, Cm8004)

HM Government (2012) *Intelligence and Security Committee Annual Report 2011–2012*, July 2012 (HM Government, Cm8403)

HM Government (2013) *CONTEST: The United Kingdom's Strategy for Countering Terrorism* (The Stationary Office, Cm8583)

HM Government (2016) *CONTEST: The United Kingdom's Strategy for Countering Terrorism* (The Stationary Office, Cm9310)

HM Government, The Cabinet Office (2011) *The UK Cyber Security Strategy: Protecting and Promoting the UK in a Digital World*

Hoffman, B. (2006) *Inside Terrorism* (2nd Edition, Columbia University Press)

Home Affairs Select Committee (2008)*A Surveillance Society? Fifth Report of Session 2007–2008* (HC 2008–2009 58-I, 8 June 2008) House of Commons, available at https://publications.parliament.uk/pa/cm200708/cmselect/cmhaff/58/58i.pdf accessed 28 March 2018

Home Affairs Select Committee, Countering Extremism, Evidence heard from Zulfiqar Karim, Bradford Council for Mosques (18 Mosques), and Fazal Dad, Senior Imam, Abu Bakr Mosque, Bradford, 12 January 2016, BBC Parliament Channel viewed 19 February 2016, available at https://www.parliament.uk/business/committees/committees-a-z/commons-select/home-affairs-committee/inquiries/parliament-2015/countering-extremism/publications accessed 12 March 2018

Home Office (2014) *User Guide to Operation of Police Powers Under the Terrorism Act 2000 and Subsequent Legislation: Arrests, Outcomes and Stops and Searches*, 6 March 2014, available at https://www.gov.uk/government/publications/user-guide-to-operation-of-police-powers-under-the-terrorism-act-2000-and-subsequent-legislation accessed 28 March 2018

Hopkins, N. (2013) UK Gathering Secret Intelligence via Covert NSA Operation, *Guardian*, 7 June 2013, available at http://www.theguardian.com/technology/2013/jun/07/uk-gathering-secret-intelligence-nsa-prism accessed 30 March 2018

Hopkins, N. and Ackermenn, S. (2013) Flexible Laws and Weak Oversight Give GCHQ Room for Manoeuvre, *Guardian*, 2 August 2013, available at http://www.theguardian.com/uk-news/2013/aug/02/gchq-laws-oversight-nsa accessed 30 March 2018

Hopkins, N. and Borger, J. (2013) Exclusive: NSA Pays £100m in Secret Funding for GCHQ, *Guardian*, 1 August 2013, available at http://www.theguardian.com/uk-news/2013/aug/01/nsa-paid-gchq-spying-edward-snowden accessed 30 March 2018

Hopkins, N., Borger, J. and Harding, L. (2013) GCHQ: Inside the Top Secret World of Britain's Biggest Spy Agency, *Guardian*, 2 August 2013, available at http://www.theguardian.com/world/interactive/2013/aug/01/gchq-spy-agency-nsa-edward-snowden accessed 30 March 2018

Horgan, J. (2009) *Walking Away from Terrorism* (Routledge)

Horne, A. and Walker, C. (2014) Lessons Learned from Political Constitutionalism? Comparing the Enactment of Control Orders and Terrorism Prevention and Investigation Measures by the UK Parliament, *Public Law*, 267–288

House of Commons, Intelligence and Security Committee (2015) *Privacy and Security: A Modern and Transparent Legal Framework*, HC 1075 2014/15, 12 March 2015

Hua, J. and Bapna, S. (2012) How Can We Deter Cyber Terrorism?, *Information Security Journal: Global Perspective*, 21(2), 102–114

Huq, A. Z., Tyler, T. R. and Schulhofer, S. J. (2011) Why Does the Public Cooperate with Law Enforcement? The Influence of the Purposes and Targets of Policing, *Psychology, Public Policy and Law*, 17(3), 419–450

Hutson, R., Long, T. and Page, M. (2009) Pathways to Violent Radicalisation in the Middle East: A Model for Future Studies of Transnational Jihad, *Rusi Journal*, 154(2), 18–26

Ilbiz, E., Kauner, C. and Anagnostakis, D. (2015) The Counterterrorism Agreements of Europol with Third Countries: Data Protection and Power Asymmetry, *Terrorism and Political Violence*, 29(6), 1–18

Imran, A. (2011) Slaying the Monster: Sentencing, *Criminal Law and Justice Weekly*, 175 (11),151–152

Ingram, H. J. (2015a) The Strategic Logic of Islamic State Information Operations, *Australian Journal of International Affairs*, 69(6), 729–752

Ingram, H. J. (2015b) Three Traits of the Islamic State's Information Warfare, *The Rusi Journal*, 159(6), 4–11

Ingram, H. J. (2016) An Analysis of Inspire and Dabiq: Lessons from AQAP and Islamic State's Propaganda War, *Studies in Conflict & Terrorism*, 40(5), 357–375

Innes, M. and Thiel, D. (2008) Policing Terror, in Newburn, T. (ed.) *Handbook of Policing* (2nd Edition, Willan)

Jackson, R. (2008) An Argument for Terrorism, *Perspectives on Terrorism*, 2(2), 1–12

Jackson, R., Jarvis, L., Gunning, J. and Smyth, M. B. (2011) *Terrorism: A Critical Introduction* (Palgrave Macmillan)

Jackson, R. and Sinclair, S. J. (2012) *Contemporary Debates on Terrorism* (Routledge)

Jenni, S. (2016) Is the Swiss Model a Brexit Solution? The UK in a Changing Europe, *The UK in a Changing Europe*, 23 March 2016, available at http://ukandeu.ac.uk/is-the-swiss-model-a-brexit-solution accessed 30 March 2018

Joffe, G. (2008) The European Union, Democracy and Counter-Terrorism in the Maghreb, *Journal of Common Market Studies*, 46(1), 147–171

Joint Committee on Human Rights, Prevention of Terrorism Bill (2005) *Report of Session 2004–2005*, 4 March, HL 68 and HC344

Joint Committee on the Draft Investigatory Powers Bill (2016) *Report of Session 2015–2016*, 11 February, HL Paper 93 and HC 651

Jones QC, A., Bowers, R. and Lodge, H. D. (2006) *Blackstone's Guide to the Terrorism Act 2006* (Oxford University Press)

Jones, R. (2000) Digital Rule: Punishment, Control and Technology, *Punishment and Society* 2(5), 5–22

Jones, S. G. (2014) *A Persistent Threat: The Evolution of al-Qaida and Other Salafi Jihadists* (RAND National Defense Research Institute), available at https://www.rand.org/

content/dam/rand/pubs/research_reports/RR600/RR637/RAND_RR637 accessed 27 March 2018

Juergensmeyer, M. (2000) *Terror in the Mind of God: The Global Rise of Religious Violence* (University of California Press)

Kaczorowska, A. (2013) *European Union Law* (3rd Edition, Routledge)

Katselli, E. (2012) International Peace and Security, Human Rights and the Courts: A Critical Reappraisal, *The International Journal of Human Rights*, 16(2), 257–277

Katz, R. (2015) How Islamic State is Still Thriving on Twitter, 11 April 2015, InSite Blog on Terrorism and Extremism, available at http://news.siteintelgroup.com/blog/index.php/entry/377-how-the-islamic-state-is-still-thriving-on-twitter accessed 30 March 2018

Kaunert, C. (2007) Without the Power of Purse or Sword: The European Arrest Warrant and the Role of the Commission, *Journal of European Integration*, 29(4), 387–404

Kaunert, C. (2009) Liberty versus Security? EU Asylum Policy and the European Commission, *Journal of Contemporary European Research*, 5(2), 148–170

Kaunert, C. (2010) Europol and EU Counterterrorism: International Security Actorness in the External Dimension, *Studies in Conflict & Terrorism*, 33(7), 652–671

Kaunert, C., Leonard, S. and McKenzie, A. (2012) The Social Construction of an EU Interest in Counter-Terrorism: US Influence and Internal Struggles in the Cases of PNR and SWIFT, *European Security*, 21(4), 474–496

Kaunert, C. and Zwolski K. (2013) *The EU as a Global Security Actor: A Comprehensive Analysis Beyond CFSP and JHA* (Palgrave Macmillan)

Kearney, J. (2016) The Security Implications of Brexit, *Compas Breakfast Briefing Summary*, available at http://www.compas.ox.ac.uk/media/160520-security-web-text.pdf accessed 30 March 2018

Keohane, D. (2008) The Absent Friend: EU Foreign Policy and Counter-Terrorism, *Journal of Common Market Studies*, 46(1), 125–146

Kepel, G. (2002) *Jihad: The Trail of Political Islam* (Harvard University Press)

Kerr, I. and Earle, J. (2013) Prediction, Preemption, Presumption: How Big Data Threatens Big Picture Privacy, *Stanford Law Review Online*, available at https://www.stanfordlawreview.org/online/privacy-and-big-data-prediction-preemption-presumption accessed 28 March 2018

Khan, A. (2014) What ISIL's English-Language Propaganda Tells Us about Its Goals, *Aljazeera*, 20 June 2014, available at http://america.aljazeera.com/watch/shows/america-tonight/articles/2014/6/19/how-isil-is-remakingitsbrandontheinternet.html accessed 30 March 2018

Khomami, N. (2015) Mohammad Emwazi: Who Were His Victims?, *Guardian*, 13 November 2015, available at http://www.theguardian.com/uk-news/2015/nov/13/mohammed-emwazi-who-were-his-victims accessed 30 March 2018

Kirby, A. (2007) London Bombers as Self-Starters: A Case Study in Indigenous Radicalisation and the Emergence of Autonomous Cliques, *Studies in Conflict and Terrorism*, 30 (Winter), 415–428

Klausen, J. (2009) British Counter-Terrorism After 7/7: Adapting Community Policing to the Fight against Domestic Terrorism, *Journal of Ethnic and Migration Studies*, 35(3) 403–420

Klausen, J. (2015) Tweeting the Jihad: Social Media Networks of Western Foreign Fighters in Syria and Iraq, *Studies in Conflict & Terrorism*, 39(1), 1–22

Knight, C. J. S. (2011) Striking Down Legislation under Bi-Polar Sovereignty, *Public Law*

Koops, B. J. (2013) Police Investigations in Internet Open Sources: Procedural Law Issues, *Computer Law and Security Review*, 29(6), 654–655

Koops, B. J., Hoepman, J. and Leenes, R. (2013) Open Source Intelligence and Privacy by Design, *Computer Law and Security Review*, 29, 676–688

LaFree, G. and Dugan, L. (2007) Introducing the Global Terrorism Database, *Terrorism and Political Violence*, 19(2), 181–204

Lambert, D. (2010) Intelligence-Led Policing in a Fusion Center, *FBI Law Enforcement Bulletin*, 79(12), 1–6

Laqueur, W. (1987) *The Age of Terrorism* (Little, Brown and Company)

Laqueur, W. (1999) *The New Terrorism: Fanaticism and the Arms of Mass Destruction* (Oxford University Press)

Lawther, C. (2010) "Securing" the Past: Policing and the Contest over Truth in Northern Ireland, *British Journal of Criminology*, 50(3) 455–473

Legislation against Terrorism, A Consultation Paper (1998) (The Stationary Office Cm4178)

Legislative Scrutiny: Counter-Terrorism and Security Bill, Fifth Report of Session 2014–15 (2015) House of Lords, House of Commons, Joint Committee on Human Rights, 12 January 2015, HL 86, HC 859

Lehrke, J. P. and Schmaker, R. (2014) Mechanisms of Convergence in Domestic Counterterrorism Regulations: American Influence, Domestic Networks and International Networks, *Studies in Conflict & Terrorism*, 37(8), 689–712

Leigh, I. (1986) A Tapper's Charter?, *Public Law*, Spring, 8–18

Leiken, R. S. (2005) *Europe's Mujahideen: Where Mass Immigration Meets Global Terrorism* April, Center for Immigration Studies

Leonard, S. and Kaunert, C. (2012) "Between a Rock and a Hard Place?": The European Union's Financial Sanctions against Suspected Terrorists, Multilateralism and Human Rights, *Cooperation and Conflict*, 47(4),473–494

Lester, A. (2005) The Utility of the Human Rights Act: A Reply to Keith Ewing, *Public Law*, 249–258

Levi, M. (2010) Combating the Financing of Terrorism: A History and Assessment of the Control of "Threat Finance", *British Journal of Criminology*, 50(4), 650–669

Lewis, N. (2005) Expanding Surveillance: Connecting Biometric Information Systems to International Police Cooperation, in Zureil, E. and Salter, M. B. (eds) *Global Surveillance and Policing: Borders, Security, Identity* (Willan)

Lewis, P. et al. (2012) Reading the Riots: Investigating England's Summer of Disorder, *Guardian shorts* and *Guardian*, Chapter 8, available at https://www.theguardian.com/info/2011/dec/15/reading-the-riots-ebook accessed 30 March 2018

Lewitt, G. (1986) Is Terrorism Worth Defining?, *Ohio Northern University Law Review*, 13, 97–98

LexisNexis® Risk Solutions (2012) Survey of Law Enforcement Personnel and Their Use of Social Media in Investigations, available at https://www.lexisnexis.com/risk/downloads/whitepaper/Infographic-Social-Media-Use-in-Law-Enforcement.pdf accessed 30 March 2018

Loader, I. (2002) Policing, Securitization and Democratization in Europe Criminal Justice, *The International Journal of Policy and Practice*, 2(2), 125–153

Lord Bingham (2007) The Rule of Law, *Cambridge Law Journal*, 66(1), 67–85

Lord Carlile of Berriew QC (2007a) Independent Reviewer of Terrorism Legislation, *The Definition of Terrorism*, March 2007, Cm7052

Lord Carlile of Berriew QC (2007b) *Report on Proposed Measures for Inclusion in a Counter Terrorism Bill*, Cm7262

Lowe, D. (2011) The Lack of Discretion in High Policing, *Policing and Society: An International Journal of Research and Policy*, 21(2), 233–247

Lowe, D. (2013) Radicalisation of Terrorist Causes: the 32CSM/IRA Threat to UK Security, in Lowe, D., Turk, A. and Das, D. (eds) *Political Violence, Terrorism and Counter-Terrorism* (Taylor & Francis)

Lowe, D. (2014) Surveillance and International Terrorism Intelligence Exchange: Balancing the Interests of National Security and Individual Liberty, *Terrorism and Political Violence*, 28(4), 653–673

Lowe, D. (2016) The European Union's Passenger Name Record Data Directive 2016/681: Is It Fit for Purpose?, *International Criminal Law Review*, 16(5), 856–884

Lynch, O. and Ryder, C. (2012) Deadliness, Organisational Change and Suicide Attacks: Understanding the Assumptions Inherent in the Use of the Term 'New Terrorism', *Critical Studies on Terrorism*, 5(2), 257–275

Lynskey, O. (2015) Beyond Privacy: The Data Protection Implications of the IP Bill, LSE Law Department Briefings on the Investigatory Powers Bill, *LSE Law Policy Briefings*, 15, *Social Science Research Network*, available at http://ssrn.com/abstract=2704299 accessed 13 March 2018

MacAskell, E., Borger, J., Davies, N. and Ball, J. (2013) GCHQ Taps Fibre-Optic Cables for Secret Access to World's Communications, *Guardian*, 21 June 2013, available at http://www.theguardian.com/uk/2013/jun/21/gchq-cables-secret-world-communications-nsa accessed 30 March 2018

Macdonald, A. (2015) EU's Tusk Warns against Federalist Push, Treaty Change, 7 September 2015, Reuters, available at http://www.reuters.com/article/us-eu-tusk-treaties-idUSKCN0R72C320150907 accessed 30 March 2018

Mahan, S. and Grist, P. L. (2013) *Terrorism in Perspective* (3rd Edition, Sage)

Mandoza, I. (2012) What's in a Name?: Challenging the Word "Islamist", *Chicago Monitor*, available at http://chicagomonitor.com/2012/05/whats-in-a-name-challenging-the-word-islamist accessed 30 March 2018

Mansfield, K. (2016) 'It is Crazy' that EU Members Would Want to Act 'Individually' Says Federalist Juncker, *Express*, 15 September 2016, available at http://www.express.co.uk/news/politics/711181/Jean-Claude-Juncker-says-crazy-EU-members-would-want-to-act-individually accessed 30 March 2018

Marong, C. (2012) Protecting the Public? Challenging the Indefinite Preventive Detention of Non-Citizens, *UCL Journal of Law and Jurisprudence*, 3(1), 115–143

Martin, A. J. (2015) *GCHQ v Privacy International*: Computer Hacking Tribunal Showdown Begins, *The Register*, 1 December 2015, available at http://www.theregister.co.uk/2015/12/01/gchq_privacy_international_investigatory_powers_tribunal accessed 30 March 2018

Martin, G. (2004) *The New Era of Terrorism: Selected Readings* (Sage)

Martin, G. (2011) *Essentials of Terrorism: Concepts and Controversies* (2nd Edition, Sage)

Martin, M. (2013) *Understanding Terrorism: Challenges, Perspectives, and Issues* (4th Edition, Sage)

Martyn, A. (2002) *The Right of Self-Defence under International Law – the Response to the Terrorist Attacks of 11 September*, Australian Law and Bills Digest Group, Parliament of Australia, available at http://www.aph.gov.au/About_Parliament/Parliamentary_Departments/Parliamentary_Library/Publications_Archive/CIB/cib0102/02CIB08 accessed 30 March 2018

Matlary, J. H. (2008) Much Ado About Little: The EU and Human Security, *International Affairs*, 84(1), 131–143

Matusitz, J. (2013) *Terrorism & Communication: A Critical Introduction* (Sage)

May, T. E. (1863) *Constitutional History of England since the Accession of King George III* (W. J. Widdleton) vol. 2

McCann, K. (2016) UK Opts Back into Europol Despite Brexit Vote, *Telegraph*, 14 November 2016, available at http://www.telegraph.co.uk/news/2016/11/14/uk-opts-back-into-europol-despite-brexit-vote accessed 24 November 2016

McCulloch, J. and Pickering, S. (2009) Pre-Crime and Counter-Terrorism: Imagining Future Crime in the "War on Terror", *British Journal of Criminology*, 49, 628–645

McKeever, D. (2010) The Human Rights Act and Anti-Terrorism in the UK: One Great Leap Forward by Parliament, but Are the Courts Able to Slow the Steady Retreat that Has Followed?, *Public Law*, January, 110–139

McKittrick, D. and McVea, D. (2001) *Making Sense of the Troubles* (Penguin Books)

Meisels, T. (2009) Defining Terrorism – a Typology, *Critical Review of International Social and Political Philosophy*, 12(3), 331–351

Middleton, B. (2013) Terrorism Prevention and Investigation Measures: Constitutional Evolution, not Revolution?, *Journal of Criminal Law*, 77(6), 562–582

Miller, C.et al. (2015) The Road to Representivity, Centre for the Analysis of Social Media at Demos/IPSOS Mori, September 2015, available at http://www.demos.co.uk/project/the-road-to-representivity accessed 28 March 2018

Milton, D. (2014) The Islamic State: An Adaptive Organisation Facing Increasing Challenges, in al-Ubaydi, M., Lahoud, N., Milton, D. and Price, B. (eds), *The Group that Calls Itself a State: Understanding the Evolution and Challenges of the Islamic State*, The Combating Terrorism Center at West Point, available at www.ctc.usma.edu accessed 30 March 2018

Mitsilegas, V. (2003) The New EU-USA Cooperation on Extradition, Mutual Legal Assistance and the Exchange of Police Data, *European Foreign Affairs Review*, 8, 515–536

Mitsilegas, V. (2010) The Transformation of Border Controls in an Era of Security: UK and EU Systems Converging?, *Journal of Immigration Asylum and Nationality Law*, 24 (3), 233–245

Mitsilegas, V. (2015) *The Criminalisation of Migration in Europe: Challenges for Human Rights and the Rule of Law* (Springer)

Moeckli, D. and King, T. (2010) Human Rights and Non-Discrimination on the "War on Terror", Publication Review, *European Journal of International Law*, 21(4), 1109–1111

Molders, S. (2005) European Arrest Warrant Act is Void – the Decision of the German Federal Constitutional Court of 18 July 2005, *German Law Journal*, 7(1), 45–58

Monar, J. (2013) EU internal security governance: the case of counter-terrorism, *European Security*, 23(2), 195–209

Monar, J. (2015) The EU as an International Counter-Terrorism Actor: Progress and Constraints, *Intelligence and National Security*, 30(2–3), 333–356

Moran, J. (2010) Evaluating Special Branch and the Use of Informant Intelligence in Northern Ireland, *Intelligence and National Security*, 25(1), 1–23

Mosendz, P. (2014) How the Head of ISIS Got His Name: Abu Bakr al-Baghdadi Chose a Name with Historic Resonance in the Muslim World, *Europe Newsweek*, 11 August 2014, available at http://europe.newsweek.com/abu-bakr-al-baghdadi-abu-dua-invisible-sheikh-awwad-ibrahim-ali-al-badri-al-282939?rm=eu accessed 28 March 2018

Moskalenko, S. and McCauley, C. (2011) The Psychology of Lone-Wolf Terrorism, *Counselling Psychology Quarterly*, 24(2), 115–126

Muller-Wille, B. (2008) The Effect of International Terrorism on EU Intelligence Co-operation, *Journal of Common Market Studies*, 46(1), 49–73

Murphy, C. C. (2015) *EU Counter-Terrorism Law: Pre-Emption and the Rule of Law* (Hart Publishing)

Murray, A. (2012) Acts of War or Acts of Terrorism? Case Comment, *Journal of Criminal Law*, 76(4), 298–302

Murray, A. and Keenan, B. (2015) *Ensuring the Rule of Law*, LSE Law Department Briefings on the Investigatory Powers Bill, LSE Law Policy Briefing, 12, Social Science Research Network, available at http://ssrn.com/abstract=2703806 accessed 30 March 2018.

Mustapha, H. (2014) *The al-Nusra Front: From Formation to Dissension*, Policy Analysis Series (Arab Centre for Research and Policy Studies)

Mythen, G. and Walklate, S. (2006) Criminology and Terrorism: Which Thesis Risk Society or Governmentality?, *British Journal of Criminology*, 46(3), 379–398

Nagesh, A. (2016) France is Probably Going to Move Our Border Back to Dover after Brexit, *Metro*, 25 June 2016, available at http://metro.co.uk/2016/06/25/france-is-probably-going-to-move-our-border-back-to-dover-after-brexit-5966133 accessed 30 March 2018

Nance, M. W. (2015) *The Terrorists of Iraq: Inside the Strategy and Tactics of the Iraqi Insurgency 2003–2014* (CRC Press)

Napoleoni, L. (2004) The New Economy of Terror: How Terrorism is Financed, *Forum on Crime and Society*, 4(1–2), 31–48

Netanyahu, B. (1985) *Terrorism: How the West Can Win* (Farrar, Straus and Giroux)

Neuburger, L. D. C. and Valentini, T. (1996) *Women and Terrorism* (Macmillan Press)

Newburn, T. (ed.) (2008) *Handbook of Policing* (Willan)

Newburn, T., Williamson, T. and Wright, A. (2008) *Handbook of Criminal Investigation* (2nd Edition, Willan)

O'Carroll, L. and Norton-Taylor, R. (2013) David Miranda Detention Prompts Outcry over 'Gross Misuse' of Terror Laws, *Guardian*, 19 August 2013, available at http://www.theguardian.com/world/2013/aug/19/david-miranda-detention-outcry-terrorism-laws accessed 30 March 2018

OFCOM (2016) The Communications Market, Telecoms and Networks, available at https://www.ofcom.org.uk/__data/assets/pdf_file/0026/26648/uk_telecoms.pdf accessed 30 March 2018

Office for Security and Counter-Terrorism (2014) *Intercept as Evidence* (Cm8989, December 2014), a report by a committee of Privy Counsellors led by the Rt. Hon. Sir John Chilcott

O'Floinn, M. and Ormerod, D. (2011) Social Networking Sites, RIPA and Criminal Investigations, *Criminal Law Review*, 10, 766–789

Ojanen, T. (2014) Privacy is more than just a Seven-Letter Word: The Court of Justice of the European Union Sets Constitutional Limits on Mass Surveillance: Court of Justice of the European Union Decision of 8 April 2014 in Joined Cases C-293/12 and C-594/12, *Digital Rights Ireland and Seitlinger and Others, European Constitutional Law Review*, 10(3), 528–541

Oltermann, P. (2013) Britain Accused of Trying to Impede EU Data Protection Law, *Guardian*, 27 September 2013, available at http://www.theguardian.com/technology/2013/sep/27/britain-eu-data-protection-law accessed 30 March 2018

Omand, D. (2012) #Intelligence, Centre for Analysis of Social Media, Demos, 24 April 2012, available at http://www.demos.co.uk/project/intelligence accessed 30 March 2018

Omand, D., Bartlett, J. and Miller, C. (for UK Cabinet Office) (2010) *A Strong Britain in an Age of Uncertainty: The National Security Strategy* (Her Majesty's Stationary Office)

Omand, D., Bartlett, J. and Miller, C. (2012) Introducing Social Media Intelligence, *Intelligence and National Security Review*, 27(6), 801–823

O'Neill, M. (2007) A Critical Analysis of the EU Legal Provisions on Terrorism, *Terrorism and Political Violence*, 20(1), 26–48

Ormerod, D. (2008) *Smith and Hogan Criminal Law* (12th Edition, Oxford University Press)

Orr, A. (2012) Terrorism: A Philosophical Discourse, *Journal of Applied Security Research*, 7(1), 93–106

Paganini, P. (2012) The Good and the Bad of the Deep Web, *The Hacker New Magazine*, 17 September 2012, available at http://securityaffairs.co/wordpress/8719/deep-web/the-good-and-the-bad-of-the-deep-web.html accessed 30 March 2018

Pantazis, C. and Pemberton, S. (2009) From the "Old" to the "New" Suspect Community: Examining the Impacts of Recent UK Counter-Terrorist Legislation, *British Journal of Criminology*, 49(5), 646–666

Pantucci, R. (2010) A Contest to Democracy? How the UK has Responded to the Current Terrorist Threat, *Democratization*, 17(2), 251–271

Papakonstantinou, V. and de Hert, P. (2009) The PNR Agreement and Transatlantic Anti-Terrorism Co-operation: No Firm Human Rights Framework of Either Side of the Atlantic, *Common Market Law Review*, 46(3), 885–919

Pape, R. A. (2003) The Strategic Logic of Suicide Terrorism, *American Political Science Review*, 97(3), 343–361

Parmer, A. (2011) Stop and Search in London: Counter-Terrorist or Counter-Productive?, *Policing & Society*, 21(4), 369–382

Patrice, J. (2016) Bombs Used by ISIS in Brussels Terror Attacks are for Sale Online, *NewsGrio*, available at http://www.newsgrio.com/articles/world/uk/244032-bombs-used-by-isis-in-brussels-terror-attacks-are-for-sale-online.html accessed 30 March 2018

Peers, S. (2011) *EU Justice and Home Affairs Law* (3rd Edition, Oxford University Press)

Perez, R. (2016) GCHQ to Fund Startups to Fight Cyber-Crime, *SC Magazine*, available at http://www.scmagazineuk.com/gchq-to-fund-startups-to-fight-cyber-crime/article/524540 accessed 30 March 2018

Perliger, A. (2012) How Democracies Respond to Terrorism: Regime Characteristics, Symbolic Power and Counterterrorism, *Security Studies*, 21(3), 490–528

Perry, M. and Negrin, H. (2008) *The Theory and Practice of Islamic Terrorism: An Anthology* (Palgrave Macmillan)

Piazza, J. (2013) Regime Age and Terrorism: Are New Democracies Prone to Terrorism? *International Interactions: Empirical and Theoretical Research in International Relations*, 39(2), 246–263

Pollard, S. (2016) The Case that Shows Why We Must Not Stay in the European Arrest Warrant, *The Spectator*, 3 September 2016, available at http://www.spectator.co.uk/2016/09/the-case-that-shows-why-we-must-not-stay-in-the-european-arrest-warrant accessed 30 March 2018

Pollinger, Z. A. (2008) Counterfeit Goods and Their Potential Financing of International Terrorism, *The Michigan Journal of Business*, 1(1), 85–102

Popham, P. (2014) Jean-Claude Juncker: The Face of Federalism, *Independent*, 6 June 2014, available at http://www.independent.co.uk/news/people/jean-claude-juncker-the-face-of-federalism-9504014.html accessed 30 March 2018

Rankin, J. (2016) Europol Chief Says Brexit Would Harm UK Crime-Fighting, *Guardian*, 22 June 2016, available at https://www.theguardian.com/politics/2016/jun/22/europol-chief-says-brexit-would-harm-uk-crime-fighting accessed 30 March 2018

Raplin, A.-J. (2011) What is Terrorism?, *Behavioural Sciences of Terrorism and Political Aggression*, 3(3), 161–175
Rashid, A. (2010) *Taliban: The Power of Militant Islam in Afghanistan and Beyond* (I. B. Tauris & Co. Ltd)
Rasmussen, D. R. (2008) Is International Travel Per Se Suspicion of Terrorism? The Dispute Between the United States and the European Union over Passenger Name Record Data Transfers, *Wisconsin International Law Journal*, 26(2), 551–590
Ratcliffe, J. (2008) *Intelligence-Led Policing* (Willan)
Ratcliffe, M., Rabenstein, C. and Staniforth, A. (2013) *Blackstone's Counter-Terrorism Handbook: Police National Legal Database* (3rd Edition, Oxford University Press)
Ratcliffe, J., Taniguchi, T. and Taylor, R. B. (2009) The Crime Reduction Effects of Public CCTV Cameras: A Multi-Method Spatial Approach, *Justice Quarterly*, 26(4), 746–770
Rees, W. (2006) *Transatlantic Counter-Terrorism Cooperation: The New Imperative* (Routledge)
Reid, A. S. and Ryder, N. (2010) For Whose Eyes Only? A Critique of the United Kingdom's Regulation of Investigatory Powers Act 2000, *Information and Communications Technology Law*, 10(2), 179–201
Reiner, R. (2010) *The Politics of the Police* (4th Edition, Oxford University Press)
Report on the Anti-Terrorism, Crime and Security Bill 2001 (2001–02 HC 351)
Reports on the Anti-Terrorism, Crime and Security Bill (2001–02 HL 37, HC 372)
Reports on the Anti-Terrorism, Crime and Security Bill (2001–02 HL 51, HC 420)
Report of the High Level Panel on Threats, Challenges and Change "A More Secure World: Our Shared Responsibility" (2004) (United Nations)
Richards, A. (2014) Conceptualizing Terrorism, *Studies in Conflict & Terrorism*, 37(3), 213–236
Richards, J. (2016) Needles in Haystacks: Law, Capability, Ethics, and Proportionality, in Big Data Intelligence-Gathering, in Bunnik, A., Cawley, A., Mulqueen, M. and Zwitter, A. (eds) *Big Data Challenges* (Palgrave Macmillan)
Rifkin, J. (2004) *The European Dream: How Europe's Vision of the Future is Quietly Eclipsing the American Dream* (Polity Press)
Roberts, A. (2015) Privacy, Data Retention and Domination: *Digital Rights Ireland Ltd v Minister for Communications*, *The Modern Law Review*, 78(3), 522–548
Robins, R. S. and Post, J. M. (1997) *Political Paranoia: The Psychopolitics of Hatred* (Yale University Press)
Rosendorff, P. and Sandler, T. (2010) Suicide Terrorism and the Backlash Effect, *Defence and Peace Economics*, 21(5–6), 443–457
Royal United Services Institute (RUSI) (2015) A Democratic Licence to Operate: Report of the Independent Surveillance Review Panel of the Independent Surveillance Review *Whitehall Reports*, 13 July 2015, available at https://rusi.org/publication/whitehall-reports/democratic-licence-operate-report-independent-surveillance-review, paragraph 3.16, accessed 13 March 2018
Rudner, M. (2006) Using Financial Intelligence against the Funding of Terrorism, *International Journal of Intelligence and CounterIntelligence*, 19(1), 32–58
Rudner, M. (2010) Hizbullah Terrorism Finance: Fund-Raising and Money-Laundering, *Studies in Conflict & Terrorism*, 33, 700–715
Rusbridger, A. (2013) David Miranda, Schedule 7 and the Danger that All Reporters Now Face, *Guardian*, 19 August 2013, available at http://www.theguardian.com/commentisfree/2013/aug/19/david-miranda-schedule7-danger-reporters accessed 30 March 2018

Ryder, N. (2007) A False Sense of Security? An Analysis of Legislative Approaches Towards the Prevention of Terrorist Finance in the United States and the United Kingdom, *Journal of Business Law*, November, 821–850

Sageman, M. (2008) *Leaderless Jihad: Terror Networks in the Twenty-First Century*, (University of Philadelphia Press)Sanchez-Cuenca, J. (2007) The Dynamics of National Terrorism: ETA and the IRA, *Terrorism and Political Violence*, 19(3), 289–306

Saner, E. (2015) Brits Abroad: Is It Against the Law to Fight ISIS?, *Guardian*, 25 February 2015, available at https://www.theguardian.com/world/shortcuts/2015/feb/25/brits-abroad-against-law-fight-isis accessed 30 March 2018

Santora, M. and Goldman, A. (2016) Ahmad Khan Rahami Was Inspired by Bin Laden, Charges Say, *New York Times*, 21 September 2016, available at http://www.nytimes.com/2016/09/21/nyregion/ahmad-khan-rahami-suspect.html accessed 30 March 2018

Santora, M., Rashbaum, W. K., Baker, A. and Goldman, A. (2016) Ahmad Khan Rahami is Arrested in Manhattan and New Jersey Bombings, *New York Times*, 19 September 2016, available at http://www.nytimes.com/2016/09/20/nyregion/nyc-nj-explosions-ahmad-khan-rahami.html?_r=0 accessed 30 March 2018

Sarma, K. (2005) Informers and the Battle against Republican Terrorism: A Review of 30 Years of Conflict, *Police Practice and Research: An International Journal*, 6(2), 165–180

Satana, N. S., Inman, M. and Birnir, J. K. (2013) Religion, Government Coalitions, and Terrorism, *Terrorism and Political Violence*, 25(1), 29–52

Saul, B. (2008) Defining 'Terrorism' to Protect Human Rights, *Sydney Law School, Legal Studies Research Paper No. 8–125*, 190–210

Saul, B. (2010) *Defining Terrorism in International Law* (Oxford University Press)Schmid, A. P. (2004) Frameworks for Conceptualising Terrorism, *Terrorism and Political Violence*, 16(2), 197–221

Schmid, A. P. (2011) *The Definition of Terrorism: The Routledge Handbook of Terrorism Research* (Routledge)

Schmid, A. P. (2013) *Radicalisation, De-Radicalisation, Counter-Radicalisation: A Conceptual Discussion and Literature Review* (International Centre for Counter-Terrorism –The Hague (ICCT))

Schmid, A. P. and Jongman, A. J. (1988) *Political Terrorism: A New Guide to Actors, Authors, Concepts, Data Bases, Theories, and Literature* (Transaction Publishers)

Schulhofer, S. J., Tyler, T. R. and Huq, A. Z. (2011) American Policing at a Crossroads: Unsustainable Policies and the Procedural Justice Alternative, *Journal of Criminal Law & Criminology*, 101(2), 335–374

Sedgwick, M. (2010) The Concept of Radicalisation as a Source of Confusion, *Terrorism and Political Violence*, 22(4), 0–0

Seib, P. (2012) Public Diplomacy versus Terrorism, *Media & Terrorism*, 14(3), 63–76

Semitsu, J. (2011) From Facebook to Mug Shot: How the Death of Social Networking Privacy Rights Revolutionized Online Government Surveillance, *Pace Law Review*, 31 (1), 291–381

Sharma, S. and MacDonald, A. (2016) British Volunteers in Syrian Kurd Forces are 'Terrorists', Turkey Says. *Middle East Eye*, 1 September 2016, available at http://www.middleeasteye.net/news/turkey-british-ypg-terrorist-syria-874419624 accessed 30 March 2018

Sheptycki, J. (2007) High Policing in the Security Control Society, *Policing*, 1(1), 25–37

Silber, M. D. and Bhatt, A. (2007) *Radicalisation in the West: The Homegrown Threat* (Police Department, Intelligence Division, New York)

Silke, A. (2008) Holy Warriors: Exploring the Psychological Processes of Jihadi Radicalisation, *European Journal of Criminology*, 5(1), 99–123

Simmons, C. H. and Mitch, J. R. (2001) Labelling Public Aggression: When is It Terrorism?, *The Journal of Social Psychology*, 125(2), 245–251

Smith, R. (1998) Criminal Exploitation of New Technologies, Australian Institute of Criminology, *Trends & Issues in Crime and Criminal Justice*, 93 (1),), 221–234

Sorell, T. (2011) Preventive Policing, Surveillance, and European Counter-Terrorism, *Criminal Justice Ethics*, 30(1), 1–22

Sottiaux, S. (2008) *Terrorism and the Limitation of Rights: The ECHR and the US Constitution* (Hart Publishing)

Sparago, M. (2007) *Terrorist Recruitment: The Crucial Case of Al Qaeda's Global Jihad Terror Network*, Center for Global Affairs, New York University, Spring, 1–56, available at http://citeseerx.ist.psu.edu/viewdoc/download;jsessionid=44D6656867332A2F925 2E59AEE771C9E?doi=10.1.1.488.1211&rep=rep1&type=pdf accessed 28 March 2018

Sparrow, A. Gabbat, A. and Quinn, B. (2013) Reactions to the Detention of David Miranda at Heathrow Airport – as It Happened, *Guardian*, 20 August 2013, available at http://www.theguardian.com/politics/blog/2013/aug/19/glenn-greenwald-partner-detained-live-reaction accessed 30 March 2018

Spigelman, J. (2010) The Forgotten Freedom: Freedom from Fear, *International & Comparative Law Quarterly*, 59(3), 543–570

Stone, J. (2016) ISIS Terrorists Used Disposable Burner Phones, Activated Just Hours Before, to Carry Out Paris Attacks, *International Business Times*, 21 March 2016, available at http://www.ibtimes.com/isis-terrorists-used-disposable-burner-phones-activa ted-just-hours-carry-out-paris-2340265 accessed 30 March 2018

Syrett, K. (2011) *The Foundations of Public Law, Principles and Problems of Power in the British Constitution* (Palgrave Macmillan)

Taheri, A. (1987) *Holy Terror: The Inside Story of Islamic Terrorism* (Sphere Books Ltd)

Taylor, J. (2010) Police Smash Romanian 'Child Trafficking Ring', *Independent*, 12 October 2010, available at http://www.independent.co.uk/news/uk/crime/poli ce-smash-romanian-child-trafficking-ring-2104694.html accessed 5 December 2016

Taylor, R. W., Caeti, T. J. D., Loper, K., Fritsch, E. J. and Liederbach, J. (2006) *Digital Crime and Digital Terrorism* (Pearson Education)

The Royal United Services Institute (RUSI) (2015)*A Democratic Licence to Operate: Report of the Independent Surveillance Review Panel of the Independent Surveillance Review*, Whitehall Reports, 13 July 2015, available at https://rusi.org/publication/whitehall-reports/democratic-licence-operate-report-independent-surveillance-review accessed 13 March 2018

The Rt. Hon. Dominic Grieve QC MP (2016) *Intelligence and Security Committee of Parliament, Report on the Draft Investigatory Powers Bill*, 9 February 2013, HC 795

The Rt. Hon Lord Lloyd of Berwick (1996) *Inquiry into Legislation against Terrorism*, Volume One (The Stationary Office, Cm3420)

The Rt. Hon. Sir Malcolm Rifkind MP (2013) *Intelligence and Security Committee, Access to Communications Data by the Intelligence and Security Agencies*, February 2013, Cm8514

The Rt. Hon. Sir Malcolm Rifkind MP (2014) *Report on the Intelligence Relating to the Murder of Fusilier Lee Rigby*, Intelligence and Security Committee of Parliament, HC 795, 2014Thomson, T. (2010) Crime Software May Help Police Predict Violent Offences, *Guardian*, 25 July 2010, available at http://www.guardian.co.uk/uk/2010/jul/25/police-software-crime-prediction accessed 30 March 2018

Thynne, K. (2009) Targeting the 'Terrorist Enemy': The Boundaries of an Armed Conflict against Transnational Terrorists, *Australian International Law Journal*, 161–187

Titcomb, J. (2016) World's Internet Traffic to Surpass One Zettabyte in 2016, *Telegraph*, 4 February 2016, available at http://www.telegraph.co.uk/technology/2016/02/04/worlds-internet-traffic-to-surpass-one-zettabyte-in-2016 accessed 30 March 2018

Tomkins, A. (2010) National Security and the Role of the Court: A Changed Landscape?, *Law Quarterly Review*, 126, 543–567

Travis, T. (2015) Snowden Leak: Governments' Hostile Reaction Fuelled Public Distrust of Spies, *Guardian*, 15 June 2015, available at https://www.theguardian.com/world/2015/jun/15/snowden-files-us-uk-government-hostile-reaction-distrust-spies accessed 30 March 2018

Travis, A., Asthana, A. and Chrisafis, A. (2016) UK and France Restate Commitment to Border Treaty after Calais Talks, *Guardian*, 30 August 2016, available at https://www.theguardian.com/world/2016/aug/30/uk-plays-down-calais-border-tensions-with-critical-ally-france accessed 30 March 2018

Trottier, D. (2012) *Social Media as Surveillance: Rethinking Visibility in a Converging World* (Ashgate Publishing)

Trottier, D. (2015) Open Source Intelligence, Social Media and Law Enforcement: Visions, Constraints and Critiques, *European Journal of Cultural Studies*, 18(4–5), 530–547

Tsukayama, H., Berman, M. and Markon, J. (2016) Terror in Orlando: 50 Killed in Shooting Rampage at Gay Club, Gunman Pledged Allegiance to ISIS, *Washington Post*, 13 June 2016, available at https://www.washingtonpost.com/news/post-nation/wp/2016/06/12/orlando-nightclub-shooting-about-20-dead-in-domestic-terror-incident-at-gay-club/?hpid=hp_hp-top-table-high_orlando-banner%3Ahomepage%2Fstory&utm_term=.8adec967a5ff accessed 30 March 2018

Tuman, J.S. (2010) *Communicating Terror: The Rhetorical Dimensions of Terrorism* (2nd Edition, Sage)

Turner, I. (2011) The Prevention of Terrorism: In Support of Control Orders, and Beyond, *Northern Ireland Law Quarterly*, 62(3), 355–359

Tzanakopoulos, A. (2013) *The Solange Argument as a Justification for Disobeying the Security Council: Countermeasures against Wrongful Sanctions* (Oxford University Press)

Tzanou. M. (2015) The War Against Terror and Transatlantic Information Sharing: Spillovers of Privacy or Spillovers of Security?, *Utrecht Journal of International and European Law*, 31(80), 87–103

United Nations General Assembly (1996a) Resolution 51/210 of 17 December 1996, Sixth session (28 January–1 February 2002), Annex II, art. 2.1

United Nations General Assembly (1996b)Resolution 51/210 of 17 December 1996, Sixth session (28 January–1 February 2002), Annex IV, art. 18

United Nations General Assembly (1994) Resolution 49/60: Declaration on Measures to Eliminate International Terrorism A/Res/60/49

United Nations General Assembly (2001) Resolution 55/25: United Nations Convention Against Transnational Organised Crime A/Res/55/2

United Nations Security Council (2004) Resolution 1566: Threats to International Peace and Security Caused by Terrorist Acts S/RES/1566

Van Wasshnova, M. R. (2008) Data Protection Conflicts Between the United States and the European Union in the War on Terror: Lessons Learned from the Existing System of Financial Information Exchange, Case Western Reserve, *Journal of International Law*, 39(3), 827–865.

Vaughan, B. and Kilcommins, S. (2008) *Terrorism, Rights and the Rule of Law* (Willan)

Vaughan-Nicols, S. (2013) Raytheon Riot: Defence Spying is Coming to Social Networks, ZDNet, 12 February 2013, available at http://www.zdnet.com/raytheon-riot-defense-spying-is-coming-to-social-networks 7000011191 accessed 30 March 2018
Vermeulen, F. (2014) Suspect Communities – Targeting Violent Extremism at the Local Level, *Terrorism and Political Violence*, 26(2), 286–306
Vilasau, M. (2007) Traffic Data Retention v Data Protection: The New European Framework, *Computer and Telecommunications Law Review*, 13(2), 52–58
Wade, M. L. (2014) The European Union as a Counter-Terrorism Actor: Right Path, Wrong Direction?, *Crime, Law and Social Change*, 62, 355–383
Walen, A. (2011) Criminalising Statements of Terrorist Intent: How to Understand the Law Governing Terrorist Threats, and Why It should be Used Instead of Long Term Preventative Detention, *The Journal of Criminal Law & Criminology*, 101(3), 803–854
Wang, Y. R. and Lumb, R. (2012) Integrating Eastern Programme Features in Western Community Policing: Balancing Individual Freedom and Collective Wellbeing, *International Journal of Police Science and Management*, 14(4), 343–361
Walker, C. (2007) The Legal Definition of "Terrorism" in United Kingdom Law and Beyond, *Public Law*, 331–352
Walker, C. (2008a) Terrorism: Terrorism Act 2000 s.57 – Direction to Jury on Defence of Possession of Items for Defensive Purposes, Case Comment, *Criminal Law Review*, 72–80
Walker, C. (2008b) Know Thine Enemy as Thyself: Discerning Friend from Foe under Anti-Terrorism Laws, *Melbourne University Law Review*, 32, 275–301
Walker, C. (2008c) Terrorism: Terrorism Act 2000 ss. 1 and 58 – Possession of Terrorist Documents, Case Comment, *Criminal Law Review*, 160–165
Walker, C. (2009) *Blackstone's Guide to the Anti-Terrorism Legislation* (2nd Edition, Oxford University Press)
Walker, C. (2010) Conscripting the Public in Terrorism Policing: Towards Safer Communities or a Police State?, *Criminal Law Review*, 441–456
Walker, C. (2011) The Judicialisation of Intelligence in Legal Process, *Public Law*, 235–237
Walker, C. (2012) The Terrorism Prevention and Investigation Measures Act 2011: One Thing but not Much the Other?, *Criminal Law Review*, 6, 421–438
Walker, C. (2013) The Reshaping of Control Orders in the United Kingdom: Time for a Fairer Go, Australia, *Melbourne University Law Review*, 37(1)
Wardlow, G. (2002) *Political Terrorism* (2nd Edition, Cambridge University Press)
Watt, N. (2013) PRISM Scandal: European Commission to Seek Privacy Guarantees from U.S., *Guardian*, 10 June 2013, available at http://www.theguardian.com/world/2013/jun/10/prism-european-commissions-privacy-guarantees accessed 30 March 2018
Weenink, A. W. (2012) Situational Prevention of Terrorism. Remarks from the Field of Counterterrorism in the Netherlands on Newman and Clarke's 'Policing Terrorism, *Trends in Organised Crime*, 15, 164–179
Welch, J. and Chakrabarti, S. (2010) The War on Terror without the Human Rights Act – What Difference has It Made?, *European Human Rights Law Review*, (6), 593–600
Whitman, J. Q. (2004) The Two Western Cultures of Privacy: Dignity versus Liberty, *Yale Law Journal*, 113, 1151–1179, available at http://digitalcommons.law.yale.edu/fss_papers/649 accessed 30 March 2018
Whittaker, D. (2012) *The Terrorism Reader* (4th Edition, Routledge)
Wilkinson, P. (2006) *Terrorism versus Democracy: The Liberal State Response* (2nd Edition, Routledge)

Williams, C. (2011) London Riots: BlackBerry Manufacturer Offers to Help Police, *Telegraph*, 8 August 2011, available at http://www.telegraph.co.uk/technology/blackberry/8689313/London-riots-BlackBerry-manufacturer-offers-to-help-police-in-any-way-we-can.html accessed 30 March 2018

Williamson, M. (2009) *Terrorism, War and International Law: The Legality of the Use of Force against Afghanistan in 2001* (Ashgate Publishing)

Willsher, K. (2016) Powerful Tributes at Funeral of Priest Killed in France Terrorist Attack, *Guardian*, 2 August 2016, available at https://www.theguardian.com/world/2016/aug/02/thousands-expected-funeral-priest-killed-in-france-terror-attack accessed 30 March 2018

Wintour, P. (2015) UK Parents to Get Power to Cancel Children's Passports over ISIS Fears, *Guardian*, 20 July 2015, available at https://www.theguardian.com/politics/2015/jul/20/uk-parents-power-cancel-childrens-passports-isis-fears accessed 24 November 2016

Wynn, K. and Blyth, K. (2011) Predicting a Riot: At What Price Privacy?, Practical Law Company, available at http://uk.practicallaw.com/9-507-6354 accessed 28 March 2018

Xhelili, B. (2012) Privacy & Terrorism Review: Where Have We Come in 10 Years?, *Journal of International Commercial Law and Technology*, 7(2), 121–135

Young, D. (1999) *Origins of the Sacred: The Ecstasies of Love and War* (St. Martin's Press)

Zedner, L. (2007) Pre-Crime and Post-Criminology?, *Theoretical Criminology*, 11(2), 720–741

Zeidan, S. (2004) Desperately Seeking Definition: The International Community's Quest for Identifying the Specter of Terrorism, *Cornell International Law Journal*, 36(3), 491–496

Zhou, H.-R. (2013) Revisiting the "Manner and Form" Theory of Parliamentary Sovereignty, *The Law Quarterly Review*, 129, 610–638

Zimmerman, M. (2015) Darknet Danger: Organs, Murder, Credit Card Info All for Sale on Internet's Underbelly, *Fox News*, available at http://www.foxnews.com/tech/2015/04/23/darknet-danger-organs-murder-credit-card-info-all-for-sale-on-internet.html accessed 30 March 2018

Zwitter, A. (1998) The Anatomy of Ideology: An Analysis of the Structure of Ideology and the Mobilisation of Terrorist (Human Security) *HUMSEC Journal*, (1), 30–46

Index

A and others v Secretary of State for the Home Department 4, 30
Abedi, Salman 159
accountability 64, 66, 129, 130; use of OSINT and SOCMINT 76
Ackerman, B. 107–8
Adebowale, Michael 85, 93
Advanced Passenger Information (API) 146, 147
Afghanistan 36, 37, 40, 42, 148
Al-Shabaab 23
algorithmic screening 78, 104, 105–6, 125, 157–8
Amazon 51
Anagnostakis, D. 150
Anderson, David 13–14, 21, 26, 29, 30, 33, 66, 75, 80, 82, 132
animal rights/liberation groups 27, 28
anonymity software 8
anti-abortion groups 27
Anti-Terrorism, Crime and Security Act 2001 4
anticipatory offences 107
anticipatory risk 106, 107
Apple 72, 86–7, 133; iMessage 50, 54; iPhone 54; Pay 54
applications service providers (ASPs) 52, 59
Argomaniz, J. 138
Armond, D. 131, 145–6, 147
asylum 16
attempt, threshold for 14
Australia 151; definition of terrorism 17, 18, 27, 32
Austria 120
al-Baghdadi, Abu Bakr (also known as Awwad Ibrahim Ali al-Badri al-Samarrai) 45

Ban Ki-moon 56
banks 54, 72; online banking 51
Bartow, A. 78
Beck, U. 105, 106
Berger, J. M. 48
Bernal, P. 71
Boer, M. D. 138–9
Bouhlel, Mohamed Lahouaiej 94
Breivik, Anders Behring 57, 94
Brexit 125, 126–7, 131, 136, 137–8, 154–5, 158; EU counterterrorism: security and intelligence 138–9; European Arrest Warrant 140–2, 145, 154; Europol 141, 142–5, 148, 154; lessons from Swiss model 139, 140, 155; Passenger Name Record data 137, 146–53, 154; Schengen Information System (SIS) 145–6, 154; UK's exit position 139
Britain First 95
Brown, C. S. D. 52, 57
bulk communications data surveillance 4, 9, 10, 60–2, 96, 111, 125, 157; broad powers with restricted use and access: evidence of necessity 84–6; bulk acquisition warrants, power to issue (s 158) 63, 68; bulk equipment interference 4, 9, 10, 28–9, 82–6, 96; bulk interception warrants (s 136) 63, 66–8, 80; bulk personal datasets (s 199) 63, 87–9; bulk powers: rationale 63–4, 90, 159; case studies 89–96; definition: content (s 261 (6) IPA) 65–6; definition: electronic communications data (RIPA) 64–5; end of encryption: national security and technical capability notices 86–7; freedom of expression 27–9; Internet connection records (ICRs) *see separate entry*; level of authorisation 69; service use information 69; subscriber information 69; traffic data 69; type of data: access and procedure 68–9

bulk equipment interference 4, 9, 10, 28–9, 82–3, 96; broad powers with restricted use and access: evidence of necessity 84–6; Code of Practice 82–3, 84; 'legalised hacking' 83–4; overseas operations 82
Bures, O. 138
Burnham, Andy 70
Bush, George W. 42

Cameron, David 26, 58, 103
Canada 142, 151; definition of terrorism 17, 18, 27, 29, 31–2, 36; *R v Khawaja* 36; *R v Spencer* 131
Cantlie, John 46
capabilities gap 7, 53, 54, 57, 63, 70, 158; privacy and 2–3
Carlile, Lord 29–30, 39, 99
Carter, D. L. 91
Carter, G. 91
Catholics, Irish and Irish descent 25
CCTV 61, 88, 105
Chakrabarti, Shami 129
Charter of Fundamental Rights of the European Union 7, 102, 120, 121–2, 126–7; Art 2: right to life 2; Art 7: private and family life 118, 120, 121–2, 131, 160; Art 8: protection of personal data 3, 114, 115, 118, 120, 121–2, 126, 158, 160; Art 19: expulsion 103; Art 45: freedom of movement and of residence 99–100; Art 52(1): scope of guaranteed rights 120
chat apps 50, 55–6
child abuse 72, 90
Choudary, Anjem 49, 77–8
Clapper, James 74
Clarke, Charles 33, 110
Clarke, R. 73
'cloud' systems 54, 65–6, 83
Coco, A. 35, 37
collection of information offence (TA 2000, s 58) 107, 108, 111–12
College of Policing 77
Comay, M. 20
communication methods of terrorists 44–6, 58–9, 156; attributing the communication 52–3; darknet 49, 51–2, 56–8, 59; emails 50, 51; encryption 50, 53–4, 55, 57, 84; Facebook 46, 49, 50, 52, 55; hashtags and followers 50; Instagram 50, 55; Internet companies' software targets terrorist material 49; Internet structure 51–2; IP addresses 52–3; media ministry, IS 46–7; messaging applications/chat apps 50, 55–6; multilingual propaganda 46, 47; networked social media campaign 50; online Islamist magazines 46, 47–8, 55, 85–6; smartphones 50–1, 52, 54, 59; Twitter 46, 48–9, 50, 52, 77; videos 46, 47, 49; YouTube 46, 49, 77
communications service providers (CSPs) 52, 53, 68
community relations: religious cause 24–5
computer network exploitation 82–4
CONTEST policy: Prevent strategies 24
control, culture of 105
Convention on the Prevention of Terrorism 108
convictions in UK for terrorist-related acts 25
corruption 72
Counter-Terrorism and Security Act 2015 (CTSA) 24, 106; IP addresses 52–3; seizure of passports and travel documents 99; temporary exclusion orders 101
Court of Justice of the European Union 3, 126, 136, 144, 147, 158; *Digital Rights Ireland* 3, 4, 8, 113, 120–1, 122, 124, 126–7, 147, 158; *Ireland v European Parliament and European Commission* 118, 120; PNR agreements between EU and US 150, 151, 152; *Schrems v Data Protection Commissioner* 134, 147, 148; temporary exclusion orders 103
courts: access to retained data 120, 122, 126, 127; judicial review *see separate entry*; judiciary *see separate entry*; temporary exclusion orders 101–2, 103
Cox, Jo 95
Crime (International Co-operation) Act 2003 38
criterion, digital rights 8, 125–6, 127–31
Crown Prosecution Service (CPS) 107; discretionary power to prosecute 40–1
cyber security 72
cybercrime 2, 55, 56, 57–8, 84, 143; equipment interference 86–7; ICR databases 72

Dabiq 46, 47–8, 85–6
darknet 2, 44, 49, 51–2, 56–8, 59, 92, 157, 160; onion routing 56
data mining 78, 96, 115, 157–8
data protection 3, 80, 81, 87, 88, 113–14, 115, 117, 126–7, 136, 158; Brexit 125,

142, 144, 154, 155, 158; Data Retention Directive (2006) 119; Directive (1995) 3, 114, 115, 116, 134, 149, 150, 153, 158; Passenger Name Record data 146, 149–50, 153; policing cooperation: EU and US intelligence 154
data retention 105, 116–17, 136, 144; criteria for new law 8, 125–6, 127–31; Data Retention Directive (2006) 4, 116, 117–23; *Digital Rights Ireland* 3, 4, 8, 113, 120–1, 122, 124, 126–7, 147, 158; European Court of Human Rights 123–5, 158; time limits 8, 9, 104, 105, 119, 125, 126, 151, 152
Data Retention (EC Directive) Regulations 2009 (SI 2009/859) 116, 121, 122
Data Retention and Investigatory Powers Act 2014 (DRIPA) 4, 121–3, 126; sunset clause 121
Davis, David 129
de Hert, P. 151
decryption 3, 111; instant messaging 8, 54, 59; Investigatory Powers Act 2016 60, 84, 86
deep/invisible web 51–2
definition of terrorism 6–7, 11–12, 156; causes 15, 17–29; concept of terrorism 12–14; discretionary power to prosecute 40–1; extra-jurisdictional effect of UK law 33–40; firearms 15, 32–3, 95; freedom of expression and causes 27–9; freedom fighter defence 34–40, 41, 42; ideological cause 15, 18, 19, 21, 26–7, 29; political cause 15, 17, 18, 19–25; political value of terrorism 41–2; racial cause 15, 18, 19, 21; religious cause 15, 18, 19, 21–7; social cause 17–18; suggested 42–3; target 15; threshold of influence 29–33; use or threat of action 15
democracy, danger to 13
dictatorships 33–4, 39
Digital Rights Ireland 3, 4, 8, 113, 120–1, 122, 124, 126–7, 147, 158
dignity 149
direct messaging 2, 55, 80
Director of Public Prosecutions (DPP) 40–1
discretionary power to prosecute 40–1
discrimination, freedom from 88
dissemination of terrorist publications offence (TA 2006, s 2) 27–9, 108, 110–11
DNA samples 123–4
'double-lock' system 9, 62, 69, 128, 129, 136
dual nationality 103
due process 41, 99

eco-terrorism 27
Edwards, L. 78–9, 80
emails 50, 51, 65, 74, 76, 81, 90, 114
EMOTIVE project 77, 78
encouragement of terrorism offence (TA 2006, s 1) 27–9, 108–10; glorification 109–10
encryption 2, 50, 53–4, 90, 95, 159, 160; darknet 57; end-to-end 54, 55, 84; equipment interference 84, 86–7; national security and technical capability notices: end of 86–7; self-starting terrorist 92; in transit 54
Eurojust 117, 141, 148, 154
European Arrest Warrant 140–2, 145, 154
European Convention on Human Rights 1950 (ECHR) 7, 36, 102, 107; Art 2: right to life 2, 125, 136, 160; Art 7: retroactivity 107; Art 8: private and family life 3, 85, 111, 123–5, 131, 134, 158, 160; Art 10: freedom of expression 27–9, 107, 109–10, 111, 125
European Court of Human Rights (ECtHR) 3, 5, 136, 144, 158; data retention 123–5, 158
European Union 17, 36, 87, 90, 96, 98, 136, 137–9; Brexit *see separate entry*; Charter of Fundamental Rights of the *see separate entry*; Commission 119, 134, 144, 149, 150, 152; Court of Justice of the *see separate entry*; Data Protection Directive (1995) 3, 114, 115, 116, 134, 149, 150, 153, 158; data retention 4, 116–23, 136; Data Retention Directive (2006) 4, 116, 117–23; definition of terrorism 18, 28, 29, 30–1, 33, 35; e-Privacy Directive (2002) 3, 76, 114–16, 118, 119, 126, 158; Framework Decision: personal data (2008) 115; Parliament 118, 144, 150, 151, 152, 153; PNR agreements with US 148–53; PNR Directive (2016) 146–7; policing cooperation with US 153–4; Schengen Area 117, 145–6; Snowden revelations 133, 134, 135; transformational trends 117; Treaty of Lisbon 115, 150, 152; Virtuoso OSINT software 75

Europol 56, 57, 117, 141, 142–5, 148, 154, 159
Evans, Lord 63–4
evidence 55
exclusion orders, temporary 101–2; international status 102–4
extra-jurisdictional effect of UK law 33–40, 86
extradition 16, 140–2, 148

Facebook 46, 49, 52, 74, 76, 78, 133, 134; analysis of 'Likes' 78–9; Messenger 50, 55; police 77; users posting notice re-affirming privacy 79
far-right extremism 95, 159
fear, culture of 105
fingerprints database 123–4
firearms 15, 32–3, 56–7, 59, 81, 95, 141; military training 98
Flickr 76–7
foreign fighters *see* Islamist terrorist training and fighting
fragmentation 53
France 17, 45–6, 47, 55, 94, 95, 143, 159
freedom of expression 107, 109–10, 111, 125; and definition of terrorism 27–9
freedom fighter defence 34–40, 41, 42
Frontex 154
Furedi, F. 105

Gale, C. J. S. 7, 41
Ganor, B. 16, 20
Garland, D. 105
Gartenstein-Ross, D. 91–2
Gearty, C. 108
Geneva Conventions: 1977 Additional Protocol I 34; Fourth 37
Germany 134; jihadi tourism 104; Red Brigades 19
Gillespie, A. 75
Gilmore, G. 150
glorification 109–10
Gmail 51
Google 49, 51, 52, 55, 57, 74, 79, 133
Goold, B. J. 131
Government Communication Head-quarters (GCHQ) 55, 58, 66, 68, 83, 84, 89, 130; Snowden revelations 132–5
Graham, R. 53–4
Greenwald, G. 133, 134
Grieve, Dominic 62, 130
Grossman, L. 91–2
Guild, E. 142, 144

Hacker, F. J. 13, 33
hacking 55, 72, 87; bulk equipment interference: 'legalised' 83–4
Haggerty, K. 73
Hague, William 133
hashes 49
Hashman and Harrup v United Kingdom 41
hashtags 50
health records 88
Hijmans, H. 116
Hillyard, P. 25
home-grown terrorists 90, 144; lone-actor terrorist 93–6, 98, 159; self-starting terrorist 92–3, 95–6, 98; traceability and typecasting 91–2
Hopkins, N. 133
hostage taking 30
Hotmail 51
human rights 9, 69, 127, 132–3, 150, 154; dignity 149; European Convention on *see separate entry*; European Court of 3, 5, 123–5, 136, 144, 158; privacy *see separate entry*; state counterterrorism and surveillance powers v 3–4; use of OSINT and SOCMINT 76; *see also* Charter of Fundamental Rights of the European Union
Human Rights Act 1998 36, 124

IBM Predictive system 77
iCloud server 54
identity 25
ideological cause 15, 18, 19, 21, 29; religious or 26–7
Ilbiz, E. 150
iMessage 50, 54
Imran, A. 108
inchoate offences 14
inciting terrorism offence (TA 2000, s 59) 108, 109
industrial action 27, 29, 30, 32, 42, 43
informants 61
Ingram, H. J. 48–9
Instagram 50, 55
instant messaging 50; decryption 8, 54, 59; London riots (2011) 76; Telegram 55, 95
Intelligence Services Act 1994 (ISA) 61, 84, 130; equipment interference warrants 83
intelligence-led policing 75, 93, 106
Interception of Communications Act 1985 (ICA) 68

international armed conflict 34, 36–7, 38, 42
International Convention for the Suppression of the Financing of Terrorism (1999) 34
International Convention for the Suppression of Terrorist Bombings (1997) 34
international criminal law 37
international humanitarian law 37, 40; 1977 Additional Protocol I to 1949 Geneva Conventions 34
international law 13; customary 27, 42; definition of terrorism 11, 12, 15–16, 27, 29, 34, 35, 37, 39–40, 42–3; statelessness 102–3
Internet connection records (ICRs) 105; definition and controversy 70–2; and open source intelligence: privacy conundrum 73–81; vulnerabilities 72
Internet service providers (ISPs) 52, 59, 86–7, 157
Internet structure 51–2
Interpol 142
Investigatory Powers Act 2016 (IPA) 2–3, 5, 8, 9, 10, 27–9, 59, 60, 61–2, 106, 107, 111, 112, 157–8; balance between individual privacy and collective security 126–9, 130, 131, 134–6; Brexit 144, 155; bulk acquisition warrants, power to issue (s 158) 63, 68; bulk equipment interference (s 176) 63, 82; bulk interception warrants (s 136) 63, 66–8; bulk personal datasets (s 199) 87; bulk powers: general rationale 63–4; definition: content (s 261(6)) 65–6; 'double-lock' system 9, 62, 69, 128, 129, 136; EU law 87, 126; Internet connection records (ICRs) 70–1; national security notices 84, 86; necessity 85; OSINT and SOCMINT data 79–80, 96; proportionality 85; removal of electronic protection (s 253) 8; technical capabilities notices 84, 86–7
Investigatory Powers Commissioner 9, 62, 68–9, 126, 128, 136
invisible/deep web 51–2
IP addresses 52–3, 69, 71
Iraq 33, 37, 38, 40, 44, 45, 46, 49, 97, 98
Ireland 87, 120
Irish Republican Army (IRA) 1, 19–20
Islamic State (IS) 4, 6, 14, 44–6, 74, 77, 90, 94; caliphate 23, 45, 46; communications *see* communication methods of terrorists; definition of terrorism 21, 23, 25, 26, 33; foreign fighters 98; Kurdish forces fighting 38–9; recruitment 47, 50
Islamist magazines, online 46, 47–8, 55, 85–6
Islamist terror threat 16–17, 24, 89
Islamist terrorist training and fighting 97–101; seizure of passports and travel documents 99–101; temporary exclusion orders 101–4
Islamophobia 24

Jabhat Fatah al-Sham (formerly al-Nusra) 23–4
Jenni, S. 139, 140
jihadi tourism 91–101; seizure of passports and travel documents 99–101; temporary exclusion orders 101–4
Jihadology website 46
Johnson, Boris 138
Joint Operations Cell (JOC) 58
Jones, A. 109
judicial commissioners 62, 68–9, 86, 113, 128–9, 136
judicial review 9, 96, 112, 113, 128, 136; seizure of passport 101
judiciary 34, 35, 107; challenge Act of Parliament 36; executive and 5, 30; independence 9, 96, 112, 129, 136
Juncker, Jean-Claude 140, 155
Justice and Security Act 2013 130

Karim, Rajib 53
Katz, R. 50
Kaunert, C. 138, 148, 150, 151
Kearney, J. 141, 143
Keenan, B. 129
Kermiche, Adel 95
Khan v UK 68
King, Eric 66–7
Klass v Germany 124
Klausen, J. 46
Kurdistan Workers' Party (PKK) 38–9

landline calls 50, 53
Lehrke, J. P. 152
Leutheusser-Schnarrenberger, Sabine 134
Lewis, Brandon 143
Lewis, Julian 24
Liberty 9, 128, 134–5, 136
Libya 97
life, right to 1–2, 3, 81, 125, 136, 159, 160
Lloyd of Berwick, Lord 16, 17–18, 21, 29
Loader, I. 142

London attacks 46, 118
London riots (2011) 74, 76
lone-actor terrorist 93–6, 98, 159
Lotus case (PCIJ) 37
Lowe, D. 149, 152
Lynskey, O. 88

McKeever, D. 14, 34–5
magazines, online Islamist 46, 47–8, 55, 85–6
Mair, Thomas 95
Martin, A. J. 83
mass data surveillance 105, 111, 125
Mateen, Omar 94
May, Sir Thomas Erskine 132
May, Theresa 70, 71, 121, 131
Merkel, Angela 134
MI5 64, 80–1, 83, 84, 85, 88–9, 90, 130; Behavioural Science Unit (BSU) 90; priority levels 92–3; Subjects of Interest: tier system 93
MI6/Secret Intelligence Service 68, 83, 84, 130
Microsoft 133
Milton, D. 46
Minority Report 106
missing trader intra-community (MTIC) fraud 89
Mitsilegas, V. 117
Morgan, J. 48
al-Muhajiroun 77
Murphy, C. C. 117, 150, 151
Murray, A. 129
Muslim community 24–5

National Action 95
National Crime Agency (NCA) 58, 81, 131, 145–6
national security notices 84, 86
necessity 66, 68, 69, 120, 132; bulk communications data surveillance 84–6, 128, 136; use of OSINT and SOCMINT 76
Netanyahu, B. 36
Neumann, P. R. 26
non-international armed conflicts 34–40
Northern Ireland 17, 20
Norway 94

O'Floinn, M. 79–80
Ogilvie, Sara 128
Omand, D. 76
open source intelligence and Internet connection records (ICRs): privacy conundrum 73–81, 96, 135
Optic Nerve 66
Ormerod, D. 79–80
Osman, Hussain 141
over-the-top (OTT) providers 53

Pantazis, C. 22, 25
Pantucci, R. 26
Papakonstantinou, V. 151
Paraguay 143
Parliament 4, 5, 9, 12, 27, 39, 61–2, 96, 112, 130–1, 136, 159; Home Affairs Select Committee 73, 131, 136; House of Lords EU Committee 153; Intelligence and Security Committee 62, 74, 81, 85, 90, 92–3, 98, 130, 136; Joint Committee of House of Lords and House of Commons on Human Rights 29, 109–11; sovereignty 35–6
Pascal, Blaise 23
Passenger Name Record data 118, 137, 146; agreements between US and EU 148–53; relationship between UK and EU 146–8, 154
passports: biometric 117, 148; seizure of travel documents and 99–101
PayPal 51
Peers, S. 141–2, 144
pejorative nature of terrorist label 14
Pemberton, S. 22, 25
Permanent Court of International Justice: *Lotus* 37
personal computers 83
personality 79, 88
Petitjean, Abdel Malik 95
PKK (Kurdistan Workers' Party) 38–9
political cause 15, 17, 18, 19–21; difference: religious or 21–5
political value of terrorism 41–2
Pollard, S. 141
possession for terrorist purposes offence (TA 2006, s 57) 107, 111–12
pre-crime measures 106, 111
predictive analytical software 74
predictive policing 106
prerogative powers 103
presumption of innocence 88
Prevent strategies 24
Prevention of Terrorism Act 1974 20, 21
Prevention of Terrorism Act 2005 6
Prevention of Terrorism (Temporary Provisions) Act 1989: definition of terrorism 17
Price, Marian 42
PRISM 133

privacy 85, 96, 111, 133; capabilities gap and 2–3; CFR (Art 7) 118, 120, 121–2, 131, 160; collective security and individual 105, 112, 113–36, 159–60; ECHR (Art 8) 3, 85, 111, 123–5, 131, 134, 158, 160; Internet connection records (ICRs) 71, 72–81; Investigatory Powers Act 2016 (IPA) 62, 86, 126–9, 130, 131, 134–6; open source intelligence and ICRs: privacy conundrum 73–81, 135; seizure of passports and travel documents 99; settings 79; social media and reasonable expectations of 79
profiling 71, 75, 77, 78, 88, 96, 147
proportionality 8, 66, 68, 69, 124, 127, 128, 132, 136, 158, 159; bulk equipment interference 85; data protection 114; national security notices 86; online Islamist magazines 85; seizure of passports and travel documents 100; technical capability notices 86; use of OSINT and SOCMINT 76
proscription 37, 38–9; Islamic State (IS) 45; al-Muhajiroun 77
Protection of Freedoms Act 2012 124
public authorities 69, 120

al-Qaeda 4, 14, 21, 23–4, 25, 37, 42, 89, 91, 94, 125; in the Arabian Peninsula (AQAP) 53, 85; encryption 53; Islamic State in Iraq 44; online magazine 46, 85
Qureshi, Yasmin 24

R (CC) v Commissioner of Police of the Metropolis and another 14, 22
R (on application of David Davis MP, Tom Watson MP, Peter Brice and Geoffrey Lewis) v Secretary of State for the Home Department 121–3
R v Coulson 65, 80, 83
R v F 33–4, 39
R v G 22, 107
R v Gul 33–4, 35, 36–8, 40
R v J 22, 107
R v K 107, 108
R v Khawaja 36
R v Spencer 131
R v Zafar 22
racial cause 15, 18, 19, 21
radicalisation 26, 58, 59, 93–4, 106, 110, 144; stages in process of 91–2
Rahami, Ahmad Khan 94
Rahman, Mohammed 77
Ramsay, Stuart 141
Raytheon's Rapid Information Overlay Technology (RIOT) 75
Regulation of Investigatory Powers Act 2000 (RIPA) 5, 60, 61, 62, 66, 106, 107, 128; categories of data 69; definition: electronic communications data 64–5; OSINT and SOCMINT data 79–80
Reid, John 28, 29, 30
religious cause 15, 18, 19; difference: political or 21–5; ideological or 26–7; ritual of making sacrifices 22–3
retention of data 105, 116–17, 136, 144; criteria for new law 8, 125–6, 127–31; Data Retention Directive (2006) 4, 116, 117–23; *Digital Rights Ireland* 3, 4, 8, 113, 120–1, 122, 124, 126–7, 147, 158; European Court of Human Rights 123–5, 158; time limits 8, 9, 104, 105, 119, 125, 126, 151, 152
Rigby, Lee 85, 92–3
right-wing groups 95
Rijpma, J. 150
risk management 90, 98, 104, 105, 107, 111
risk society: resulting increase in state powers 105–6
Romania 141, 143
Rugby Football Union v Consolidated Information Services Ltd 121–2
rule of law 6–7, 11, 19, 40, 42, 124, 129, 133, 134, 138, 149, 150, 159
Russia 142

S and Marper v UK 123–4
Salafism 26
Schengen Area 117, 145; Information System (SIS) 145–6, 154
Schmaker, R. 152
Schmid, A. P. 20, 22, 23
Scirocco, A. 116
Secret Intelligence Service/MI6 68, 83, 84, 130
Security Service Act 1989 (SSA) 61, 84, 89
Security Service/MI5 64, 81, 83, 84, 85, 88–9, 90, 130; Behavioural Science Unit (BSU) 90; priority levels 92–3; Subjects of Interest: tier system 93
self-determination 34, 43
self-starting terrorist 92–3, 95–6, 98
Semitsu, J. 78
separation of powers 129
service use information 69

Sexual Offences Act 2003 36, 40–1
sexuality 71, 78
Al-Shabaab 23–4
'Silk Road' 56
Skype 52, 53
smartphones 2, 50–1, 52, 54, 59, 65, 71, 81, 96; equipment interference 83–4, 86–7
Snowden revelations 132–5, 154
social cause 17–18
social control 73
social graph 78
Social Media Intelligence (SMI or SOCMINT) 73–81, 96, 135; civil litigation 73, 74; privacy settings 79; reliability of content 79
Somalia 97
Sony 72
Soufan Centre 97–8
sovereignty, parliamentary 35–6
Spain 118, 143; Euzkadi Ta Askatasuna (ETA) 19
state terrorism 40, 41–2
statelessness 102–3
statistics: arrests 159; convictions in UK for terrorist-related act 25; Internet 74; IS foreign fighters 98, 99; IS investigation 78; landlines 50; open source intelligence 74; social media intelligence 77; use of communications data 72, 81
statutory interpretation 19
Steel and others v United Kingdom 41
Straw, Jack 13, 27
strikes 27, 30
subscriber information 69
surveillance, mass data 105, 111, 125
surveillance society, fears of 132–5
Switzerland 139, 140, 155
Syria 38–9, 44, 45, 46, 49, 97, 98, 99

Takfir 26
TalkTalk 72
technical capability notices 8, 84, 86–7
temporary exclusion orders 101–2; international status 102–4
Terrorism Act 2000 5, 13, 14–15, 16, 22, 36, 38, 39; collection of information (s 58) 107, 108, 111–12; definition of terrorism (s 1) 7, 15, 17, 20, 27, 28, 32–4, 42, 156; discretionary power to DPP (s 117) 40, 41; inciting terrorism (s 59) 108, 109; possession for terrorist purposes (s 57) 107, 111–12; proscription (Sch 2) 37, 38
Terrorism Act 2006 5, 34, 111–12; dissemination of terrorist publications (s 2) 27–9, 108, 110–11; encouragement of terrorism (s 1) 27–9, 108–10
Terrorism Prevention and Investigation Measures Act 2011 (TPIMs) 6
test: digital rights criterion 8, 125–6, 127–31
text messaging 50, 65
threshold of influence: definition of terrorism 29–33
Tilley, N. 75
time limits: Passenger Name Record data 151, 152; retention of data 8, 9, 104, 105, 119, 125, 126, 151, 152; seizure of passports and travel documents 99; temporary exclusion orders 101, 102
Tor 56, 57
traffic data 69
transparency 62, 64, 129, 134
travel documents and passports, seizure of 99–101
triadic concept 6, 13, 33
Trottier, D. 73, 76
trust: privacy and 131–5; building public 9
Tunisia 45
Turkey 38–9, 142
Twitter 46, 48–9, 50, 52, 74, 77; EMOTIVE project 77; London riots (2011) 76

United Nations: Charter 34; General Assembly 15–16, 34, 39–40; Office on Drugs and Crime (UNODC) 142; Security Council Resolution 1566 28
United States 90, 94, 137–8, 142, 154; 9/11 attack 4, 37, 91, 115, 148; Aviation and Transport Security Act 2001 148–9; definition of terrorism 17, 29, 42; EU and US: PNR agreements 148–53; EU and US: policing cooperation 153–4; FBI 17, 29; Foreign Intelligence Services Act 1978 134; liberty 149; National Security Agency 132–5; Omnibus Crime Control and Safe Streets Act 87; Snowden revelations 132–5, 154; social media intelligence 76
Urquhart, L. 78–9, 80

Van Wasshnova, M. R. 149
Vaz, Keith 49

Voice Over Internet Protocol (VOIP) 53
voicemail messages 80

Wahhabism 26
Wainwright, Rob 96
Walker, C. 19, 20, 39, 106
war crimes 37, 40
War Damages Act 1965 36
website addresses: url up to first slash 69, 70–1
Whatsapp 8, 52, 55
Wiegand, I. 138–9
Wilkinson, P. 12, 19
Wireless Telegraphy Act 2006 61
World Customs Organisation (WCO) 142

Yemen 97
YouTube 46, 49, 74, 77

Zakharov v Russia 124
al-Zarqawi, Abu Musab 44
Zwolski, K. 148, 150, 151

For Product Safety Concerns and Information please contact our EU representative GPSR@taylorandfrancis.com
Taylor & Francis Verlag GmbH, Kaufingerstraße 24, 80331 München, Germany

www.ingramcontent.com/pod-product-compliance
Ingram Content Group UK Ltd.
Pitfield, Milton Keynes, MK11 3LW, UK
UKHW022127190926
475702UK00013B/1683
9780367588861